Governance and Nationbuilding

Governance and Nationbuilding

The Failure of International Intervention

Kate Jenkins

Visiting Professor, Government Department, London School of Economics and Chairman, KJA Ltd.

William Plowden

Visiting Professor, Government Department, London School of Economics

Edward Elgar

Cheltenham, UK • Northampton, MA, USA

Published by
Edward Elgar Publishing Limited
Glensanda House
Montpellier Parade
Cheltenham
Glos GL50 1UA
UK

Edward Elgar Publishing, Inc.
136 West Street
Suite 202
Northampton
Massachusetts 01060
USA

A catalogue record for this book
is available from the British Library

Library of Congress Cataloguing in Publication Data

Jenkins, Kate.
Governance and nationbuilding : the failure of international intervention / Kate Jenkins, William Plowden.
p. cm.
Includes bibliographical references and index.
1. Nation-building. 2. Intervention (International law) 3. Developing countries—Politics and government. 4. International relations. 5. Conflict management—Developing countries. 6. United States—Foreign relations—2001– I. Plowden, William, 1935– II. Title.
JZ6300.J46 2006
327.1'1—dc22

2006007961

ISBN-13: 978 1 84542 191 5
ISBN-10: 1 84542 191 4

Printed and bound in Great Britain by MPG Books Ltd, Bodmin, Cornwall

Contents

Acknowledgements

We are grateful to a number of people who helped us at different stages of this study. Bob Ainscow, Robert Cassen, Nigel Forman, Nicholas Monck and Kate Mortimer were valuable members of an informal advisory group; several of them read and commented on a draft version of the text. Others for whose advice we are grateful include Bob Bonwitt; Claire Cameron, Don McGregor and colleagues at PAI; Stephen Catchpole; Andrew Edwards; Roger Hay; Michael Johnson; Professor George Jones; Nick Manning; Alex Matheson; Derry Ormond; Neil Parison; Steve Rankin; Trevor Robinson; Roger Riddell; David Steedman; Sally Timpson; two anonymous reviewers. We are also grateful to the Government Department at the London School of Economics for appointing us as Visiting Professors.

KJ
WJLP

Abbreviations

DAC	Development Assistance Committee – of OECD
DANIDA	Danish International Development Agency
DfID	Department for International Development
IMF	International Monetary Fund
ODA	Overseas Development Administration
OECD	Organisation for Economic Cooperation and Development
OED	Operations Evaluation Department, World Bank
SIDA	Swedish International Development Cooperation Agency
UNDP	United Nations Development Programme

Forms of government are forged mainly in the fire of practice, not in the vacuum of theory. They respond to national character and to national realities. There is great good in the Russian national character, and the realities of that country scream out today for a form of administration more considerate of that good. Let us hope that it will come. But when Soviet power has run its course, or when its personalities and spirit begin to change (for the ultimate outcome could be one or the other), let us not hover nervously over the people who come after, applying litmus papers daily to their political complexions to find out whether they answer to our concept of 'democratic'. Give them time; let them be Russians; let them work out their internal problems in their own manner. The ways by which peoples advance toward dignity and enlightenment in government are things that constitute the deepest and most intimate processes of national life. There is nothing less understandable to foreigners, nothing in which foreign interference can do less good.

George F. Kennan
Foreign Affairs, Spring 1951

1. Nationbuilding and governance

In the early years of the twenty-first century two concepts moved from research theses and the learned journals to the mass media and into public discourse. 'Nationbuilding' is a term much used by apologists for the shambles in Iraq and Afghanistan, and by their critics. It is relatively new, though the practice has a longer history. 'Governance', a term long familiar to political scientists, almost overnight in the summer of 2005 became central to public and political debate about poverty in Africa.

These terms are linked, in the sense that success in achieving the first requires high standards of the second. They also have in common a deceptive simplicity, which conceals wide disagreement about what they actually mean, and remarkable reluctance on the part of many of those who use them to acknowledge the extreme difficulty of giving practical effect to the ideas behind them. Attempts to build nations, and to improve governance, are often regarded as being 'new' endeavours: in fact there is a long history of activities whose underlying aims and philosophy are strikingly similar, which have largely failed to realize their objectives – and from which much can be learned. That is the theme of this book.

NATIONBUILDING

Definitions

Nationbuilding can be defined in different ways. It invariably involves intervention by an outside power in the internal workings of a state. It is frequently seen as being associated with some form of military activity and, often closely linked to this, with 'regime change' – the regime in question being hostile or dangerous to the intervening power. In some cases the regime may already have changed. Nationbuilding is undertaken either to bring peace or to reconstruct a society badly damaged by internal conflict. Most of its advocates would agree that 'nation' means 'democratic nation'; they see the activity as a necessary component of a wider task of 'spreading democracy'. It is regarded as a crucial way of reinforcing or indeed creating the fabric for a solid and peaceable international order. It is now regarded by many of those involved as a major instrument in an interventionist foreign policy. Before he was first elected, George W. Bush declared, in October 2000, 'I don't think our troops ought to be used for what's called nation-building'. However, since he became President he has been active in making the case for bringing about regime change, and the consequent constitutional and political change. By early 2004 he was saying, 'The best way to secure America for the long term is to promote freedom and a free society and to encourage democracy [in Iraq]'. By early 2005, in his second inauguration speech and elsewhere, he had elevated spreading democracy worldwide to the status of a major element in US foreign policy: nationbuilding comes hard on the heels of determination to spread democracy.

Whether or not the first step in nationbuilding is military action or regime change, one conviction underlying intervention is that international help is essential; there is inadequate domestic capacity to deal with the situation and outside help is needed to jump-start the process which will bring better government, a more stable state, economic and social development and a more constructive participation in the international community. The concept has a longer pedigree than the Bush administrations. Nationbuilding has for some time been regarded as an appropriate response where the state machine has collapsed for other reasons – war and civil war, civil disorder, famine or other catastrophe. The United Nations has in recent years been closely involved in many crises in states with political or social problems which are apparently not resolvable internally. The United States has increasingly seen nationbuilding as an activity to be led by itself. Afghanistan and Iraq are the most recent, dramatic and contentious examples of nationbuilding following military intervention.

Much of the related comment and literature on nationbuilding reflects the US dominance in this field. Many American commentators take the argument further and assume that therefore the only feasible form of nationbuilding must be US-led; the activity must be in the hands of the only single power today capable of deploying the resources needed. One recent analysis suggested three criteria for deciding whether or not an activity constitutes nationbuilding. There should be: (1) an American armed intervention that led to regime change or the survival of a regime that would otherwise have collapsed; (2) the deployment of a large number of US troops on the ground; and (3) the use of American military and civilian personnel in the administration of the target countries (Pei and Kasper, 2003). This is a description of an invasion. Nationbuilding as thus defined is no more than the occupation of another country by force.

Advocates of nationbuilding would like to see it as one major routine weapon in the US foreign policy armoury. But, as just defined, its scope is limited; the US role is primarily military. This reflects a certain realism about the feasibility of trying to do more. Even Donald Rumsfeld, the US Secretary for Defense in charge of the invasion of Iraq, is on record as saying, 'I don't know people who are smart enough … to tell other countries the kind of arrangements they ought to have to govern themselves' (Woodward, 2002).

But Donald Rumsfeld is now in a minority in the nationbuilding camp. The term is frequently used to mean something more ambitious than military invasion, occupation and administration. Many advocates of nationbuilding argue that a central part of the process is indeed telling other countries how to run themselves, combined with pressing on them the institutions and processes that will enable them to do so. Some see this wider role as more or less exclusively one for the United States, explicitly or implicitly:

> In most cases, [post-colonial countries'] only hope for the future would seem to be intervention by a foreign power capable of constructing the basic institutional foundations that are indispensable for economic development. (Ferguson, 2004)

> Countries have to be able to construct state institutions not just within their own borders but in other more disorganised and dangerous countries as well … we insist that we are promoting democracy, self-government and human rights … the art of state-building will be a key component of national power. (Fukuyama, 2004b)

Other commentators are less unilateral: 'Nation-building should be a multilateral undertaking, managed by the United Nations. It must involve the locals' (Pei and Kasper, 2003).

Most US commentators argue, or imply, with Fukuyama, that the ultimate aim of nationbuilding is the creation of democratic states (Dobbins et al., 2003). They would presumably not think it sufficient to replace an oppressive dictatorship with an ostensibly benevolent one, although in practice many dictatorships, oppressive and relatively benevolent alike, are quietly tolerated while others, apparently no worse, are singled out for intervention. The term 'democracy' is central to the rhetoric of the United States and its allies, although what the word means in practice is far from clear. There is little consensus as to whether this type of government takes, or should be expected to take, the same form in all circumstances and in all parts of the world.

One of the most basic issues is whether democracy is a matter of institutions or of values or some combination of both. It is difficult to define ways of measuring the degree of progress towards democracy in a country, and impossible to find measures on which all agree. In practice a choice is necessary about which components of a democratic state are the most important and which, on the realistic assumption that everything cannot be done at once, should be put in place first. A more difficult conceptual question is whether democracy can be defined by processes, for example free elections, or by outcomes such as enhanced human rights. In practice elections are widely favoured as a significant indicator, no doubt because they are concrete, observable, relatively measurable and achievable in the short term. Elections in Afghanistan and Iraq have been presented by the international media and by the governments of the intervening powers as evidence that the process of rebuilding is well under way and that it has been endorsed by the citizens concerned.

The simple act of an election says nothing about the conditions of the election or the consequences that flow from it, including the behaviour of the victors. Under pressure, advocates of 'democracy promotion' can be flexible, even evasive. Paul Wolfowitz, responding to critics who mocked his alleged aspiration to build a Jeffersonian democracy in Iraq, said:

> It's something of a test. We can't be sure they'll pass. And they're not going to pass with an A-plus. I mean, if they do Romanian democracy and the country doesn't break up that'll be pretty good. (Boyer, 2004)

In this instance responsibility seems to lie firmly with 'them' and not with 'us'; Wolfowitz's remarks raise the question of who sets the test and awards the marks – an uncomfortable issue for anyone involved, especially if, like Wolfowitz, they don't have to live with the consequences of success or failure.

An ever more difficult practical question is whether democratic processes are so important in principle that they should be encouraged regardless of the outcomes. Elections are the most obvious example of this. It is entirely possible that free and fair elections may bring to power a government pledged to confiscate the assets of all Western-owned businesses, or a hostile theocratic state. At the very least, elections may have a destabilizing effect on previously smoothly-running autocracies. It has been suggested that aid donors, aware of such possibilities, have in some cases been half-hearted about encouraging the process of democratization through to its logical conclusions (Brown, 2001, 2004).

Even the best-conducted, totally scandal-free election will not guarantee a viable and sustainable nation. It has been argued that the conditions required are more complex – a sense of hope, wide participation in political decision-making and community affairs, expanded civil liberties and tangible benefits (Jennings, 2003). These qualities are hardly likely to emerge directly from external intervention, especially where military intervention has had consequences for the inhabitants as devastating as those of a major war. 'Tangible benefits' sound simple enough, but usually require major construction or reconstruction of infrastructure – roads, water and sewerage systems and distribution systems of all kinds which take planning, time and huge investment to achieve.

There is active and widespread debate about both the legitimacy and the feasibility of this kind of intervention. Critics of the nation builders argue that it is arrogant to suppose that outsiders can build nations or spread democracy, and that they infringe upon the sovereignty of other states in doing so. They argue that the nation builders assume a proven and successful capacity for political and institutional engineering which is unjustified by history or by current events. For example:

> The United States has rightly set itself the mission of ensuring that Afghanistan is not a safe haven … for anti-American terrorists. It is another matter altogether to take on the mission of turning Afghanistan into a civil society. (Cabe, 2002)

Both sides refer to the reconstruction of Germany and Japan after 1945: 'Germany and Japan show that the task takes far longer than politicians are willing to contemplate' (Jennings, 2003).

Views about the character of the task and the details of what needs to be done can vary with ideology:

> Few national undertakings are as complex, costly, and time consuming as reconstructing the governing institutions of foreign societies … The rule of law, property rights, free markets, and an entrepreneurial culture are what are necessary for economic success. Afghanistan has none of these things. And well-meaning senators in Washington can't make it otherwise.' (Dempsey, 2004)

The warnings of history are often unfashionable but in this case it has been argued that they are unequivocal: 'Historically, nation-building attempts by outside powers are notable mainly for their bitter disappointments, not their triumphs' (Pei and Kasper, 2003).

Much of the debate has been dominated by the US preoccupation with pre-emptive security and the need to demonstrate that military intervention with the right objectives can lead to beneficial results. Parallel to this discussion is the continuing debate about the chronological and causal relationships between democracy and economic growth, fuelled by the experience of the former Communist states since 1989. Which of these states of affairs is cause and which effect, which is a necessary and which a sufficient condition for either of the others and, probably most significantly, what is the optimum sequence of introducing them? Amartya Sen has argued, 'there is strong evidence that economic and political freedoms help to reinforce one another' and, in effect, that political freedom is an essential condition for economic development (Sen, 1999).

This claim seems to be more convincingly demonstrated in the medium to long term. Short-term correlations are much harder to find. A survey of ten African countries found no relationship between formal democratic institutions and economic reform. Two prominent reformers – Rawlings of Ghana and Museveni of Uganda – came to power through military coups. By contrast in Zambia Kaunda was replaced by a democratic government, but this government made little progress with reform (Devarajan et al., 2001). The recent experience of Ghana suggests that democratization does not necessarily generate good economic policy (Tsikata, 2001). The current example of China shows that economic growth is possible without democratization. India has managed to combine growth with widespread corruption.

For all the apparent sophistication of the analysis of the requirements of a 'rebuilt nation', many of the assertions conceal more than they reveal. One could and should ask what constitutes a 'sense of hope' in a nation emerging from dictatorship, how significant it is and what exactly should be done to develop it. What practical steps are needed to create a sense of national identity in a society fragmented by tribal divisions? Objective analysts and committed liberals alike may agree that expanded civil liberties are an essential component of a democratic society, but neither have much to say about the corrective actions needed or about the priorities which should be observed. Most commentators are also cagey about where responsibility for this kind of development should lie, and whether it should be a function for local people or for outsiders.

The first stage in a nationbuilding exercise – regime change, whether or not preceded by military intervention – is relatively speaking fairly straightforward. The problems begin with the second stage. The ability to create or recreate a nation requires the ability also to create the institutions necessary for its effective functioning, and which bestow legitimacy on its rulers – electoral systems, or other arrangements for choosing the rulers, legislatures, the apparatus of the executive, legal and judicial systems, police, sub-national government, taxation systems, defence capability and public services of all kinds. All these are activities which demand a high degree of understanding and experience of the existing conditions and the unspoken assumptions which make up the fabric of a society.

A recent analysis of the situation in Afghanistan noted that:

> Afghans are hopeful this time round … [But] Afghans continue to worry about commanders, crime and the lack of dependable police. They see corruption and a culture of impunity undermining the promising new government, and they worry about Kabul's inability to deliver to the provinces, where most people live … They prioritize education and the rule of law. (Courtney et al., 2005)

One of the more sophisticated commentators on democratization has observed: 'Before a country can become a democracy it must have coherent, effective administration' (Carothers, 2003b). This proposition is useful as a statement of intent. It recognizes that elections alone do not make a democracy. But many questions are begged. The kind of administration, how developed it needs to be and who should develop it are all issues which demand knowledge and preferably experience if much time and effort are not to be wasted. The terminology of nationbuilding often fails to address this point but concentrates on the intangible benefits, not the practical improvements needed for an acceptable standard of living. In post-war Iraq the citizens' most frequent complaints have been about the lack of essential services – water, electricity, security. Without these essentials the higher-order benefits of civil society, a sense of nationhood or indeed a sense of hope, are dwarfed by the ordeals of the day-to-day. The tasks involved are not simply operational; they demand hardware, people, managerial skills, trust and a culture of public service which has to be built up over time.

At this level arise many of the important issues that can critically affect the outcome of intervention. The proposition that uncongenial regimes can be removed and replaced by others modelled on Western democracy has great political appeal, but the details of what must be done next are difficult to specify and lengthy to explain – and, for some, frankly boring. The list of issues to be covered, the people to be involved, costs, budgets and priorities: these are all the familiar elements of any project, however large or small. In addition complex and difficult questions arise about the sequencing of events. There is still little understanding of how to establish the institutions needed, whatever they may be. A recent RAND study concluded that although US armed forces had dramatically improved their fighting capability in recent years:

> ... there has been no comparable increase in the capacity of US armed forces or of US civilian agencies to conduct postcombat stabilisation and reconstruction operations ... Institutional resistance in departments of State and Defense neither of which regard nation-building among their core missions, has also been an obstacle. As a result, successive administrations have treated each new mission as if it were the first and, more importantly, as if it were the last. (Dobbins et al., 2003)

In attempting to describe what has to be done and when, the ability, and indeed the apparent desire, of most commentators to offer useful advice diminishes to zero. One of the most prominent summarizes what he sees as the important and challenging second stage of nationbuilding, following the initial intervention. He sees the task as being 'creating self-sustaining political and economic institutions that will ultimately create competent democratic governance and economic growth' (Fukuyama, 2004b). His proposals for achieving this new world consist exclusively of the creation, by the United States, of a 'central authority backed by a permanent staff', with adequate authority to coordinate other agencies, ties with similar agencies elsewhere, and 'clear civilian control'. The list of tasks sound more like ends than means, goals rather than processes, aspirations rather than proposals. The author has nothing to say about what such an authority should do, let alone about how it should acquire the necessary 'authority' and how it should use its powers once they have been acquired.

A major example of the difficulty of imposing political systems and ways of behaviour on people who do not want them was the almost total failure of the Soviet Union to create nations in its own image in its main sphere of influence in Central and Eastern Europe. The structures and ways of thinking built up by force over 50 years were swept away almost overnight after 1989. What was left behind were not successfully functioning nations but largely dysfunctional public sector institutions and, among the public, a deep residue of mistrust of governments and all their works. This mistrust continues to complicate the tasks of those trying now to build modern democracies in the former Soviet territories.

GOVERNANCE

Definitions

Theoretically, a 'rebuilt' nation should include an effective state, working harmoniously with the community as a whole. In the closing years of the twentieth century those working in development frequently used the term 'governance' to cover this area of activity. Governance applies to the activities of governments, whether democratically elected or brought to power by a military coup. The central issues are competence, efficiency and effectiveness, and the capacity to provide citizens with the necessities of life – protection from foreign powers, security, food and drink, a legal system, health care, education and other basic services.

But governance, as conventionally used, goes much wider than this. It also includes the network of institutions and relationships through which citizens express their views, articulate their sectional interests, communicate with governments and try to ensure that their preferences are reflected in public policy. It covers the political as well as the administrative processes of a country; the relationships between politicians and between politicians and citizens are an important dimension. It covers not only civil services and Cabinets, local authorities and public corporations, but also legislatures, electoral systems and their working, and the often literally innumerable population of voluntary or non-governmental organizations which are lumped together under the heading 'civil society'. It is, increasingly, seen as including corruption (and its prevention) and transparency (or its absence). Beyond this, attempts to clarify more precisely the term 'governance' have demonstrated that it is as difficult to define satisfactorily as is nationbuilding and, similarly, tends to be used in several different ways.

This book focuses on what might be thought to be the more manageable sense of governance – the effective state defined in narrower terms above. It might be supposed that the activities covered there are relatively easy to define, to compare across national boundaries and to improve according to well-understood principles and familiar models. Nothing could be further from the truth. The theme of this book is that experience has demonstrated all too clearly how difficult are definition, comparison and institutional transfer. A large volume of literature supports this proposition (for example, Rose, 1993; Minogue et al., 1998; McCourt and Minogue, 2001; Page, 2003), but still the efforts to develop governance as an internationally negotiable commodity continue unabated, and still – as outlined below – they fail to produce the results intended.

Once the epithet 'good' is linked to governance, or to government, the way is clear to enquire about how these institutions work, severally and collectively. Improving governance, and creating 'good governance', became a major element in overseas aid programmes from the 1980s onwards. Over 20 years' experience show clearly that efforts to achieve these objectives raise as many problems as does building the nation which needs governance. These problems had not been solved when, in 2004–2005, the quality of governance suddenly became a front-page issue, of concern not just to aid professionals but to the whole of the global community concerned with alleviating poverty in developing countries in general and in Africa in particular.

Africa

The Commission for Africa was established in the spring of 2004 to review the needs and the future of sub-Saharan Africa. It reported in March 2005. The Commission's report declared unequivocally:

> Without progress in governance, all other reforms will have limited impact. While there have been improvements in many African countries, weakness in governance and capacity is the central cause of Africa's difficult experience over the last decades.

The report called for changes in donor behaviour; it also urged African governments to take a more strategic approach to public sector reform, to increase their own commitment to reform and to take the lead in improving their own accountability. It had much to say about building up professional skills and developing incentives to retain and to recall skilled Africans rather than importing expensive expatriates. All this was to be done in the context of governments' own poverty reduction strategies. The report did not say what should happen in the absence of such strategies (DfID, 2005).

Later the same year public attention focused on the annual meeting of the rich countries' club, the G8, held in July 2005 near Edinburgh. In 2003 the member states of the New Partnership for Africa's Development (NEPAD) had set up a process of 'peer review' of each other's governance. This had been suggested when NEPAD was first established in 2001. The goal was to improve the governance of African states by setting up a system of regular reviews of each country by other states, with particular emphasis on human rights, democratic decision-making, economic and political management. The first two subjects, Rwanda and Ghana, had not yet been reviewed when a major, worldwide public campaign began in 2004 to 'Make Poverty History'. This merged with pressure on the G8 to agree at their meeting in July 2005 to debt relief for the world's poorest countries and to large increases in aid to Africa.

Much of the public discussion before the G8 meeting suggested that increases in debt relief would be conditional on African commitments to improve governance. Precisely what was covered by this term, how improvements were to be made, and how long the process might take, were not discussed. The final communiqué after the G8 meeting committed the G8 to help to strengthen the African Union and NEPAD, 'including through ... appropriate and coordinated support to African countries in the implementation of their good governance national strategies, including their country action plans for implementation of the African Peer Review Mechanism recommendations'.

The G8 discussions had been vague about what was covered by the term 'governance'. The final communiqué must have given the impression to many readers that a new problem had been identified and that, agreement having been reached on what to do, work on solving it could now proceed without further delay. But, like nationbuilding, improving governance – or rather, government – has a long history.

This history shows that practical understanding of the processes involved in reforming and improving government, in any country, has always been limited, and continues to be so. Its absence has never deterred would-be reformers who have taken little interest in trying to learn from their own or others' experience. The central theme of this book is that while the record of reformers attempting to improve governments in their own countries has been, to put it politely, at best mixed, the story of outside interventions aimed at reform in other countries is much more depressing.

Theory and Practice

There has never been any shortage of theory about government itself. Political Science departments are full of descriptive treatises on democracy, constitutional government and public administration, but academic analysis, however sophisticated, has rarely had much to say about the practical process of bringing about change in government. The practice of reforming or reorganizing governments is well developed and sometimes overdeveloped in many countries. In Britain the pace of change accelerated during the second half of the twentieth century, to a rate at which it became virtually impossible for those involved to analyse and learn from the experience. The result was that little was learned. Enthusiasts for reform and their advisers have tended to be much clearer about the destinations they would like to reach than about the routes for reaching them, let alone about the obstacles likely to be encountered. Machiavelli has been much cited but rarely heeded.

The gap between theory and practice is even more substantial when what is being attempted is to transfer techniques of governing between different social and political cultures – whether the activity has been shoring up crumbling ex-colonial administrations, modernizing inadequate education systems or eliminating endemic corruption. The absence of any kind of intellectual or practical framework for thinking about and managing the processes of reform has constantly bedevilled international activities in governance reform.

Precedents

There is a widely held belief that external intervention of this kind is a recent phenomenon. The same small number of detailed examples are regularly cited – Kosovo, Somalia, post-1945 Germany and Japan, Afghanistan and Iraq. In fact nationbuilding, and the sudden focus on 'governance' in Africa, are only the latest and most extreme examples of activities with a long history, which furnish a great deal of highly relevant experience. These activities raise issues of principle and of practice almost identical to those which have arisen in connection with nationbuilding, and which will arise in any efforts to implement the aims of the G8. What is surprising, both about the nationbuilding debate and about the campaign for better governance in Africa, is how little reference has been made to this history. Part of the purpose of this book is to summarize and to review that experience, to describe the problems that have arisen and to show why we should not be surprised by the practical difficulties encountered.

Rather than returning to the same half-dozen examples, reference might be made to the hundreds of case-studies of efforts by the developed countries to spread the institutions and skills of government, and sometimes to develop democracy, in the less-developed world, through various forms of technical assistance, in conditions which in many cases have been close to crisis. The aid agencies have spent millions of dollars, pounds, yen, francs and other currencies for these purposes; thousands of experts of different kinds have been employed. The donor agencies of the developed nations have sought to reform existing organizations and to create new ones, to develop new skills among those who work in them, to change the latter's behaviour and, often, to promote new value systems. They have however continued and reinforced relationships between the developed and the less-developed nations in which, for much of their history, the latter have been the passive recipients of programmes and policies planned and implemented by the former. This relationship has meant, as one commentator has remarked, that in public sector reform:

> ... to a degree unparalleled in history, outsiders have introduced, even imposed, reforms intended to change the way that sovereign governments organise themselves and spend their money. (Berg, 2000b)

Consequences

These activities now occupy a major sector of the global 'aid industry', a multinational undertaking which has acquired a momentum, a rationale and interests of its own which are only partly congruent with the interests of its clients. Some activities were well planned initially, but unsuccessful in practice. Some, as with other aid activities, were misconceived in the first place. They took little account of local conditions or of the most effective sequence in which to try to introduce changes. They rested on overoptimistic assumptions about the ability of institutions to influence people's behaviour and about the time it would take to put working organizations into operation. The results of much of this intervention have been haphazard and sometimes perverse. Many countries, especially in Africa, are no better governed today than they were 30 years ago. Well-meant and sometimes well-planned programmes of public sector reform have been derailed by events, sometimes unpredictable, but in many cases completely to be expected. Even where there have been results, the timescales have been glacial. Where expectations have been unrealistically high, disappointments have been correspondingly great.

There are important lessons to be learnt. Changing the processes, institutions and, sometimes, the underlying values of a government is extraordinarily difficult; bringing about lasting change takes a long time; there are few unambiguous success stories; above all there is no recognized and successful approach. In fact, like the State Department according to the RAND study mentioned above, we do not know how to do it.

Much of this argument is familiar to those professionally involved. There are shelves of critical reviews of projects and programmes in all parts of the world. But this lack of success is little discussed or understood outside the professional group concerned with these issues. When the issues have been discussed, the debate has been conducted in technical terms among experts. Even they have been unable to develop any real understanding of the relationships between inputs and outcomes. Furthermore, when the conclusions of the debate have been negative, these conclusions appear to have been largely ignored by those working in the field. The shelves of reports are seldom disturbed. Lessons of experience have too rarely been learned. Still less has there has been any 'read across' from these activities to the activity of nationbuilding – or in the opposite direction. Evaluators, critics and commentators have been functioning busily in a parallel universe which seems to connect hardly at all with the world of practice; in that world donors, consultants and their clients carry on doing things in much the same way as they did a generation ago.

And yet, in 2005, the principal aid donors took on a major new commitment directed to precisely this area. The rhetoric of the G8 communiqué implied that African states had now developed the will to improve their governance, that putting their resolution into practice was a fairly straightforward matter and that if the donors' help was needed, they knew what to do.

This book reviews the copious evidence that suggests the donors do not in fact know what to do – or that, if they do, they have so far been incapable of acting on that knowledge. The authors have been involved in trying to improve the processes of government in less-developed countries for the past 15 years. They brought to those activities many years of previous experience working in or close to the centre of British government, where they have observed at first hand the remarkable capacity of a well-entrenched bureaucracy to withstand even the most convinced reformer. The origin of this book was a growing belief that although the objectives of their work were mostly admirable, and the intended changes often highly desirable, much of what they were employed to do was unlikely to have any lasting impact. It reflects their concern that although much is now known about the reasons for this failure to achieve the desired outcomes, the knowledge has been neither effectively applied to the development process nor shared with a wider public, including the legislators who should be monitoring the national and international agencies, and the citizens whose taxes are financing the activities in question.

This book is divided into three sections; Chapters 2, 3, and 4 deal with the post-imperial experience of reforming government, the donors who supply the expertise and the recipients who use it. Chapters 5, 6, 7 and 8 deal with the system which donors and recipients operate to support and sustain the reform process, with the findings of evaluations of activities in this field, and with the differences in local context and culture which militate against global solutions. Chapter 9 draws some conclusions from the discussion in the earlier chapters and suggests new approaches which might help to improve the quality and effectiveness of attempts at nationbuilding and reform.

2. Empire and influence

In the second half of the twentieth century the work of the international community on governance has grown from small beginnings into today's global business. This book focuses mainly on that period. But there are important cases of earlier interventions, some extending over many years, from which important lessons might have been learned. The contexts have varied: the US in South and Central America, the UK and France in their former colonies, especially in sub-Saharan Africa, and other bilateral donors and international institutions worldwide. It is still not too late to assess these examples and to distil lessons which are relevant for today and tomorrow.

EMPIRES

Empire and Government

In the first half of the twentieth century the imperial powers started to develop in their colonies some of the skills and systems needed for effective government under continuing imperial rule. Before the war Britain had instituted a process of 'colonial development', which meant in practice modest social and economic development within a colonial framework. The 1929 Colonial Development Act was followed by the 1940 Colonial Development and Welfare Act. Preparation for independence outside the Empire was not the policy of the British government until the 1950s. Britain, like other colonial powers, paid relatively little attention to the need for countries to develop a capacity to create and manage independent government and administrative systems, as well as the necessary social and economic institutions, until just before independence. In the rush to independence after the 1939–45 war there was little time to build the capacity and organizations of independent states.

France began to subsidize the development of infrastructure and education in its African colonies after 1945. The underlying principle was that any assistance would not be continued for a colony rash enough to declare its independence. This principle was applied in 1958 when Guinea, uniquely, voted for independence. After 1960, when other colonies also decided to become independent, the principle was revoked and assistance continued (Lancaster, 1999).

Hasty efforts were made to prepare some colonies for self-government when independence was clearly imminent. In India the British, under pressure, gradually opened up positions in the Indian Civil Service (ICS) to Indians, who initially had to travel to Britain even to take the entrance examination. The last British appointments to the ICS were made in 1942. By independence in 1947 Indians filled over half the 1250 places in the ICS. In many African countries the transfer of responsibility was more grudging and less far-reaching. In West Africa, the system of 'indirect rule' was developed by Lord Lugard in Uganda and Nigeria. Under this system the paramount chiefs were constituted into a 'native authority', responsible for traditional and customary institutions and practices, under the control of the colonial district commissioner. The connection between the colonial idea of how local government should work and what already was in place when colonization took place was frequently tenuous. Colonial administrators appear to have assumed that chiefs had similar powers to those of the feudal landlords with which they were familiar in Europe. The complex and widely differing local patterns of tribal government were replaced by a colonial system described as 'custom'; this gave chiefs authority which did not necessarily reflect tribal custom, and which was then reinforced by tax-gathering and policing functions.

This system thus reinforced or, in some cases, created a structure of sub-national government which was the antithesis of the well-developed British system of elected and accountable local authorities praised by J.S. Mill as the nursery of representative government. Even in the Gold Coast, perhaps the most prosperous and best-developed British African colony, local arrangements introduced in the 1920s had reinforced the powers of the chiefs, subject to the control of the central government; as late as 1951 the ministries of defence, external affairs, finance and justice were controlled by British officials not answerable to the legislature. Although a 1919 development plan had emphasised the importance of education in preparing Africans to replace Europeans in civil service posts, these arrangements applied only to the lower grades.

Before the end of the colonial period there was a belated recognition that in Africa, in the longer term, formal systems of local government might be preferable to relying on the chiefs, and might be essential for economic development. In 1947 the Colonial Secretary sent a dispatch to the governors of the African colonies. He said that the key to success in political, social and economic advancement was 'the development of an efficient and democratic system of local government' (Hicks, 1961). A report prepared for the Fabian Colonial Bureau in 1950 advocated strengthening local government systems, especially in Africa. It concluded that such a policy would run up against a stone wall – 'the absence of local initiative and a sense of local responsibility'. It was unsure of the reasons for this situation. It might be the fault of the authorities who had previously 'preferred good government to self-government; it may be inherent in the colonial system; or it may be due to popular ignorance and lethargy'. The report recommended that the authorities should now start devolving power as far as possible, even if the cost were an obvious sacrifice of efficiency (Hinden, 1950).

The moves were belated and modest. Courses were run at Oxford to train British officials in local government finance, 'in order that they should pass on what they had learned to the people themselves ... as a preparation for Independence' (Hicks, 1961). Some efforts were made by the British government to encourage the training of people with the relevant skills for government in the colonies before they became independent. In the Gold Coast it was not until the early 1950s, with independence looming, that the colonial government embarked on a crash programme to train Africans for senior posts. Senior colonial officials from British colonies were represented at a conference held in Cambridge in 1955, chaired by the Colonial Office, on the development of local government in the colonies – one of the early examples of attempts to widen debate about government.

Independence and Government

From the 1950s the normal operations of colonial government were overtaken by the urgent need to develop institutions to form the basis of the governments in the newly independent states (Iliffe, 1995). There was little or no systematic preparation of any country for independence, much less of the detailed process of setting up and running suitable institutions for government. The British Colonial Office approached the task by providing a constitution, a legislative assembly and some development plans. It was under the development plans that the first temporary 'experts' to assist in the early process of independence were appointed; in some cases they replaced competent African officials (Mamdani, 1996). This appears to be the beginning of the era of the long-term expatriate adviser, whose influential role was, by the end of the century, generally decried. Expatriate advisers were even more conspicuous in the former French colonies, where advisers effectively replaced colonial administrators, with little or no loss of influence by the French government. In Côte d'Ivoire in the 1960s and 1970s one of the distinctive features of government was the influence of French technical assistance over the system of decision-making in the administration as well as in the President's office. There were virtually no Ivoirian nationals in the position of adviser in any part of the government.

In the British Empire the guiding assumption seems to have been that the post-imperial position would be a continuation of the past. Neither the British government nor the newly independent governments appear to have made an assessment of how their model plans might work in practice in the light of what was likely to happen in any specific country. Most institutions were inadequate for the tasks of running a newly independent country; the necessary skills had not been developed nor the necessary experience acquired. One bequest of colonial rule, perhaps unsurprisingly, was undemocratic governments, and bureaucracies that emphasized hierarchy, compliance and discipline, and ignored public accountability, responsiveness and participation. The political structures could be and were established, but the detail of administration – rules and trained employees, the processes of government, the day-to-day functioning of public institutions and the responsibility for public accountability – all needed detailed planning and the skills which could cope with an altered pattern of power and decision-taking. The procedures the colonial powers left in place in Africa were 'not congruent with African reality' (Peterson in Grindle, 1997).

The imperial models of government hastily patched up in London and Paris bore little relationship to the reality of life in a newly independent state. For example, the constitution provided for the Solomon Islands in the South Pacific, a latecomer to independence, had extensive penalties for dealing with crimes committed against railways even though there were no railways – nor were there likely to be in an archipelago of small islands. The Commonwealth Office simply gave the new government at independence a legal system drawing on the Indian criminal code as a model, ignoring both its physical characteristics and its economic structure – a fragmented island economy based mainly on barter with entrenched and diverse local customs. It was over a decade before a new legal code, suited to the needs of the independent state, was introduced.

In some countries in Africa, Malaysia and parts of India, newly independent from the British Empire, the new governments inherited the arrangements based on local chiefs. The authority which 'custom' gave to tribal chiefs was further enhanced by the forms of democracy which came with independence. It has been argued that the structure built up under colonial rule in effect enhanced tribal or geographic development rather than the individual and egalitarian social structures of a Western-style democracy (Mamdani, 1996; Illiffe, 1995).

The governments of the newly independent countries were in many ways as artificial as the colonial structures had been. Post-colonial assistance was mainly concerned with training officials in the skills they needed to manage the institutions they had inherited. Since these institutions were modelled closely, and in many cases uncritically, on those of the former colonial power, the training provided derived closely from practices in the colonial government and was often provided by expatriates – many of whom were current or former officials in the colonial government itself. In Britain the first training courses started in the 1950s. At the request of the Foreign Office the University of Manchester launched a course in administration, for officials from South-East Asia, in 1958 (Clarke, 1999). The new activities were epitomized in the activities of the Royal Institute of Public Administration (RIPA). The RIPA had organized the 1955 conference on local government. In 1959 RIPA organized another Cambridge conference on Administrative Organisation for Economic Development. Over 60 representatives of 30 Commonwealth countries took part.

RIPA's conferences were followed by training courses. In 1972 RIPA's director-general artlessly described the expansion of these activities:

> A phenomenon of the late 1950s was the number of officially sponsored visitors to Britain in search of instruction in public administration skills. They would say, in effect, 'I believe that the British are good administrators. I wish to be a good administrator. Where do I take the course?' (Nottage, 1972)

In the years that followed the number of such activities increased rapidly. In 1960 the director of the RIPA was invited by the Foreign and Commonwealth Office to visit several countries in South-East Asia and to give lectures on British public administration. He did so in Singapore, Malaya, Cambodia, Laos and the Philippines. The following year RIPA held a 13-week training course in Britain, on the Practice of Administration in Central Government. India, Nigeria, Tanganyika, Indonesia, Thailand and the United Arab Republic were among the ten countries that sent officials to take part. The director of the course, which was repeated in several subsequent years, was a recently retired Treasury official.

The same year the Secretary for Technical Cooperation set up a committee chaired by Lord Bridges, the former Cabinet Secretary, to investigate the facilities in Britain for training public servants from overseas countries and to consider what might be done to develop suitable training. One result was that in 1964 RIPA launched a course on Techniques of Instruction; in its first year this attracted 17 participants from nine Commonwealth countries. A shorter course was run on 'practical administration' for officials from overseas, who were taking part at the invitation of the British government in year-long courses based on those originally devised for colonial officials. In effect the British government and British institutions continued to train officials of Commonwealth countries as though the processes of public administration had been unaffected by the upheaval of independence.

During the 1960s the indefatigable RIPA expanded its empire and ran further courses on management services, personnel management and the training and recruitment of government officials. It operated in Nigeria, Indonesia, Peru, Iran, Zambia and Nepal. The numbers of participants taking part in UK-based courses rose into the high hundreds. Directors of studies for these courses were often retired colonial officials who had subsequently worked in the UK public service.

It is hardly surprising that for many newly independent countries a continuity of administrative style marked the early years after independence. The first wave of civil service reform broadly reinforced the structures and processes inherited from colonial days, only slowly replacing expatriates with locally based professionals and creating new structures to try to meet the needs of the developing state. Many African Commonwealth countries were influenced by the modest reforms taking place elsewhere in the Commonwealth. 'Senior African civil servants, now retired, look back at this period as a golden age, when things worked, pay befitted the status of a public officer, and the public service was often the dominant partner in the relationship with ministers' (Stevens and Teggeman, 2004). In India continuity with the Empire was even more marked. A later commentator compared the old ICS with the current Indian Administrative Service. 'It was expected that with independence they would be Indian in thinking and action. The general perception is that the Indian civil service has changed hardly a bit in terms of attitudes, mores and culture' (Mishra, 1997).

THE UNITED STATES AND LATIN AMERICA

Britain and France, as imperial powers, saw a major change in their concern for the governance of many countries in Africa and Asia during the 1940s, 1950s and 1960s, as former colonies became independent and tried to develop governance systems appropriate to their new status. On the other side of the world there was a remarkable continuity in the relationships between the United States, itself a former colony but never formally an imperial power, and the countries of Latin America. Unlike much of Asia, Africa and India, Latin America, which had successfully fought its wars of independence with Spain and Portugal in the nineteenth century, consisted largely of independent sovereign states. At the turn of the twentieth century many of them combined economic potential with severe social and political inequality. The consequent political instability threatened both their own future prosperity and that of their neighbours and trading partners.

Britain had major economic and commercial interests throughout Latin America, notably in Argentina and Chile, but in general remained detached from Latin American politics. Not so the United States, which throughout the twentieth century was deeply concerned not with the style or competence of Latin American governments, but with their degree of friendliness and amenability towards the United States, and with their potential for destabilizing the region. This concern was expressed in a campaign which lasted through virtually the whole of the twentieth century – and beyond – to spread the institutions and practices of democracy to Latin American countries. The underlying assumptions were that democracy would encourage stability and economic growth, which would benefit the United States. The emphasis given to democracy was used to justify direct intervention, sometimes backed with military force, in the internal affairs of independent states; the sincerity of the American desire for democracy in the fullest sense, and the immediate aims of such intervention, varied both over time and between individual episodes. The history of these interventions, summarized below, is excellently told and analysed in Lowenthal (1991).

There were variations, too, in the institutions on which intervention was focused. By far the most common focus was electoral systems and elections; but security services (military and police) were often targeted. So were trade unions and, more recently, non-governmental organizations and the multifarious activities that have since come to be labelled 'civil society'.

Even before the beginning of the twentieth century the United States tried to set up an electoral system in Cuba, following the defeat of the imperial power, Spain. Subsequent American policy was to establish a stable self-governing republic, which could manage its own affairs without further outside help. To safeguard the future US position, however, an amendment to the new Cuban constitution gave the United States 'the right to intervene for … the maintenance of a government adequate for the protection of life, property and individual liberty'. This right was exercised in 1906, when violent protests against the Cuban government led President Roosevelt to send troops to Cuba; military occupation did not end until 1909, by which time the United States had been directly involved in annulling the results of the last election, passing new electoral legislation, registering voters and supervising a further election.

This pattern was to be familiar for the rest of the century. Sometimes on a US initiative, sometimes at the request of unstable incumbent governments or frustrated oppositions, US politicians, diplomats and, from time to time, Marines would be directly involved in setting up and managing elections, or trying to nullify the results of manifestly fraudulent ones, supporting government or opposition parties, generally attempting to maintain law and order. In some places – Haiti, Nicaragua, the Dominican Republic – US troops were on Latin American soil for years. In the earlier part of the century a nominally guiding principle was the Wilson Doctrine, whereby the United States would not recognise unconstitutional governments.

However, this principle, like subsequent policies of the kind, was inconsistently applied. There were occasions when political stability, however illegitimate or merely unappealing the regime imposing it, was thought preferable to instability or the prospect of an anti-American government. This was especially true both during the Second World War and during the height of the Cold War, when Washington was anxious to support Latin American regimes thought to be hostile, respectively, to Fascism or Communism. Greater importance was often attached to the existence of an electoral system and the holding of elections than to the outcome of these processes or to the behaviour in office of the governments which were elected. Apart from the brief interlude of the Carter administration, human rights have been low on the priority list of official US support for democracy in Latin America.

The inconsistency of the US approach derived in part from the primacy given to the wider US foreign policy agenda. The effects were damaging both to the longer-term development of democratic political institutions and sometimes to the welfare of the citizens of the countries involved. The havoc wrought by the 'contras' in Nicaragua is a striking recent example. But damage was also done both to the cause of 'democracy promotion' and to the status of the United States more widely. The emphasis on elections as a symbol of democratic respectability impeded constructive thinking about the conditions needed to ensure that democracy could take root without repeated US intervention. In some cases US policy-makers were convinced that local circumstances made democratic elections impossible; it was often said that Haitians, in particular, were congenitally incapable of reasoned self-government (Drake, 1993). In general, the US support for democratization did not extend to encouraging the more fundamental social, economic and political changes which would ensure a sound basis for future democracy. Indeed, such changes were sometimes actively discouraged.

The one major exception to this uneven support for democracy was the brief flowering of the Alliance for Progress under the Kennedy administration in the early 1960s. The first goal was declared to be the need to 'improve and strengthen democratic institutions through application of the principle of self-determination by the people'; the basic principle of the alliance was the conviction that 'free men working through the institutions of representative democracy can best satisfy man's aspirations, including those for work, home and land, health and schools.' The most radical of the changes proposed was for land reform: unjust structures and systems of land tenure and use were to be replaced by an equitable system of property supported by timely and adequate credit.

The Alliance failed, partly because its immensely ambitious programme proved unrealizable in the face of only lukewarm support in some of the countries at which it was directed, and partly because, as on earlier occasions, *realpolitik* led to US support for some Latin American regimes which were completely out of sympathy with the Alliance's principles. In any case, it is questionable how sound the conceptual basis of the programme was. It was not clear what the links were between democratization and the specific reforms outlined in the programme, nor how they were to be brought about. The programme did not confront the fact that land reform was bound to be resisted by the ruling elites whose backing was essential for the programme's success.

The Alliance faced immense problems from the start, because of the sheer scale on which its activities were envisaged. More recent examples of US intervention in Latin American countries have been less ambitious in scope, indeed almost simplistic, and more limited in scale. But the outcomes of these more modest actions do not offer much comfort, and few positive lessons, for nation builders elsewhere. The invasions of Grenada in 1983, Panama in 1989, and Haiti in 1994 all demonstrated the application of overwhelming military force to minuscule countries. With the possible exception of Grenada, where the action was taken for once not unilaterally but at the request of neighbouring countries, it is hard to see any long-term improvements in the countries' governance. Despite the gradual replacement, during the last years of the twentieth century, of the more outrageous Latin American regimes by others with a plausibly democratic veneer, it is equally hard to attribute these changes to the many decades of US intervention. Indeed, even if the gross excesses of Galtieri's Argentina or Pinochet's Chile are now things of the past, Latin American standards of governance remain depressingly low. 'Enhancing governance and strengthening accountability remain the defining challenges of Latin American unstable democracies' (Santiso, 2003).

GERMANY AND JAPAN AFTER 1945

There are, by contrast, two examples of military action followed by nationbuilding which are often cited as demonstrating that nationbuilding is indeed possible in principle and in practice. These are the reconstructions of Germany and Japan after 1945. The nature of the reconstruction, and its relevance, is not entirely consistent with the accepted story. As one distinguished journalist put it in a private discussion of the difficulties facing Afghanistan and Iraq: 'I don't understand the problem. We did it after the war, didn't we? Japan and Germany are clear examples.' It is widely believed that the victorious allies approached each defeated country with a clear preconceived plan, which was imposed on each according to schedule and which led, in short order, to the development of two of the world's strongest economies and most stable nations. The detailed history of post-war Germany and Japan shows a rather different picture. Not only did reconstruction involve changes of plan, compromise and adaptation, but the successful outcome was a function of the victors' contribution of the total destruction of the incumbent regime followed by the imposition of a framework of stability; reliance on key people inherited from the old defeated regime, however tarnished they might be; and the recipient countries' own inherent skills, values and institutional capacity.

In Germany the work was carried out by the Allies and in Japan by the US acting alone. Using today's terminology, the war had created 'regime change' – but it was regime collapse, not simply change, that had to be managed. The initial policy of the Allies was, first, to eliminate all traces and influence of the previous regimes and, second, to build democratic institutions, a model apparently followed in Iraq.

Germany

In Germany the US directive which guided the occupying regime declared that Germans 'must be made to understand that all necessary steps will be taken to guarantee against a third attempt by them to conquer the world', and that Germany would 'be not occupied for the purpose of liberation but as a defeated nation'. Both aims required intervention at all levels of local and national government. But in due course a policy which had been punitive, indeed vindictive, in intent, was significantly modified in response to the need to work with and through people living locally rather than by military diktat. As one commentator has remarked, this 'required a deep compromise on regime change' (Pei and Kasper, 2003).

The Allies targeted demilitarization of the German public service by reforming the personnel structure and encouraging promotion on merit from the lower ranks. Persuasion was tried first and then legislation; both were ignored by the Adenauer administration, which later introduced its own legislation to re-establish the pre-war stratified structure. Indeed, priority was given to hiring former officials from the higher ranks of the Prussian and Third Reich ministries, many with long-standing connections with the Nazis. It has been estimated that by the late 1940s more than 60 per cent of those employed by the federal government had been officials in the Nazi government. More than 90 per cent of Germans blacklisted in the US government's original plan for post-war Germany were eventually rehabilitated (Garner, 1997).

At the local level the military government tended to look for Germans with some administrative experience and with 'cooperative and respectful attitudes', rather than social democrats with less experience and often with their own agendas. This tended to mean, as at the national level, rehiring many people who had been closely associated with the previous regime (Boehling, 1996).

Japan

In Japan, General McArthur was determined to modernize the feudal culture and to introduce democracy. The phrase much used was 'democratic revolution from above'. In contrast with Germany, where the Allies had initially governed directly, in their four separate zones, in Japan the Americans were in sole command – and MacArthur was in unchallenged command of the American occupying forces. However, American ignorance of Japanese language and culture meant that they had to govern indirectly – through the existing bureaucracy, which they left more or less intact. Less than 2 per cent of key people linked to the previous regime were ultimately purged. The people responsible for implementing the changes were not the American victors, but predominantly the same bureaucrats who had been responsible under the previous defeated regime (Dower, 1999).

The Emperor was the other key institution left unchallenged, his continued presence giving legitimacy to the new regime. Some of MacArthur's proposals were at first resisted strongly; some were wholly or partly abandoned in the face of the resistance of the Japanese government. The influence of the Emperor was important in publicly encouraging acceptance of the changes which were introduced; within two years there were signs of greater public enthusiasm and support for some of the changes.

In Japan in 1945 the Americans inherited and largely perpetuated an industrial and financial system which had been built up in the 1930s for waging total war. After the war this system was adapted to the purposes of total commercial war. It was indeed the Americans themselves who set up the supreme embodiment and key instrument of this policy, the later much-feared Ministry of International Trade and Industry. Their failure to bring the industrial bureaucracy under control has been labelled 'a major act of omission' (Dower, 1999). The combination of institution-building and the promotion of social and economic welfare appear to have contributed to creating the conditions for economic and social success. In both countries there was widespread – if not universal – acceptance that a new government system was necessary. For most of the population, survival under unprecedented conditions of deprivation and dislocation meant that the details of government institutions were relatively insignificant. The new government had to be created in conditions of social and economic collapse with a population suffering from extreme trauma and starvation.

In both Germany and Japan sustained effort, backed initially by military force, produced new patterns of government and, especially in Japan, a constitution much more nearly democratic than had been seen before. The development of new governments and new systems of democracy in both countries has over time produced recognizable modern states. However, in both countries the strength of the changes depended heavily on local determination to succeed and, in many cases, the re-establishment of the old hierarchies, even if their objectives and policies had changed. More fundamentally, it has been argued that both countries had characteristics that made them suitable candidates for nationbuilding: a relatively strong social identity, high ethnic homogeneity and relative socio-economic equality (Pei and Kasper, 2003).

AID AND GOVERNMENT

These different types of external intervention in the structure and the processes of governments – the US in South America, post-Second World War reconstruction, and the post-colonial experience – all had potentially important lessons for those who, starting in the 1980s, attempted to modernize and, sometimes, to 'democratise' the governments of other countries. The Bretton Woods discussions of 1944 were held to set up a system for regulating the world economy. These later attempts developed within the framework of the general principle, established at Bretton Woods, that richer nations could and should provide assistance to poorer nations. The institutional expressions of this were the International Monetary Fund and the World Bank. The United Nations, which was established the following year, set up its own specialized agency for development, the United Nations Development Programme (UNDP), in 1965. Like other donors, the UNDP was later powerfully influenced by the report of the Independent Commission on International Development, chaired by former German Chancellor Willy Brandt (1980).

By the 1970s both the patterns of relationships, and the quality and quantity of aid flows, between the developed and the developing countries were a function of history, politics, economics and international relations. One fact was clear. In many countries, notably in sub-Saharan Africa, the optimism of the early post-independence years was cooling; despite domestic resources and external aid, political and economic development was going backwards rather than forwards. Much of the aid, whether provided as grants or as loans, was manifestly being wasted; in some countries aid money was itself said to be a major contributor to corruption (Hanlon, 2002). By the 1990s fingers were beginning to be pointed at the quality of governance. A statement by the World Bank can stand for many such:

> Dysfunctional and ineffective public institutions … and weak governance are increasingly seen to be at the heart of the economic development challenge … it became evident in the 1990s that policy reforms are less likely to succeed when public institutions and governance are weak … While 'first generation' economic reforms have proceeded rapidly in many settings over the past 15 years, institutional reform has moved far more slowly, and weak institutions have become the main constraint to more robust and sustained growth … (World Bank 2000)

What this statement fails to reveal is how extensive the attempts in the 1980s and 1990s to reform institutions had been – and how largely unsuccessful. There might have been lessons, positive and negative, to be learned from the largely unsuccessful interventions by the United States in parts of Latin America, from the irrelevance of the systems and structures of government bequeathed to former British and French colonies in Africa and elsewhere, and from the strikingly successful but locally driven reconstructions of Germany and Japan after 1945. The more general lesson might have been that methods of governance introduced from outside and from another context and culture will grow few roots and are unlikely to be sustainable. The lessons were not learned. The rest of this book looks in greater detail at some of these attempts at institutional reform and at the lessons for the future.

3. The providers: the donors

In the debates about aid and development most weight is carried by the international institutions – the World Bank, the UNDP and the European Union (EU) – even though most aid money in all areas is spent by 'bilateral' donors through their own separate aid agencies. Although in recent years total aid expenditure has risen, bilateral spending accounts for over 70 per cent of the total. In 2003 about $50 billion was spent bilaterally on all aid and about $19 billion through multilateral programmes. Most countries run their own programmes while contributing to multilateral programmes as well.

Non-governmental organizations (NGOs) are increasingly involved in the delivery of aid. The figures produced by the Development Assistance Committee (DAC) at OECD suggest that NGOs spend about 12 per cent of technical cooperation funds and take responsibility for a large share of emergency aid. More recent calculations indicate that if to private donations are added funds transferred to NGOs by official donors, to run both their own programmes and the donors' programmes, NGOs are now responsible for nearly a quarter of all official development assistance.[1]

Aid for government itself is a small proportion of the total. The realization of the significance of government has come only slowly to the aid community. Aid for government has been growing as donors begin to recognize that the effective implementation of most of their policies and expenditure on development depends heavily on the capacity and quality of the governments with which they deal. But it was only in the debates on Africa, in the course of preparations for the G8 summit in 2005, that the international community finally recognized publicly that what it referred to as 'governance' was central to the success or failure of development.

THE INTERNATIONAL ORGANIZATIONS

The World Bank

The World Bank has been interested in government for at least 20 years, if its own publications are to be taken at face value. But in the 1980s the Bank's interest in government was distinctly negative. Its assumption of principle, sustained by the views of the IMF (International Monetary Fund), was that there should be as little government as possible. Largely as a result of this the Bank was slow to develop any serious analytical capability for thinking about government; it was committing loans on government long before it started to develop such a capability in the late 1990s.

The Bank set up a 'public sector management team' in the early 1980s; in 1983 the Bank's *World Development Report* highlighted, for the first time in the Bank's thinking, a significant role for better government in the development process. In 1989 in its report on sub-Saharan Africa it focused explicitly on the role to be played by better government. It declared that 'underlying the litany of Africa's development problems is a crisis of governance'. 'Governance' was then defined as including the state's institutional arrangements, the processes for formulating policy, decision-making and implementation, information flows within government and the overall relations between citizens and government (World Bank, 1989). The Bank's first development report expressly dealing with good government was *Governance and Development* in 1991. As a former staff member noted: 'By [the early 1990s] there was a growing appreciation that policy depended on institutions for implementation – but no one had figured out how to build those institutions successfully in inhospitable political and social climates' (Einhorn, 2001).

Members of the Bank's public sector management team worked on government issues in the central project staff and later in the Africa, Latin America and Caribbean regions. The regional groups had significant numbers of public sector specialists throughout the 1990s; other regions have followed since. But despite the thinking and discussion associated with this work, the Bank admitted that before 1996 work on government was often left to individual staff members and mid-level managers, that a substantial number of specialists was not built up until 1997, and that only after 1996 was 'systematic management attention' given to the relevant issues – by which time its experts had, in practice, been dealing with it in recipient countries for several years (World Bank, 2001a). A striking feature of the history of the development of aid to government has been the repeated public admissions by the World Bank that its capability in preceding periods has not been adequate for the tasks it was trying to perform.

The Bank acknowledged that 'from the late 1980s through the mid-1990s, the subject [of public sector management] received little attention' (World Bank, 2004a). Its first major strategy paper on public sector reform was issued only in 2000. The Bank's weakness in this field was revealed in its work in specific countries: in 2002 the Russian government commented that:

> until 1998, the Bank did not pay proper attention to the issues of providing proper quality of the state administration system, including management of state resources

> and reform of the civil service and legal system. This considerably worsened the efficiency of the Bank-financed programs. (Zanini, 2002)

The Bank's public concern with the quality of government was intensified when it developed an official interest in corruption. In 1996 the Bank's president, James Wolfensohn, spoke publicly about the 'cancer of corruption' which he saw as undermining development. The 1996 and 1997 *World Development Reports* discussed the issue, and in 1997 the Bank approved a comprehensive anti-corruption strategy. Corruption, said the Bank, hampered economic growth, discouraged public and private investment and worsened poverty. It also placed disproportionate burdens on the poor.

Developing countries, the Bank's clients, are also among its shareholders. This fact often inhibits frank speaking, if not rigorous analysis, when the Bank is considering whether or not specific interventions are likely to be effective. Unlike most of the other aid agencies, the Bank lends, it does not give, except in very limited cases. This means that its support carries with it the tail of debt, repayments and debt relief which present so many problems in later years. Recipient governments may find themselves with debts incurred by their predecessors for projects with whose objectives they may not agree and which may well be no longer relevant or useful.

In spite of these difficulties the Bank lends a lot of money for improvements in government. Having started giving the matter 'systematic management attention' in 1996, the Bank lent \$2 billion for 'public sector governance' in 2000, and \$3.4 billion in 2004. This was equivalent to about 17 per cent of its total lending; the percentage varied among the Bank's regions, from a low of 2 per cent in the Middle East and North Africa to a high of 25 per cent in Europe and Central Asia. In Africa, between 1995 and 2004 the Bank lent \$9 billion and provided \$900 million in grants and administrative budget to support public sector capacity-building (World Bank, 2005). Lending was divided into four areas: public sector management, accountability (especially of public sector officials), legal framework development, and transparency and information. Public sector governance accounted for 8 per cent of the Bank's 'active project portfolio' (World Bank, 2004d).

Notably, democracy is not on the Bank's list of topics for lending, even by implication; a commitment to democratic institutions is not a precondition for borrowing, nor is a commitment to the UN principles on human rights. Until the mid-1990s the Bank distinguished specifically between democracy and good government. During the late 1980s and the early 1990s, World Bank policy was dominated by IMF-led policies of enforcing 'structural adjustments' on recipient countries to reduce the size and economic influence of the public sector and to open up a private sector for economic development. In this scenario government was 'bad' in the sense that it could act as a drag on economic development; the emphasis was on reducing the scale of government and its demands on national resources. This was the basis for the pressure, hardly relaxed since, for privatization.

Not until the late 1990s was serious attention focused on the need for better state institutions – which might mean more and different government, rather than less government. In 1997 the Bank's annual *World Development Report* took as its theme 'the state in a changing world'. This report declared, in terms not surprising to those who had been involved in attempts at public sector reform, at home or abroad, during the 1970s, 1980s and 1990s, that, 'For human welfare to be advanced, the state's capability … must be increased.'

Four years later, anyone aware of the efforts, worldwide, to improve standards of public sector management during the 1980s and 1990s might have been equally surprised to see that a 2001 Bank study of aid and reform in Uganda thought it worth making the point that 'institutional capacity is a very important determinant of success in implementation' (Holmgren et al., 1999). In 2004 the Bank's *World Development Report* took as its theme 'making services work for poor people', and devoted much of the report to discussions of aspects of what used to be called public administration.

The Bank generates and makes available a considerable amount of research findings and evaluations of its own projects. Both are freely available in published form and often, free of charge, on the internet. This policy of openness is admirable. However, it is far from clear to the observer that there is any connection between the research and evaluation that is undertaken and the actions of the Bank, and of its subcontractors, on the ground. Neither of the authors, in the course of several projects funded by the Bank, have ever had their attention drawn to a single one of the Bank's research reports, books or papers. The Bank itself acknowledged, after more than a decade of activity on government, that it had failed to keep up with the enormous amount of thinking and activity going on elsewhere in this area:

> The Bank has been slow in mainstreaming the new thinking about institutions and the role of the state which gained prominence in the past decade. (World Bank, 2000)

Staffing patterns have reflected and, doubtless, contributed to this weakness. A commentator noted that in 1996 the Bank's staff of 6500 included very few anthropologists, sociologists or political scientists, 'despite the fact that much of its work has extensive social and political ramifications' (Lancaster, 1999). A few years later the Bank admitted that traditionally it had

> lacked a sufficient number of specialized staff with extensive knowledge and practical in-country reform experience in … public financial management (tax policy, tax administration, expenditure policy, budget process, information systems,

> accounting, auditing); administrative and civil service reform (policymaking, service delivery, agency structure, and civil service regulation, pay and employment); legal and judicial reform; subnational government reform; and regulatory and public enterprise reform. ... (World Bank, 1999a)

In 2000 it suggested that these shortages reflected, in part, 'the lower demand for these skills in the past given the limited emphasis placed on institution-building goals' (World Bank, 2000). In 2005 the Bank, remarkably, still did not record the educational qualifications of its governance team; an official told the authors that the team was 'highly multi-disciplinary – economics, public finance, public administration, political science, law, international affairs – attracting both deep thematic and broader governance specialists'.

There are many critics of the Bank's work on governance. It has been said, for instance, that the Bank has 'failed to develop a coherent and consistent approach to key governance issues', that its definition of the subject is vague and hard to operationalize and that it lacks adequate expertise (Ahrens, 2001). The Bank itself has repeatedly acknowledged that much of its work in this area has been ineffective. 'Bank-supported civil service reforms were largely ineffective in achieving sustainable results in down-sizing, capacity-building and institutional reform' (World Bank, 1999a). The Bank's internal analysis of 124 civil service reform activities between 1980 and 1997 found that only 33 per cent of completed activities had achieved satisfactory outcomes (World Bank, 1999a). 'Have Bank interventions helped make governments work better?' asked a Bank staff member in 1999. She answered her own question: 'Despite some progress, the answer is "probably not"' (Nunberg, 1999). More fundamentally, the Bank has been criticised for its *de facto* support of incumbent regimes, regardless of their quality as governments, and for its repeated failure to enforce its own conditions for lending (Hibou, 2002). (This issue is discussed in Chapter 5.)

The Bank, like the IMF, has repeatedly been under fire for advocating the principles of good government to its member states while too often ignoring these itself. The Bank has been criticized for its non-transparent decision-making processes, for the closed nature of the appointment of its president and for having only two African executive directors to represent 46 sub-Saharan countries (Woods, 2000; Corpwatch, 2003). Joseph Stiglitz remarked that 'underlying the problems of the IMF and the other international institutions is the problem of governance ... [The institutions] are not representative of the nations they serve' (Stiglitz, 2002).

The International Monetary Fund

The International Monetary Fund (IMF), whose role was originally focused on reforming recipient countries' economic activities, has moved into the government arena. It has been explicitly involved with promoting good government since the mid-1990s. In 1996 it declared that the framework for prosperous economies included 'promoting good governance in all its aspects, including ensuring the rule of law, improving the efficiency and accountability of the public sector and tackling corruption' (IMF, 1997a). Its managing director, Michel Camdessus, was more explicit:

> Our approach is to concentrate on those aspects of good governance which are most closely related to our surveillance over macro economic policies – namely the transparency of government accounts, the effectiveness of public resource management and the stability and transparency of the economic and regulatory environment for private sector activity. (July 1997)

A 1997 internal 'Guidance Note' (IMF, 1997b) stated that the IMF should focus on areas of its 'traditional purview and expertise', and that for subjects in which it did not have a comparative advantage – public enterprise and civil service reform, property rights – it should rely on the expertise of other institutions, especially the World Bank. But a few years later the IMF declared that 'governance and corruption ... are now clearly seen as issues to be addressed as an integral part of economic analysis and policy discussion, be it by the Fund and other International Organisations or by national governments' (Schiller, 2000). By then the IMF was also involved in judicial reform, legislative strengthening and decentralization.

It has been suggested that none of the international development banks have effective processes for institution-building. 'If anything they have an even greater tendency than democracy promoters to sponsor elaborate institutional designs created by external consultants and to rely on formalistic top down methods' (Carothers, 1999). The IMF has been much criticized not only for what are seen as its 'anti-poor' policies but also for being dominated by economists and being largely unqualified to pronounce on matters of government. Its interest in this field has been criticized as 'legitimiz[ing] the IMF's power grabs of the last several decades' and furthering the foreign policy interests of the United States (Welch, 1998).

The United Nations

The United Nations has a different focus and a different approach. Since its foundation it has been concerned with democratic rights and liberties. The United Nations Development Programme (UNDP) was set up in 1965, as the result of an amalgamation of the UN Special Fund and the Expanded Programme of Technical Assistance which had been set up in 1949. It focused initially on poverty reduction through providing for basic needs such as water, food, housing, health care and education. 'Consideration was rarely given', acknowledged the UNDP 30 years later, 'to the capacity of the recipient government agency, nor the policy environment in which it operated' (UNDP, 1998). By 1988 it was spending $60 million on government; in that year a management development programme was launched to help with sustainable improvements in the public sector. Between 1992 and 1996 the UNDP spent a total of $1.3 billion on good government, public resources management and coordination.

By 1995 the programme was spending a third of its total resources on government issues in Africa, the Arab states, Eastern Europe and the former Soviet Union, with a smaller proportion going to Asia and the Pacific region. The expenditure was primarily on aid management and coordination. Expenditure in Latin America and the Caribbean was mainly on planning and policy formulation. Its global programmes were concentrating on decentralization and strengthening civil society as well. In 2003 the UNDP was supporting 380 public administration projects in 112 countries; 31 per cent of them were in Europe and the former Soviet Union, only 12.6 per cent in Africa.

The UNDP produced two reports on the significance of government. In 1994 in 'Initiatives for change' and in 1997 in 'Governance for sustainable human development' it drew attention to the link between competent systems of government and sustainable development. It argued that the hard grind of development could not succeed without the kind of infrastructure provided by a competent and incorrupt government. Again competence and a lack of corruption appear higher priorities than democracy and human rights. Compared with the World Bank and the IMF, both seen by many as tools of the G8 powers, the UNDP tends to have much easier relationships with its client governments. It sees its own institutional strengths as being its impartiality, its customer orientation, its long-term perspective, its experience, the trust of its clients and its ubiquity (UNDP, 1997). A senior official who moved from the Bank to UNDP commented how much freer he was to raise issues with governments than he had been when working under the auspices of the World Bank (Denny, 2000).

The European Union

The European Union is the world's second-largest multilateral donor, providing about 12 per cent of all international financial aid. It has long had an aid programme of a traditional kind, initially based on the first Lomé Convention of 1975 – a programme of development cooperation with 72 countries in Africa, the Caribbean and the Pacific. The third programme, Lomé III (1985–90) pledged EU commitment to human dignity and economic, social and cultural rights. The fourth, Lomé IV (1990–2000), stipulated that democracy, human rights and the rule of law were preconditions for development cooperation with the EU. The levels of expenditure are substantial: of the EU's nearly $5 billion aid in 2000, $1.5 billion went to sub-Saharan Africa, $1 billion to Europe.

Forty per cent of EU aid goes to Africa. Just over 40 per cent goes to the poorest countries (down from 70 per cent in 1990). All this activity and the associated expenditure are not necessarily highly regarded. EU aid activities have been widely criticized as incoherent, bureaucratic and ineffective. Clare Short, when the minister in charge of DfID, described its development programme as 'an embarrassment' and inadequately focused on alleviating poverty (Short, 2002). Others agree. 'It has become almost impossible to navigate the complex labyrinth of the Commission bureaucracy and in particular its foreign aid apparatus whose Kafkaesque structures and procedures are beyond comprehension' (Santiso, 2002b). Consultants complain that the processes for letting contracts are complex, perverse and sometimes corrupt.

The EU's canvas is unlike that of any other donor. As in Germany after 1945, the countries of central Europe after the fall of Communism replaced their discredited governments; they reached back, in some cases, to their earlier experience of more or less democratic rule. The new rulers wanted modern democratic government, they wanted to be accepted into the European Union and they were eager for all the help they could get. The EU made money and expertise available and specified the criteria it would use to decide whether applicant countries were ready for membership. The purpose of the PHARE programme was to help the candidate countries to prepare for accession by institution-building and adopting the legal structures of the European Union's *acquis communautaire*. The TACIS programme was launched in 1991, directed towards the component countries of the former USSR. Once again, its main aim has been to assist the transition process. Between 2000 and 2006 the total budget for the programme of support for the applicant countries was set at 11 billion euros.

The governments of the applicant countries to the east of the EU, unlike most of the traditional aid recipient countries, were under intense political and social pressure to achieve whatever was necessary to obtain entry to the EU in the shortest possible time. For most of them these requirements included radical changes to their government institutions. The public pressure for entry was such that they were able to put the full range of the EU's agreements into operation with little opposition. In 1991 the EU's funding support was focused on Poland and Hungary, but by 1996 it had been extended to all ten applicant states. Association agreements with these countries contained provisions on democracy, human rights and the rule of law. In 1992 further clauses provided that accession and financial aid would be available only to states complying with democratic principles, human rights, the rule of law and a market economy. The Copenhagen agreement of 1993 provided that 'the associated countries in central and eastern Europe that so desire shall become members of the European Union'. Accession could take place as soon as applicants could 'assume the obligations of membership by satisfying the economic and political conditions required'. The conditions were written into the Copenhagen agreement.

By 1997 the EU's requirements for membership were spelt out in greater detail:

> A country cannot be considered stable if the respective rights and obligations of institutions such as the Presidency, the constitutional court or the central referendum commission can be put into question by the government itself and the legitimate role of the opposition in parliamentary committees is not accepted. (European Commission, 1997)

In 1997 Slovakia was excluded from the initial round for entry after the Commission concluded that it did not meet the Copenhagen conditions 'because of the instability of Slovakia's institutions, their lack of rootedness in political life and the shortcomings in the functioning of its democracy' (European Commission, 1997).

The EU's objective at the start of the PHARE programme had been to provide assistance with the costs of transition according to needs perceived by the recipient countries, but over time the criteria changed significantly to 'providing assistance to candidate countries to meet the goals set by the EU'. The progress achieved by the candidate countries against these goals was monitored by EU experts whose reports determined the future for applicant countries.

The EU, as donor, was less rigorous in its dealings with the former Communist bloc states that were not attempting to become applicants for membership of the EU. It emphasized the need to reinvigorate civil society and restructure the state apparatus but, despite a vote in the European Parliament requiring that the development of democracy should be one of the aims of assistance to these states, the proportion of total aid spent on 'democracy' was small. Unlike in the applicant states, democracy was not a precondition for support from the EU.

The question arises of how far applicant countries were expected to meet standards which were not met by established EU members. The system set up by the Council of Europe in 1998 to monitor compliance by existing member states with the European Charter of Fundamental Rights found in some EU countries 'political interference especially concerning judges; cases of corruption – largely due to poor salaries and status; a shortage of resources; frequent delays and an alarming proximity of prosecution and judiciary'

(Kennedy 2004). The issue of how far donors set standards for 'recipient' countries that are not met in the donor states and institutions is by no means uniquely a problem in the EU. It also arises in connection with the policies and activities of many of the donor agencies.

Organization for Economic Cooperation and Development (OECD)

Distinct from the big multinational donor organizations is the Organization for Economic Cooperation and Development (OECD), based in Paris and consisting of members from the world's wealthier states. Members meet and set standards of economic development. It is essentially a large-scale research and discussion group, which builds its publications on its own research and on the reports of member states. It has reflected the growing interest in the management of government over the past 20 years in its research and working groups, in which member states can present and compare their experiences. It has a specialized public sector research unit, PUMA. Unlike the World Bank or the EU, PUMA has provided assistance in response to demand and without strings. Within the ambit of PUMA there is a specialized programme, SIGMA, which has concentrated on the needs of the ex-Communist bloc countries, particularly the applicant countries to the EU, under contract to the EU programme PHARE. It has worked with the EU candidate countries, the western Balkan countries and Russia.

OECD, recognizing the extent of development work being undertaken by its members, has a formal committee – the Development Assistance Committee (DAC) – which acts as a coordinating body for aid and development activity. One of DAC's roles is to pull together information about activity and expenditure by its members on development aid. It also publishes advice and guidance on aspects of development, drawn up by specialized committees of its members, and holds conferences and workshops on specific topics. It is generally recognized as providing the best available information on aid activity generally, although, in common with many donors, its statistics do not separate out expenditure and activity specifically about government. Although OECD has no specific budget for development work, the work of its expert committees is published and used as a benchmark by many donors.

For example, OECD has published guidelines on poverty reduction, on strengthening trade capacity for development and on helping to prevent violent conflict. The problem OECD faces with such work is that there are few countries who are recipients within OECD; by definition, if a country is receiving aid on any scale it is unlikely to have made it to membership of OECD – although this is not the case with technical cooperation where some activity has continued in some OECD member states, for example Mexico and Brazil. OECD's analyses of development issues tend therefore to be focused on the perceptions of donor states rather than on a full understanding of the views of both sides of the development relationship.

BILATERAL DONORS

The major bilateral donors in volume terms are the United States, Japan, France, Germany, Britain and the Netherlands, followed by Italy, Canada, Sweden, Norway, Spain. The ranking by percentage of GNP is led by Norway, followed by Denmark, Netherlands, Luxembourg, Sweden, Belgium, France, Ireland, Switzerland, Finland and Britain. The big bilateral donors – Germany, Japan, US, Britain and the Scandinavian countries – both contribute people and money to the international organizations and run their own programmes. These donors inevitably operate in different ways from the big multilateral organizations. They have greater operational flexibility but they have to work to their own domestic political agenda as well as taking part in multilateral policy development and projects.

Different donors tend to concentrate on particular areas. In the 1990s 73 per cent of Swedish assistance went to projects dealing with the executive, as compared with Britain's 30 per cent. Britain and the US both spent over 30 per cent of their totals on legal systems, as compared with Sweden's 10 per cent (Crawford, 2000). Japan stands out from most of the other bilateral donors in its reluctance to promote democratization through its aid activities. 'Japan has as a principle refrained from attaching political conditions to its aid', the Foreign Ministry stated in 1991 (Akaha, 2002).

There is also considerable differentiation by country and region. The distribution of aid says as much about the donor's history as its current political priorities. Thus Britain's top ten recipients of total aid are India, Serbia and Montenegro, Tanzania, Mozambique, Bangladesh, Ghana, Uganda, Afghanistan, Zambia and Malawi – eight Commonwealth countries out of ten. For France, the list reads Côte d'Ivoire, French Polynesia, New Caledonia, Morocco, Egypt, Poland, Cameroon, Senegal and Mayotte, seven ex-colonies out of nine. The United States' list has Egypt, Russia, Israel, Pakistan, Serbia, Colombia, Ukraine, Jordan, Peru and Afghanistan. There are four countries on the German list that do not feature high up in the priorities for expenditure of the US, France and the UK: China, Bolivia, Indonesia and Turkey (OECD DAC, 2003).

Britain

Although Britain has had an aid programme of sorts since the 1920s, this initially consisted mainly of grants and loans to British colonies under the

Colonial Development Act of 1929 and the Colonial Development and Welfare Act of 1940. The link to colonial interests and responsibilities was clear and unambiguous. As the colonies of the old empire moved to independence, the structure of the programme reflected, in part, recognition of the need to bolster their competence as they took over responsibility for their own government both nationally and locally. In the 1960s levels of financial aid reflected the British government's belief that former colonies should be able to meet their capital needs through borrowing – a policy which conspicuously failed to solve the financial problems of several new states (Browne, 1990). Aid support reflected the similarity in systems between Britain and many of its ex-colonies, which leant heavily on what was known as 'the Westminster model' of public administration; many people assumed, logically, that Westminster, or Britain, was the best place to obtain the training to operate it. In the 1970s the theme of much of the aid programme dealing with public administration was training; in the 1980s it included institutional development; and since the 1990s 'good governance' has featured significantly. The focus on poverty reduction after 1997 altered the emphasis of the British approach but the Department for International Development (DfID) continued to include projects on government within its overall programme.

The British government's aid department has been variously known over the years as the Ministry for Overseas Development (ODM), the Overseas Development Administration (ODA) and, since 1997, the Department for International Development (DfID). The changes in name reflect the political fortunes of the aid budget in Britain. Labour governments have made the aid department a full ministry with its minister a member of the Cabinet; the Conservatives prefer to have the aid process managed within the responsibility of the Foreign and Commonwealth Office. Britain is now unusual in having a separate and senior ministry with a Cabinet minister in charge dealing solely with aid. The department has been remarkable by British standards for two interrelated factors – the lack of movement of its senior staff around Whitehall and, especially in its earlier years, their relative and, for the British civil service, unusual enthusiasm for their tasks. This enthusiasm may be reflected in its development in recent years. By the twenty-first century DfID had grown to cover formal programmes in 71 countries and territories. 'A lot of countries', as the International Development Committee commented drily, welcoming a DfID assurance that the number would be reduced in future (Select Committee on International Development, 2002). The average number for the 22 major bilateral donors in 2000 was 95 (World Bank, 2004a). The most widely dispersed portfolio appears to be that of Canada, which in 2005 was involved in 155 different countries (Mulley et al., 2005).

For some years the department was also remarkable in distinguishing government as a speciality, which was reflected in the structure of the organization. The staff included dedicated 'governance advisers' who were grouped into a 'governance' division working both in London and overseas. In 2005 there were still some 80 such advisers. However, those working in the UK are now divided between geographical sections and about 20 'policy teams', focusing on issues such as corruption, migration, urban and rural development. As with much of the British civil service, many of the governance advisers drew their expertise from being 'responsible' for the topic within the organization rather than from substantial personal knowledge or experience in their role. The specialized division focusing on governance is now part of a larger division concerned with governance, conflict and social development.

The publicity surrounding the Thatcher government's changes to public administration in Britain had an impact on the content of the aid programme. Recipient countries were eager to obtain information on what was being introduced in Britain, and in some cases to try some of the changes for themselves with help from Britain. This interest was demonstrated by the flow of visitors, many funded by the aid programme, from governments worldwide to see what the Thatcher 'revolution' meant in practice. Budgets, management accounting, privatization, outsourcing and executive agencies all attracted attention, so much so that the civil servants responsible for these changes had to make specific time available in their schedules to fit in the many visitors.

In the early 1990s the Conservative government began to discuss the significance of the quality of government for the effectiveness of the aid programme. The Foreign Secretary, Douglas Hurd, first publicly referred to the link between good government and development. He said that programmes should take account of potential recipients' record on government, by which he meant the competence of their government institutions as well as their democratic credentials (Hurd, 1990). In 1992 the Minister for Overseas Development argued that the policy of promoting good government was not an excuse to cut the aid programme nor an attempt to promote Westminster-style democracy. It was neither neo-capitalist nor neo-colonialist. It was designed to promote pluralist systems – which in political terms meant democracy. 'We firmly believe that democratic reforms are necessary in many countries for broad based sustainable development' (Chalker, 1991).

British Council

The British Council, which is primarily the cultural agency of the British government, has also been involved in promoting good government, either under the auspices of the aid ministry or on its own. The British Council's key areas in the governance field are human rights, access to justice, corruption, and supporting open and accountable government. It has a governance programme in about 90 of the 110 countries in which it is active, spending about £16 million in this area annually. It operates governance projects for other donors through its development services department. Elsewhere in this study there are references to some specific programmes or projects supported by the Council. To take the example of one country, Mexico, projects there were aimed at strengthening public administration, the rule of law, human rights and the role of the media and civil society in development. There, as ever, strong emphasis was placed on practice in Britain, with the focus on civil service careers, the so-called 'Best Value' initiative, health service reform, children's rights and citizenship and the criminal justice system.

The British Council organizes conferences and seminars, dispatches experts to help governments rethink their policies on government, and provides lecturers for discussions at colleges of public administration. It has run large-scale contracts for ODA/DfID and provides essential in-country back-up and support where the aid ministry does not have its own offices. In doing this it effectively extends the local reach of DfID and the Foreign and Commonwealth Office while carrying out its primary function to spread understanding of British culture. In 1995 the Council issued a leaflet on good government which said, rather despairingly, that 'good government cannot be precisely defined. It is a set of ideas about the legitimacy, competence and accountability of government, about respect for human rights and the law which together add up to what most people expect from those who rule over them' (Goldsworthy, 1995).

In Britain as in many other countries a change of government produces a new aid policy. Since 1997 the British government's aid programme has been focused on poverty alleviation as a primary objective. Britain has played a significant part in the elevation of poverty alleviation as a priority for the donor community. The United Nations Millennium Development Goals (discussed below) have given expression to this priority. Projects aimed at improving government still feature prominently in the programme, but they are now explicitly seen as instrumental to poverty reduction. In 1997 the new Labour aid minister said:

> In the past DfID promoted good government by supporting the strengthening of government as a good in itself … in the future we will look at government from the perspective of poor and disadvantaged people. We act to strengthen government institutions so that they can better serve those with the greatest need. (Short, 1997)

Four years later the connection between good government and other objectives was made clearer. Clare Short's introduction to *Making Government Work for Poor People* stated uncompromisingly:

> Building the institutions of an effective, democratic modern state is the most important condition for sustainable development ... We are determined to avoid the hectoring attitudes of the past that were often associated with the term 'good governance'. Too often OECD governments were simply trying to replicate their own institutions or to blame governments for the fact that they lacked the capacity to do what was needed. (DfID, 2001b)

By 1999 the British Council too had 'repositioned' itself. The Council's focus was that of the government: spreading the values of human rights, civil liberties, democracy, the rule of law and good government as part of an ethical foreign policy which 'placed human rights at the centre'. The Council's new programme was called 'Governance and Society'.

Britain was also involved in the expansion of the EU to the east of Europe. It established a modest programme of assistance to the applicant countries, to the other former Communist countries and to the Soviet Union. The expenditure, channelled through the 'Know How Fund', was based in the Foreign Office but managed jointly with the aid department. The fund had a representative in the British Embassy in each country involved in the programme.

OTHER DONORS

There are many other donors – not all linked directly to governments but drawing funds from a range of sources to support specialized interests in specific areas. The US and Germany have a long tradition of research institutes, funded often by private trust funds, and the numbers of research institutes interested in aid and government issues has risen in recent years in many countries.

Stiftungen

In Germany, the independent donors include the party foundations, or *Stiftungen*. One result of their partisan background is that they make no secret of their political views. One of the most prominent is the longest-established, the Friedrich Ebert Stiftung, set up in 1925 and banned by the Nazis, embodying the values of social democratic parties. It describes itself as 'committed to the ideas and basic values of social democracy'. It is funded mainly by the German government, to a total value of some 110 million euro a year. It has offices in 70 developing countries, where it aims to support democratization and strengthen civil society. In Latin America it has funded a regular annual training programme on government management and strategic policy-making for senior officials from all countries in the region.

The Konrad Adenauer Stiftung is a post-war creation. It is similar in most ways to Friedrich Ebert, though it is linked to the Christian democratic wing of politics. It operates in over 100 countries worldwide, with a total spend of over 100 million DM. In Asia, it has organized conferences on human rights, Shariah law and democracy, the rule of law and corruption. In the early 1990s it set up offices in the Baltic states and Lithuania, where it concentrated on helping Christian democrat and conservative political parties, briefing them on the rule of law, party democracy and the working of a social market economy. A Lithuanian observer described the foundation as 'not only … observing and analysing the political processes in our country, but … also … actively involved in them'. When the two Lithuanian conservative parties, which had formed the majority coalition between 1996 and 2000, lost heavily in the elections and subsequently split, this defeat was described as 'a painful experience for the … Foundation'. Thereafter the foundation worked actively to reunite the centre-right parties (Jonaityte, n.d.).

Open Society Institute

Better known than the German foundations is the newer system of organizations with broadly similar aims, set up or supported by the financier George Soros. His Open Society Institute (OSI) is described as a 'private operating and grant making foundation', whose aims are to shape public policy to promote democratic governance, human rights, and economic, legal and social reform. The OSI was created in 1993 to support foundations already established in Central and Eastern Europe to help countries to make the transition from Communism. The Soros Foundations network now covers more than 60 countries, spending some $400 million a year. In 2004 it set up AfriMAP, a project whose purpose is to monitor African states' compliance with the standards adopted by the African Union in good governance, democracy, human rights and the rule of law. AFRIMAP is starting its work in four countries: Senegal, South Africa, Mozambique and Ghana.

Ford Foundation

Many other foundations are active around the fringes of the government field. The Ford Foundation boasts that it has been promoting democratic values since its foundation, and has focused directly on public management. In Egypt in the 1950s it made grants to establish national planning and development agencies and to train staff for them. Later, it funded efforts to strengthen the rule of law and to protect human rights, providing legal assistance and funding monitoring activities. More recently, it has focused more on non-governmental institutions and activities grouped under the broad heading of 'civil society'.

One recent grant was to a US school of public policy 'to conduct research and policy dialogues on the standards of accountability for international economic advisers engaged in development and nation-building activities'.

Project Liberty

In the 1990s there was a proliferation of activities and organizations, many based at universities, think-tanks and research centres, to promote the skills of government, especially in the newly democratizing countries of East and Central Europe. One example was 'Project Liberty', based at the Kennedy School of Government at Harvard. Funded by several major US charitable foundations, and directed by the former British Cabinet minister Shirley Williams, the project expressed its aims as helping the newly elected leaders of its target countries in building stable pluralist democracies and creating an environment for economic growth, improving the technical competence and policy-making skills of government officials, and creating an East–West network. In the early 1990s Project Liberty held conferences and workshops on privatization, decentralization and the role of women in politics and enterprise, in Poland, the Czech Republic and elsewhere. It ran training programmes in several countries, and a series of classes and lectures in Ukraine. The visiting team was usually led by Shirley Williams, included a number of Harvard academics and others, and made much use of the Harvard case-study method of teaching. In Ukraine the students politely suggested it would be helpful in future to use examples from Ukraine rather than North America (private information).

Westminster Foundation for Democracy

The Westminster Foundation for Democracy (WFD) is a small-scale, multi-party equivalent to a German *Stiftung*. Its history strikingly illustrates two major themes which are only too familiar in organizations working to improve government. First, how good intentions and a conviction of the desirability of the objectives can militate against systematic thinking and good management and, second, how strong is the organizational urge to compete, even when collaboration might be more effective.

WFD was set up in 1992, when the initial excitement at the fall of Communism was strong and donors were starting to show a greater interest in government. It is technically what is called in the UK a 'quango', a non-departmental public body, funded directly by the Foreign and Commonwealth Office (FCO). Its aim is to achieve sustainable political change in emerging democracies, working with political parties and other partners. Half of its grant is spent on projects devised within WFD, and half on projects put forward by the British political parties who provide eight members – a majority of the WFD's 14-strong governing board.

WFD has worked in Sierra Leone, Bosnia and Herzegovina among other countries. By 2004 it had received nearly £40 million in government grants, including funding from DfID, other public sector bodies and the private sector. But ten years after its establishment WFD was in chaos. In 2002 it was described as being 'at crisis point', its effectiveness was open to question, its financial and management systems were said to be close to breakdown. The FCO commissioned a review to examine whether the WFD was needed at all and, if so, whether it was structured and working on the right lines.

The report, published on the FCO website, reveals all too clearly how, when 'democracy' is the theme, prudent management practices can fly out of the window (Foreign and Commonwealth Office, 2005). The report suggests an almost complete lack of understanding, by those who planned WFD activities, of the complexity of the problems in this field and the difficulty of making any impact on them. In 2003–2004 WFD ran 341 projects in 62 different countries – in Europe, Africa and elsewhere. The average spend per project was about £9000 – down from £11 700 in 2000–2001. Case studies showed projects started, suspended, restarted, sometimes left incomplete and sometimes producing no final report. Grant-making was mostly reactive, with no guiding framework of programmes country by country. There was no effective evaluation scheme. The report noted that 'To date, WFD has been mostly reliant on anecdotal evidence for assessing the impact of its work.' Cooperation with the two other major government-funded bodies working in this field, DfID and the British Council, was described as 'sporadic'. WFD's relationship with the British Embassy in Belgrade had been 'quite distant'. On the other hand it was noted that the FCO, whose six programmes in its Global Opportunities Fund include 'Democracy and Good Governance', had done nothing to address the strategic relationships between these programmes and WFD (Foreign and Commonwealth Office, 2005).

WFD published its response to the report in March 2005. It objected to the report's focus on the whole of WFD's lifespan, rather than on the most recent two years when its working arrangements, it said, had been greatly improved. In April the FCO announced a three-month consultation exercise on the future of WFD (FCO, 2005). But the report implies that, if WFD continues in existence, whatever improvements may be made in its management, its strategy will still be open to question. WFD would, like so many other organizations in this field, be likely to continue to pursue its own objectives regardless of the wider context or the activities of its 'competitors'. For example, in Kenya, where its total budget in 2003–2004 was £78 000, WFD is reported to have identified three draft objectives: promoting representative democracy, engaging the electorate, and promoting effective political communication. As if these objectives were not sufficiently ambitious, WFD has suggested a further longer-term objective, subject to funding being available: 'promoting the growth of an independent and professional civil service'. There is no suggestion either that any of these objectives might be thought somewhat ambitious even for a large organization, or that others might already be active in the same area. In 2001 the World Bank launched a Public Sector Management Technical Assistance Project in Kenya with a total value of $15 million. It is hard to see what value WFD could possibly add with its chaotic management and modest budget, and no apparent specialist skill.

Donor Inconsistency

In the area of government, as with aid in general, the nature and the scale of donor activities depends only partly, and sometimes very little, on any objective characteristics of the recipients. Aid is, however reluctant many aid enthusiasts may be to recognize it, an instrument of foreign policy; as such it is likely to be used to further national policies towards particular countries and within the international community. The common thread which links the recipients is the donors' subjective belief – collective or individual – that in each case there is a 'problem' which can best be addressed by the loan or donation of finance. But the problem can have many aspects. It may be internal or external in character, it may be commercial, humanitarian, geo-strategic or political. The weight given to characteristics of each type may differ at different times, or between different donors: it will depend, not on the needs of the recipients, but on the wider domestic and foreign policy aims of the government which funds the donor. For no country is altruism the sole basis of its aid programme – including activities focused on improving government. One of the most thoughtful studies of the moral and political bases of international aid concluded, in the early 1990s, that 'probably about one-third of aid can be attributed to direct donor self-interest' (Lumsdaine, 1993). This is crucial to understanding why countries' and multilateral aid programmes take the form that they do, and why donor coordination, widely accepted in principle, is so hard to achieve in practice. It also partly explains the wide fluctuations over time in the flow of aid to particular countries or regions. One group of countries, of which the Congo is an outstanding example, experienced the consequences of shifts in the geo-political situation during the period between the 1960s and the 1990s, when they were seen by the capitalist and the socialist powers as crucial to the conduct of the Cold War, although their role was usually more passive than active. In the late 1980s Tanzania, a major recipient of aid from the UK, found its aid reduced sharply during the Thatcher government because of its role as a 'frontline' state advocating independence for countries in southern Africa and criticizing Western economic ties with South Africa. Official doubts about Tanzania diminished with the change of UK government in 1997; since then UK aid to Tanzania has doubled – although, to put the UK contribution in context, it has been estimated that Tanzania receives aid donations from at least 50 different sources. In the early twenty-first century the countries of Central Asia emerged from centuries of global obscurity as the West, using aid among other instruments, attempted to build relationships with them to contain the spread of terrorism from the Islamic states to the south.

Donors will often have different criteria for helping, or ceasing to help, particular countries. These criteria may often be expressed in the conditions laid down for providing assistance – conditions which increasingly refer to standards of government. The example of Zambia is instructive. In the 1980s, as Zambia sank further into a morass of debt and corruption, and cancelled its agreements with the multinational institutions, the bilateral donors increased their support. In the 1990s the bilateral donors, focusing on the quality of government among other aspects of Zambia, took exception to the government's activities and cut back their aid support. The multinationals, more concerned with economic performance, were impressed by Zambian economic reforms and simultaneously increased their contributions (Devarajan et al., 2001). Much the same has been true of Uganda, rated among the most corrupt countries in the world. 'Donors prefer to ignore this and hold on to official growth indicators, which enable them to keep betting on a winning horse' (Doornbos, 2003). Other countries have been subject to considerable pressure to develop multi-party competition, while Uganda's 'no-party' regime was for many years implicitly tolerated.

Criteria are applied differently to different recipients. Numerous small countries have been reproached and, in some cases, had aid suspended for violations of electoral procedures or for levels of corruption which, for example, in China, have passed largely unremarked. Democracy promotion tends to take second place to more conventional objectives of foreign policy. Encouraging democracy was not the primary purpose of US support for Marcos of the Philippines, Selassie in Ethiopia and the Shah in Iran; the USA and other donors were willing to condone some distinctly undemocratic behaviour by aid recipients, such as Nyerere in Tanzania, Mengistu in Ethiopia and Mugabe in Zimbabwe (Schraeder, 2002).

It has been remarked of the EU that 'Europe has never decided whether it wants development aid to be an instrument of its diplomacy or an autonomous policy with its own objectives and rationale' (Santiso, 2002b). Much the same is true of most other donors.

One country which has never disguised its attitude to its aid programme is Japan, much of whose aid goes to other Asian countries. It has always unambiguously used aid as an instrument for achieving foreign policy objectives – never more clearly than when the head of its fisheries ministry, discussing Japanese efforts to secure support for its opposition to the international ban on whaling, told an Australian television reporter:

> Japan does not have military powers, unlike the US or Australia ... Japanese means are simply diplomatic communication and overseas development aid. So, in order to get appreciation of Japan's position, it is natural that we must resort to those two major tools. I think there is nothing wrong. (BBC News, 2001)

Lack of Donor Coordination

The ambiguity of the donors' aims and objectives, together with pressure from domestic agendas, economic and trade issues, contribute significantly to one familiar problem – the much-criticised lack of coordination between donors and their programmes. Donor agencies, bluntly, need projects to survive, and in practice are in constant competition with each other for the influence that can lead to the best projects, the closest relationship with senior officials and the projects most likely to succeed. Successful projects enhance individual prestige, build up the size and budget of the donor agency, please the politicians at home and generate positive international recognition. With different interests, different procedures, different timescales and reporting requirements, the donors collectively place immense burdens on their often overstretched clients. They also often fail to maximize the benefits of their own programmes by failing to coordinate them with those of other donors, and indeed by failing even to inform other donors of their intentions and activities.

In this situation obtaining the contract is more important than finishing the project. A Nicaraguan minister of planning had 300 visits from donors in a single year; it was only when he asked them to bring the evaluations from their earlier projects with them that the importuning visitors were reduced to a small trickle (private information). The Tanzanian government receives over 1000 donor delegations a year and has to prepare about 2000 reports to donors (World Bank, 2004d).

The next chapter considers the host nations – the recipients – how they figure in the process of donor politics and policies and how their relationships with the major donors work in practice.

NOTE

1. This comprises the funds provided by governments and official agents of donor countries, including contributions to NGOs. It does not include either private flows or money raised privately by NGOs (Browne, 1990). These figures were kindly supplied by Roger Riddell.

4. The recipients: the host nations

The donor organizations provide most of the resources in the relationships that determine the distribution of aid to improve government. People in Washington, Paris, London, Geneva, Brussels, Tokyo and Berlin decide what money should go where, who should compete for it and who should win the contracts to spend it. Even though the money may be borrowed from the bank, as in the case of the World Bank, the client gets little say in what happens. Although the donors are fond of expressions like 'partner'or 'local champion' it is commonly clear to all involved that it is the donor managing the project. In the case of the Bank, a project will often be labelled 'a World Bank project' – even though the Kenyan or Ecuadorean taxpayer will eventually foot the bill.

Billions of dollars are directed annually at the perceived problems of the recipient countries, some – though not all – the poorest on the planet. As mentioned above they share, above all else, the belief on the part of the donors that there is a problem which can best be addressed by the loan or donation of aid.

VARIATIONS AMONG RECIPIENTS

The Development Assistance Committee (DAC) of OECD provides lists each year of the countries which receive support. It shows where the aid comes from by donor and the totals each recipient country received. The top ten recipients of aid of all kinds, including government, from the countries reported by the DAC in 2002–2003 were, in order, Congo, China, India, Pakistan, Serbia and Montenegro, Egypt, Mozambique, Afghanistan, Russia. Some but by no means all of these states are manifestly poor. Assistance is also given to 'middle-income countries' including not only Russia but also Chile, Colombia, Georgia, the Czech Republic – nearly 100 in all. The justification for including this group, as expressed by DfID, is that their 'governance systems have not responded quickly enough to [political] changes. This has meant dysfunctional governance including political systems which exclude the poor, corruption, and civil society structures which fail to address the needs of the poor' (DfID, 2001c). In the recent past, over 40 per cent of UK aid expenditure has gone to these countries. This expenditure has recently and understandably come under considerable challenge, not least because of the inadequacy of the definition and the relative wealth of the countries in the group (Eyben and Lister, 2004). Current DfID policy is to reduce the share of aid going to the middle income countries, so that by 2005–2006 90 per cent will go to the low-income countries (DfID, 2003b).

The recipients, even more than the donors, are not 'a community' and vary significantly in a number of critical dimensions. Failure to take account of the scale and the significance of these variations is a major reason why many of the efforts to spread good governance are so irrelevant and ineffective. The needs of the recipients of aid or technical assistance can be very different. This observation may seem obvious but it needs to be stated because the donors tend to think in labels. A recipient country may be faced with a suggestion for a project which fits a worldwide donor programme, but which is neither appropriate nor a priority for the recipient. A country may be in a situation of civil or international conflict, post-conflict recovery, in economic crisis, in political crisis or simply have a stable but inadequate government which has difficulty responding to local needs. Even in the increasingly familiar chaos of post-conflict recovery, where the need for state-building is manifest, no simple model can apply. The degree of support will need to vary according to the nature of the conflict and the residual strength of governmental institutions as well as to all the cultural nuances which make up a nation. Thus Afghanistan was, and is, a deeply primitive society which has never developed the institutions of a nation-state; Iraq, by contrast, was a relatively wealthy and sophisticated society in which the authority of the state, however flawed its political foundations, had been well established for three-quarters of a century. One of the most damaging aspects of the American-led invasion of Iraq was the sustained onslaught which followed on many crucial state institutions, most notably the security services.

State institutions may be impressive on paper but ineffective in practice. A recent analysis of failures of economic reform in Latin America concluded that:

> Enhancing governance and strengthening accountability remain the defining challenges of Latin American unstable democracies. Government ineffectiveness and ineptness are a major source of ungovernability. The states in Latin America lack the capacity to assert an authoritative presence of law and order. (Santiso, 2003)

Brazil, for all its sophistication, has seen corruption scandals which have destroyed the credibility of one administration after another. It has been commented that whatever the superficial appearance of African states, beneath the surface old networks still rule. Networks, moreover, that cannot perform the tasks that need to be performed today:

> Africa's states do not have administrative structures that reach from the government to the people. Even if governments are committed to delivering books to schools or drugs to clinics, few outside Botswana and South Africa could deliver them. There is simply a lack of human capacity and infrastructure. (Dowden, 2005)

Geography and history are among the main influences which shape governments and affect the impact of attempts to change how they work. Recipient countries vary in every dimension – in physical size, history, population, culture, geography and government structure. The simple issue of size alone indicates how different these countries are. Contrast on the one hand Russia with its 145 million inhabitants, 17 million square kilometres, 89 federal sub-units and 11 time zones with Western Samoa's 162000 people and 1700 square kilometres, or Dominica's 72000 people and 750 square kilometres. All these countries, and many more in between, are clients for advice about government; but the geographical contexts vary so greatly that the advice must take account of this.

Many recipient countries share a colonial past, but all colonies were not equal any more than all empires were run in the same fashion. For some, colonial rule was relatively short. The British Empire had its main period of expansion in the eighteenth and nineteenth centuries, the Spanish and Portuguese in the sixteenth and seventeenth centuries. In Africa barely two generations have passed since most of today's sovereign states were colonies of Britain, France or Portugal. From their former rulers they inherited not only common languages, but also systems of government and many of the assumptions that go with them. A World Bank publication observed that 'in several countries, particularly in South Asia and Africa, the colonial imprint is still evident in administrative systems, land and property rights, and state–society relations. This legacy … can often limit the options available to contemporary reformers of public management systems' (Girishankar, 2001). The extreme form of patrimonial state prevalent in Zaire/Congo for much of its post-independence history has been seen as part of the heritage of the despotic personal regime of King Leopold of Belgium (Kiakwama and Chevallier, 2001).

Much the same is true of those large parts of Central and Eastern Europe and Central Asia which were, even more recently, part of the Russian Empire. Many of these countries have found it difficult to emerge from the patterns of behaviour which were a legacy of decades of Soviet rule. The visibility of the colonial past of many countries can make it too easy to forget the pre-colonial legacy, whether of Mughal emperors, Zulu tribes or Mayan civilizations. All have an impact on the way that citizens of their successor states view their government.

In some parts of their Empire, notably the Indian subcontinent, the British left well-developed institutions of government which could be adapted to serve the purposes of the newly independent states. This was much less true in Africa, where countries inherited governments and public services of widely differing quality. Ghana had one of the best in Africa, with many local professionals in senior positions, while in Tanzania and Zambia there were so few local graduates that it was difficult to fill the posts that were vacated by expatriates. But hurried though the end of the British Empire was, the departing power did at least attempt to hand over some kind of system in running order. Elsewhere, different attitudes prevailed. Symptomatic of the attitudes which informed the Portuguese in their African empire, before their belated scramble out in 1974, is the multi-storey hotel building which still stands unfinished on the beach in Maputo.

Externally some imperial connections have endured. Countries inherited continuing relationships not only with former colonial powers, as Mozambique with Portugal, but also with other former members of the same empire, for example Mozambique with Brazil. Many countries of the British Commonwealth after 40 or 50 years of independence still preserve signs of their past in civil service grades and styles of official behaviour, in some places continuing to use the rule books left behind by the British. Commonwealth countries share an inherited language and at least traces of an approach to governance. The fairly relaxed approach to rules and the need for legislation which characterizes 'Westminster-style' democracies with informal rules, leaning heavily on custom and practice, contrasts acutely with countries with constitutions based on the Code Napoleon or heavily constrained by legal structures that can be changed only by constitutional amendment. This difference has helped to build bridges between Commonwealth countries, while making the fault lines within the European Union all the more obvious.

Russia, by contrast, is itself a former imperial power, not unlike Britain or Portugal; many senior Russian officials are still smarting under the recent loss of empire and of great power status, humiliated by the assumption that they need advice from outsiders and often reluctant to accept the changes the outsiders suggest. In the early years after the fall of Communism many outside advisers working on projects in Russia had been somewhat hastily transferred from other regions of the world, including Africa; some did not find it easy to adapt their style to this different context.

In this mix of influences language is one of the most evident legacies. The patterns of Spanish and Portuguese exploration and conquest are clear from the languages of South America, although English is increasingly the predominant second language. In Africa and India, English is common, particularly in government. The international organizations also operate mainly in English so that, for example, Angola has greater difficulty in dealing with outside advisers who do not understand Portuguese than does its neighbour, South Africa, where English is the principal language of government.

A country's political and social history, including the extent of its experience of well-managed government or of democratic institutions, directly affect the institutions and style of its government. The familiar grouping of 'Central and Eastern Europe' includes the Czech Republic which, as part of the old Czechoslovakia, was once one of the most culturally and politically advanced states of Europe with 20 years' experience of fully functioning democracy. Even under Communist rule in the 1950s and 1960s it had a vibrant underground cultural and intellectual life, linked to a highly sophisticated and effective dissident movement. However, the same group includes Romania which, after the collapse of the Hapsburg Empire, suffered a period of corrupt and dissolute monarchy and, after 1945, was governed by Communist rulers who became increasingly notorious for corruption and extremism. In some cases politics can be more significant than geography.

The larger grouping of 'former Communist states' includes Russia, the collective experience of whose citizens had embraced 60 years of totalitarianism following upon centuries of Tsarist tyranny. It also includes the republics of Central Asia, recently components of the same union, and for centuries before that governed by primitive and arbitrary despots. The presidents of Turkmenistan or Uzbekistan are autocrats whose style of governing would be completely recognizable by the independent khans who ruled for centuries before the Russians came, and whose status as aid recipients owes much more to their geo-strategic significance than to their own interest in improving their governance. But it also includes the tiny Baltic states; though successively dominated by Nazi Germany and by the USSR, these managed to preserve quite remarkable degrees of distinctive nationalism and receptiveness to the principles of democratic self-government.

Elsewhere, other variations in the nature of countries' history and political systems affect both their attitudes to government and their capacity to implement advice. In Latin America the historically common resort to military dictatorships has left some countries little time to develop experience and appreciate the nature of multi-party politics. In South-East Asia, Vietnam is one of the few countries in the world still ruled by a Communist Party where independent civil society organizations are virtually unknown.

Variations in resources of all kinds among the recipient countries are wide. Material wealth as measured by GDP per head has enormous variations: Haiti's $50 or Sierra Leone's $130 compare with Brazil's $3490 or Hungary's $4550 (2003 figures). Within countries too the distribution of wealth is far from equal, and in many countries is getting worse. The capacity to improve the economic base of many countries has been severely damaged by the condition of their infrastructure. Years of war in some African countries have smashed almost beyond repair roads, railways, telephone networks and other resources crucial to the business of governing and building an economy.

Human resources, because of the condition of many education systems, are also a constraining factor – and in many countries a critical one. Some countries combine low levels of schooling and literacy with some highly educated elites. Again history or economics has given rise to wide differences. In Mozambique, the Portuguese did not see any need to educate Africans; illiteracy in Mozambique still runs at about 60 per cent. Compare this level with Zimbabwe's literacy rate of 90 per cent in the 1990s – although this may be very different in 2005. In Brazil, literally thousands of Brazilians have graduated from American business and public management schools with masters degrees or doctorates, while children in the *favelas* are fortunate if they get two or three years' schooling, a symptom of Brazil's huge gulf between rich and poor. Other Latin American countries are in a similar position; in the 1980s and 1990s ministers of finance in Argentina, Chile, Colombia, Ecuador, Mexico and Peru had economics PhDs, although overall education standards – with the single exception of Chile – were low (Grindle, 1996).

In African countries, even where efforts over the years have started to build up a professional class with the skills needed for work in a modern economy and in government, as elsewhere the number of people available is subject to a constant process of attrition because of the impact of AIDS – a continuing threat to the whole of the developing world.

The effectiveness of outside interventions can be affected by the condition of the existing institutions of government and the physical infrastructure which supports them – whether staff, office equipment, buildings or internal systems. Even in post-conflict situations much of this may survive. Events such as the American dismissal of the Iraqi army, or the widespread physical destruction wrought by former colonial powers as they left their African colonies, are fortunately rare. Varying patterns were seen in four Southern European states as they made the transition from dictatorship to democracy: in Spain competent, non-partisan bureaucrats stayed on and largely managed the transition; in Portugal, there were widespread purges in a bureaucracy closely identified with the old regime; in Greece there were limited purges; in Italy after 1943 pro-Fascist officials were simply allowed to fade from the scene (Sotiropoulos, 2004). In Czechoslovakia after 1989, purges in the judiciary greatly hampered later attempts to use the courts to establish and confirm citizens' property rights.

RELATIONSHIPS BETWEEN RECIPIENTS AND DONORS

Material resources directly affect another important variable – the extent of a country's dependence on aid and its independence of the donors and their prescriptions. Aid is equivalent to 24 per cent of central government expenditure in Bolivia, 77 per cent in Uganda and even more in Mozambique where this ratio peaked at 150 per cent in 1998–99. In some countries the major donors – the World Bank, the European Union and the main bilateral donors – have been established and active for years. They are effectively participants in the process of government, and as significant in that role as any minister. Some countries are in the middle of their second, fifth – or in one recent case in southern Africa, their tenth – civil service reform project. Relationships between the donors involved and their trusted intermediaries in the recipient government are closer than many relationships within the government itself.

Recipients have faced problems in handling offers of external advice. After 1989 countries in Eastern Europe were not only the recipients of some generally well-managed programmes of assistance, notably the UK 'Know How Fund', but were also the targets for large numbers of Western consultants trying, not always scrupulously, to secure profitable contracts to advise them on such matters. By the turn of the century there had been a certain amount of disillusion on both sides, but much had been learned – both about governance and about how to use advice (Struyk, 1997; British Embassy Warsaw, 2002). Both Poland and the Czech Republic declined the proposals of the World Bank for assistance and turned elsewhere for support.

Globally, there are a large number of donors: many countries are the recipients of advice and assistance from a bewilderingly long list. Tanzania has received aid from more than 50 bilateral donors. In Zambia in the 1980s the main bilateral donors included Canada, Denmark, Finland, Germany, Japan, Netherlands, Norway, Sweden, the UK and the USA. Each of these relationships has to be managed individually. The economic and political self-confidence to refuse assistance is relatively rare, especially when there are pressures to conform to the demands of the international community. Post-apartheid South Africa was particularly robust about external advice. At a World Bank conference on sub-Saharan Africa in 1995 the newly appointed officials were blunt in discussion with one of the authors: 'we'll take free advice if it makes sense but we are not paying for anything – we can do it ourselves'. Carol Lancaster reports a very similar episode (Lancaster, 1999).

Many recipient countries find the processes of aid difficult and, in some cases, humiliating. Being not only lent or given money but, more significantly, being told explicitly what to do with it, can be damaging to their sense of nationhood and deeply offensive. Even more damaging is the apparent irrationality of the distribution of project funding which may depend on the particular interests of an ambassador, or domestic political pressure on a donor in some distant country. The personal preferences of a diplomat are one thing, the pressures of geo-politics may be another, but the results can be similar – a sudden surge in interest in and support for a particular topic which may have nothing to do with what is happening in the recipient country.

In their dealings with recipients, donors are continually hampered by their past history and by the strains of a rich–poor relationship. These strains are in large measure a consequence of the gulf between the employees of a wealthy and powerful international body and their counterparts in a recipient country. The donors – bilateral as well as multinational – do not always seem to the recipients as disinterestedly benevolent as they might wish to appear. A recent article in an African newspaper expressed a familiar viewpoint:

> Traditionally, Africa's development partners have been the wealthy nations of the west, most of whom colonised the continent in the past … The same wealthy nations have over time set up funding and lending institutions that have grown over time into empires of their own. Such institutions that readily come to mind … are DfID of Britain, USAID of the USA, SIDA of Sweden, CIDA of Canada, GTZ of Germany, the World Bank and the IMF among others. What [the New African Partnership] is championing is the philosophy of home-grown partnerships as opposed to total dependence on foreign partners whose interests and priorities may not necessarily rank Africa's issues on the top of their agenda … (Okungu, 2005)

Geography and history can both influence what might be called the 'status' of less-developed countries as actual or potential recipients of aid. During the Cold War the United States was more concerned even than before to maintain friendly regimes, however undemocratic, in Latin America. Latterly and improbably, Uzbekistan has had considerable status due to its geographical position in Central Asia. Similar considerations have bolstered the relationship between the Philippines and the US, and between France and the Côte d'Ivoire.

Compared to the donors there is little material available on the record about the views of the recipients. They have fewer resources for research and fewer opportunities to express their views; complete frankness on their part may risk jeopardizing future possible sources of funding. Unusually, in the mid-1990s the British Council ran two private conferences in England to discuss 'public sector reform' for ministers and senior officials from countries from every continent. This provided an opportunity for an open and general discussion of what had been achieved over decades of intervention in their countries. Many of them had had to cope with IMF prescriptions for structural adjustment. The discussions were held without any representatives of the donors and, apart from the independent facilitators, no one else was present. The group's conclusions were forthright – and were of a kind seldom heard from so senior a group.

The participants agreed that reform was difficult to manage and that they had problems, common to many of them, with the process of reform, but the main message was that there was a steady and consistent pattern of experience with donors that gave cause for concern. They argued that the donor agencies did not appear to understand the nature of the problems to be handled in reforming a state. They had unrealistic views of the sequence to be followed, the timescales involved or the means of measuring success or failure. As serious was the inability of their experts to anticipate problems that had arisen, or to warn of possible difficulties. In the early 1990s the donors were trying to support institution-building and to reduce the scale of public spending and employment. In most cases they had exaggerated the effectiveness of improved institutions and had seriously underestimated the resource and transaction costs of the changes involved in restructuring the public sector.

The participants in both seminars were emphatic that recipient governments could not look to the donors for expertise, or even competence, on government reform. This was despite the fact that the donors had been working at reform programmes in many parts of the world for decades. They argued that the staff of the donor agencies did not appear to the recipients to have any method for learning from experience – potentially one of the most valuable benefits from having external help.

The experiences described by this group were much the same whether the individuals came from large or small governments, countries in crisis or countries with reasonably stable governments and economies. Their experiences were also broadly the same with all donor agencies. The problems mentioned seemed to be inherent in the nature of the relationship as well as a consequence of poor management by either side. One minister had been startled in a recent election when groups of electors had brushed aside all the party propaganda and had simply demanded better public services. Another from another continent nodded her head: 'We found the same thing, the management of public services was what really enraged our electors.' There was a division between ministers and officials. Ministers appeared optimistic that reform was possible and would be difficult but could be achieved. Some officials shook their heads in despair; they argued that senior officials knew what was needed but political support vanished at the first sign of trouble and, in most cases, trouble was inevitable. The international agencies could provide useful pressure, but too often governments, inexperienced in this field and threatened with economic sanctions by the IMF, were pushed into accepting a reform programme that they knew was unrealistic or unsuited to local conditions.

In 1996 a group of African countries presented their analysis of the position in their countries at a meeting with the president of the World Bank. They began by stating: 'if there is one obvious lesson to be drawn from the experience of the generation after independence in Africa it is the crucial importance of establishing good governance'. But they went on to say:

> there are severe capacity constraints in literally all sectors in almost all countries, characterised by a shortage of skilled staff and weak institutional environments ... [E]ven where skills are available they are under utilised because of poor deployment, a weak institutional environment, lack of morale, or political interference in administration and the assignment of responsibilities.

The group pointed out that adjustment programmes had been specific in terms of wage bill limits and reduction in civil service employment – the relatively easy part of structural adjustment – 'but are usually vague or even silent on how to implement restraints without further damage to morale and the effectiveness of the public service'.

The report of this meeting points out that this 'erosion' of capacity is all the more remarkable in the context of the multiple civil service reform and capacity development initiatives supported by donor agencies during the 1980s and 1990s. The report records that it had been estimated in 1992 that there were approximately 100000 expatriate advisers working in the public sectors of sub-Saharan African countries, at an annual cost of more than $4 billion – the period to which the African leaders were referring (OECD, 2000).

Inevitably donors have to make assumptions about recipients. Difficulties arise when assumptions are wrong or derive from misunderstandings. One source of difficulties is the working assumption that any specific recipient government can be regarded and treated as a single actor – and that, as a result, a government's apparent commitment to change will be recognized as binding by all the organizations and interests which form part of the government and need to be involved. This assumption presupposes a degree of internal discipline and cohesiveness, which is unlikely to be present within the governments of most countries and perhaps especially those with a crisis of governance. The consequence is that elaborate plans may be made and finance committed to a reform programme which has no guarantee of acceptance by those not directly involved in the planning, but on whose support its success depends. Even where an official commitment to reform is sincere and widely shared, circumstances and personalities change. A change of minister or senior official can wreck a project which appears to be going well, by simply putting it down the order of priorities and therefore depriving it of critical support.

In any case, recipients do not necessarily share the views of donors on what is an optimal political solution. People may agree for tactical reasons that they are in favour of democracy. But, as experience in the countries of the former USSR has shown, democracy may take very different forms in different countries; apparently free elections can lead to very different results. Problems can arise from the interpretation put on expressions which are, on the face of it, in common currency. For example, in Romania, a few years after the fall of the Ceausescu regime the government was anxious to establish a modern approach to administration. They wanted to demonstrate how much government had changed; it was now run for the benefit of the people, not for that of the old state bureaucrats. OECD sent in Western European experts to help. A discussion of customer service was met with blank expressions; the eagerness of the local Companies Registration Office to modernize was tempered by a strong resistance to changing familiar patterns of working.

'Of course we want to give citizens what they want,' they assured one of the authors.

'How will you be changing what you do?' she asked.

'We will change nothing', was the reply. 'If citizens are unhappy they are now free to complain.'

Together with coordination, 'partnership' or 'ownership' is one of the themes most emphasized in the literature over recent years. The first is seen as the means to the second. The importance of involving recipient countries in the planning and implementation of change is acknowledged by donors; so is the case for ensuring that plans and programmes are not simply foisted on recipients by donors, but are genuinely 'owned' by the former. The papers produced by OECD, the World Bank and DfID emphasize that they are aware that they need to hear from and work with recipient countries. An OECD workshop on evaluation in Tokyo in September 2000 concluded: 'Several important challenges were laid down … in particular the need for much fuller involvement of developing country partners in the evaluation and learning process.'

Unfortunately, there are too many instances where the mantra of partnership with recipients simply does not translate into action. For example, the workshop in Tokyo, mentioned above, was led by the Japanese government under the auspices of OECD. Of the 91 participants, only 11 were from recipient countries, representing six countries. In the report of 115 pages, six pages dealt with 'involving partners', even though the recommendations for recipients – insisting on involvement in evaluations, developing a culture of recognizing the value of evaluations – are difficult enough for the donors to achieve within their own organizations, much more so for the recipients. A major bilateral aid agency recently commissioned a report on the effectiveness of their aid on governance, but explicitly forbade the expert writing the report from discussing the question with any recipient countries. Another recent report on the capacity of recipients to manage capacity development projects says blandly, 'it has not been possible during the course of the study to consult or exchange ideas with any of the recipient governments or institutions'. The list of those consulted in this instance runs to three pages, 14 institutions and 49 people, the bibliography to 34 pages (OECD, 2000). There is no suggestion in the text that that this gap detracts from the validity of the conclusions.

The development of 'pro-poor strategies' by donors threatens to introduce a more, not less, prescriptive approach into their relationships with recipients. In many ways it is logical of the donors thus explicitly to focus their policies on poverty, and on poverty reduction as the desired outcome of activities relating to government. But insistence on poverty reduction does not necessarily take account of recipients' existing economic and social policies. It risks reducing local ownership – especially in cases where poverty reduction is not high on the government's agenda. One country moving fairly into the middle range of development on hearing of this change was incensed at this challenge, as they saw it, to their priorities. In the Ministry of Finance, they were dismissive: 'That's not our priority, it just not how we look at the issue. It's no help to us' (private information).

Some of the flavour of relations between donors and other bodies they deal with come through in a report by DfID in 2001 on the workings of the Commonwealth Secretariat, a small institution which provides assistance to members of the Commonwealth who share common systems and much common history. The tone is kindly but undeniably patronizing. The report is called an 'institutional strategy paper' and was produced by DfID to show how the department 'aims to achieve our objectives in partnership with the institutions concerned'. The report however loses all tone of partnership very quickly. In its summary the writer said:

> The Commonwealth Secretariat's development activities cover a broad agenda. The programmes are disparate and lack focus. In some areas the CS assistance lacks the critical mass to make a significant impact. With limited resources the CS needs to play to its strengths in a limited number of areas whilst building on strategic partnerships with other international bodies to deliver support to its members. The governance arrangements for the CS are cumbersome and hamper effectiveness. There is a need for governance and administrative structures to be streamlined.

The report spoke warmly of the value of the Commonwealth Secretariat, despite being only 'a small player in the development field'. Its membership was diverse, but shared a common heritage in, among other things, administrative and legal structures. It had a commitment and mechanisms to promote democracy, the rule of law, just and honest government and fundamental human rights. It could promote South–South cooperation.

However, the paper continued, these advantages were often not fully exploited. The fragmentation of the Commonwealth inhibited its members from working together or from developing effective relationships with other international development agencies. The Secretariat, with its own clumsy governance arrangements, and a proliferation of unconstructive committees and meetings, did too little to pull things together, not least because its limited resources were too widely spread. The Commonwealth could play a particular role in promoting 'democratic and effective government, rule of law, conflict resolution and the promotion of human rights', and in developing a 'focused programme in this area'. And so on. In spite of the jargon-ridden language the message throughout the report was clear. If the Commonwealth Secretariat smartened up a bit it might help DfID achieve its targets; there appeared to be no mention of any targets the Secretariat might have of its own (DfID, 2001a).

Attempts to develop a partnership approach often come up against the problem of conflicting priorities. This goes back a long way. It was observed by the Americans in Latin America in the 1920s, where a diplomat observed that local politicians did not want the democratic system they were being offered; they wanted power. The combination of domestic pressures on the donors, and their confidence in their own prescriptions, can lead them to ignore the views of recipients and to propose changes that do not necessarily meet local needs. Failure to regard the other parties' views as significant or worth listening to is unlikely to foster a sense of partnership.

The relationship between donor and recipient is bound to be an uneasy one. It is bedevilled by different priorities, policies and cultures. It is hampered by the large flows of money. It is to the credit of the people who work directly together in recipient countries that they can overcome these obstacles to achieve some positive results. The following chapters consider the systems that operate to provide assistance to recipient countries and the evaluation of the effectiveness of that assistance.

5. The system and its objectives

In the early post-war years aid tended to focus on achieving specific development objectives in the recipient countries – improved transport links, economic development, better education and welfare. The possibility of improving the quality of government was seldom explored, even though almost all aid was processed through government agencies. Furthermore, whatever the formal objectives of aid policies, the process of implementation, in general or in detail, was seldom seen by the donors as a matter of concern.

Where changes in government institutions were in question, the prescriptions were not complex. Especially in Africa, the dominant donor view was that the public sector was consuming an excessive share of national resources. The main need, therefore, was to reduce its size and cost. Civil service 'reform' programmes concentrated on reducing the numbers directly employed by the state and the size of the wage bill, with a secondary emphasis on improving human resource management, raising real wages and 'decompressing' salary scales to ensure that those at the top were paid significantly and adequately more than their subordinates. The capability of the state and the quality of the services which it provided were not matters of concern. Where the programmes of reform succeeded in reducing numbers the consequence was, as many commentators have argued, that state capability was negatively affected. But all too often even objectives simply defined numerically were not met.

FOCUSING ON GOVERNMENT

As aid budgets increased in size, questions of public sector management became more significant, stimulated in part by the recognition of weaknesses in their own public sector institutions by the governments of the developed world. In Britain in the 1980s the Thatcher administration developed an increasingly radical agenda for reforming the management of government. Progress in Britain was watched and to some extent copied by other countries where institutional weaknesses were posing similar problems – poor budgetary control and ineffective implementation of social welfare programmes. The efforts of the British government to improve the financial and managerial competence of the public sector demonstrated how much there was to be done even in the most developed economies. In less-developed economies the donors, frustrated by the unresponsiveness of institutions and activities at one level, were tempted to see the causes of failure to reform elsewhere and to turn their attention there. Observing this one commentator said:

> it was as if the donors were going up the ladder of causation, from projects to policies to the way in which countries were governed. The concept was variously interpreted; in its most narrow sense it referred mainly to public administration; at its broadest it embraced issues of human rights and democratisation. (Cassen, 1994)

The main practical question has long been which aspects of government were key and, more recently, how 'good' was to be defined. For the World Bank, which has invested substantial resources in drafting definitions, the main relevant dimensions were originally, in 1992, public sector management, accountability, the legal framework for development, information and transparency. From 1996–97 the Bank started to place a new and heavy emphasis on corruption, and its eradication. In 2003 the Bank listed three critical dimensions of government – the processes of selecting, monitoring and replacing governments; the capacity to formulate and implement sound policies and to deliver public services; and the respect of citizens for the state and for the institutions that govern economic and social interactions among them. They 'unbundled' these into six concepts which they considered measurable: voice and external accountability; political stability and lack of violence, crime and terrorism; government effectiveness; lack of regulatory burden; rule of law; control of corruption. These concepts were then used to select hundreds of indicators, worldwide, derived from surveys of citizens, experts, firms and others, and which were analysed as proxies for various aspects of governance (World Bank, 2003a).

For the British Overseas Development Administration (1993) good government was legitimate, in the sense that it allowed citizen participation and rested on their consent; it was accountable, which required the existence of specific internal processes, and the existence of free media; it was competent, in both making and implementing policies; and it respected human rights and the rule of law.

By 2001 DfID's paper *Making Government Work for Poor People* had a more elaborate account. It listed seven key capabilities which it saw as essential to the quality of democratic government. They were:

- To operate political systems which provide opportunities for all poor and disadvantaged people to influence government policy and practice.
- To provide macroeconomic stability and to facilitate private sector investment.

- To implement pro-poor policy and to raise, allocate and account for public resources accordingly.
- To guarantee the equitable and universal provision of effective basic services.
- To ensure personal safety and security with access to justice for all.
- To manage national security arrangements accountably and to resolve differences between communities before they develop into violent conflicts.
- To develop honest and accountable government that can combat corruption. (DfID, 2001b)

These were, in effect, stringent and wide-ranging government-related conditions, which would have to be met before further aid would be provided.

The UNDP has said that 'Good Governance addresses the allocation and management of resources to respond to collective problems; it is characterized by participation, transparency, accountability, rule of law, effectiveness and equity.' Its longer definition is a telling illustration of how the definition becomes more difficult as the authors struggle for greater precision:

> the exercise of economic, political and administrative authority to manage a country's affairs at all levels. It comprises the mechanisms, processes and institutions through which citizens and groups articulate their interests, exercise their legal rights, meet their obligations and mediate their differences … Governance has three legs: economic, political and administrative … Political governance is the process of decision-making to formulate policy. Administrative governance is the system of policy implementation. (UNDP, 1997)

The DAC has its own definition of governance, which overlaps largely with those above, but has so far been unable to agree on indicators of good government.

A term which entered the development discourse in the 1990s is 'capacity-building'. It is worth mentioning here less because it has serious analytical and descriptive value than because otherwise its somewhat haphazard occurrence in the official and academic literature (see for example World Bank, 2005) might puzzle the casual reader. One writer has suggested that it refers more to an alternative approach to the development process, rather than describing a specific set of activities. He himself uses the term to mean creating 'the long-term capacity of developing countries to analyze and address their own development problems', so as ultimately to make donors superfluous (Schacter, 2000b).

The emphasis on government as a focus for aid efforts developed in parallel with the growing weight given, by the World Bank and the IMF in particular, to conditions for adjustment loans. In the 1960s and 1970s conditions were aimed mainly at improvements in the management of money and credit, government expenditure and revenue and exchange rates. Later, detailed loan conditions focused on specific expenditure cuts, for example in military spending, government administration, public sector pensions and environmental protection. In the 1980s the new emphasis on improving public sector management was reflected in loan conditions which embraced virtually all aspects of government – privatization of public enterprises, tariff reductions and trade liberalization, civil service reform, reform of public expenditure procedures, public procurement and local government, human rights and justice systems, citizen involvement in decision-making, transparency and competition in political processes. In April 2005 the British government cancelled £5 million out of £40 million aid promised to Uganda for 2004–2005, justifying this change in policy on its view that 'insufficient progress had been made towards establishing a fair basis for a multi-party system'.

Conditionality in this sense has been much criticized – on the grounds that it constitutes excessive interference in countries' internal affairs, that conditions are likely to be imposed on the very countries least able to meet them, that as a result they are too often not enforced, and that attempts to compel changes by external pressure virtually guarantees that without local 'ownership', they will not be sustained. In late 2004 the UK government – having perhaps forgotten the highly conditional tone of its earlier prescriptions in *Making Government Work for Poor People* – issued a discussion paper on conditionality, declaring that 'we believe that it is inappropriate and ineffective for donors to impose policies on developing countries. Instead, we argue that successful aid relationships are based on mutual commitment and dialogue, transparency and accountability' (DfID, FCO, Treasury, 2004). The World Bank announced its own review of conditionality in early 2005, and invited comments.

It has been suggested that with the collapse of Communism the donors, led by the World Bank, wanted a new basis for the conditions with which they controlled the use of their financial assistance. This was the genesis of 'good governance' – a flexible and highly ambiguous term which could be used both to legitimize their intervention in the internal management of recipient states, and to distinguish between states deemed to be deserving and others – 'a political tool justifying and rationalising choices that are made on other, possibly arbitrary grounds' (Doornbos, 2003). This interpretation may be correct, but if so, it suggests a degree of purpose and coordination by the donors that has rarely been manifested in other contexts.

The focus on governance as a theme in aid programmes added a new dimension to attempts to assess the effectiveness of aid. The arguments about this have raged for years. In governance the difficulty is compounded by the nature of the subject matter and the reluctance of the donors to recognize it as of a different order from many traditional aid projects where most inputs and outputs are visible and often measurable. The complexity of what is attempted, the ambiguity of objectives, the timescales involved and the frequently uncertain relationships between cause and effect combine greatly to complicate the task of analysing the effectiveness of the activities involved.

There is also the continuing uncertainty as whether the quality of government should be judged by results or by process. It is far from clear how, for example, exceptional competence in policy-making might be identified, and how far it would excuse an authoritarian style of government which allows for minimal participation. If what citizens want is clean and crime-free streets, does it matter if this is achieved by draconian penalties for littering and imprisonment without trial for suspected robbers? A consultant with long and recent experience of Pakistan expressed the firm view that that country was much better governed under the military dictatorship of General Musharraf than under the chaotic, deeply corrupt, nominally democratic administrations that preceded him.

It is salutary to recall Lee Kuan Yew's musings on this theme. 'People of all countries need good government. What is good government? This depends on the values of a people … Whilst democracy and human rights are worth-while ideas, we should be clear that the real objective is good government' (Sebastian, 1999). Amartya Sen and, recently, spokesmen for the donors have argued that this apparent choice is not a real one: economic growth, development and the consequent material benefits are fostered by democratic government and by proper respect for human rights (Sen, 2000).

On the other hand, there is much room for debate about the universality of approaches to government. As the Israeli academic Yehezkel Dror has put it:

> Different countries need quite different governance systems in terms of both principles and structure. Governance in such different democracies as India and the Netherlands is and has to be different in significant respects. Countries with different political ideologies and theologies, such as China and Iran, have and require unique governance set-ups … (Dror, 2001)

It has been suggested that for many leaders in Asia, 'western concern for areas such as human rights … are seen as unwarranted interference at best and as revealing ulterior motives at worst' (Sung Yoo, 1999).

The donors have used the 'good governance' label for some time and appear content to continue to use it despite its defects as a means of defining a set of objectives or indeed outcomes. It has raised suspicions about the underlying objectives of programmes of government improvement:

> Donors often have strong pre-conceived notions of what constitutes 'good' governance. This often results in local traditions and accountabilities being undervalued and undermined ... Donors take an 'Alice in Wonderland' approach to governance, so that it means whatever a donor wants it to mean ... Many in the South ... are asking whether the donor concerns for 'good' governance are no more than repackaged structural adjustment programmes ... (Reality of Aid, 2004)

POVERTY REDUCTION

Indeed as a new set of concepts giving overriding priority to poverty reduction came to the fore they did not replace good government but simply supplemented it in the donors' armoury and, more significantly, added a dimension focusing on outcomes. The donors' new insistence on poverty reduction, as the primary objective of aid programmes of all kinds, laid more emphasis than before on government. Since 1999 borrowing countries have been under pressure to produce Poverty Reduction Strategy Papers (PRSPs). These are strategic documents describing the economic, structural and social policies to be carried out over a three-year period with the aim of reducing poverty in their countries. The PRS process has been controversial from the first. It assumes an overriding priority in the recipient country to eliminate poverty. It presupposes a capacity for comprehensive planning on a scale which the developed countries have long abandoned as impracticable for themselves – although donor assistance is, of course, available to help with this. As a World Bank paper pointed out, 'poverty reduction requires governance reforms that the poorest countries are in the weakest position to undertake' (Shah, 2002). A joint Bank–IMF review made the same point even more clearly:

> The development of PRSPs is a major challenge for low-income countries, both in terms of analysis and organisation. Besides managing a complex policy dialogue with development partners, low-income country governments have to put together an integrated medium-term economic and poverty reduction strategy, complete with short- and long-term goals and monitoring systems; *these are a set of tasks that few industrial countries could systematically do well.* (emphasis added) (IMF/World Bank, 2002)

The same issues are raised by the Millennium Development Goals (MDGs), although their scope is even wider. The eight MDGs were agreed at the UN Millennium Summit in September 2000. All 191 UN member states have since signed up to them as goals to be achieved by 2015. The goals were to eradicate extreme poverty and hunger; achieve universal primary education; promote gender equality and empower women; reduce child mortality; improve maternal health; combat HIV/AIDS, malaria and other diseases; ensure environmental sustainability; develop a global partnership for development.

These goals are supported by more detailed targets, with some quantities and some intermediate dates – for example, for the 'child mortality' goal, 'reduce by two thirds the mortality rate among children under five'. Some of the targets are unmeasurable – for the environmental sustainability goal, 'achieve significant improvement in lives of at least 100 million slum dwellers, by 2020'. DfID has described the goals as being part of 'a wider attempt to encourage the international community to stop talking about making a difference in the developing world and join forces to start doing something about it'. It has commented that although 'some significant progress is being made towards meeting some of the targets in some of the affected countries, in many cases progress is patchy, too slow or non-existent'. (DfID, n.d.(c)).

In the past there would have been little discussion about the means for achieving objectives such as the MDGs; a mere statement of aims so self-evidently desirable would have been thought sufficient, and questions about implementation would have been left unanswered. Today there is growing emphasis on government, and a belated recognition that goals of any kind will not be reached unless countries have the public institutions and the skills necessary to use resources – indigenous and external – effectively. Symptomatic is a chapter in a 2005 UN publication, explicitly entitled 'Governance to achieve the Millennium Development Goals'. The first sentence of this chapter states: 'The successful scale-up of investment strategies to achieve the Millennium Development Goals requires a commitment to good governance' (UNDP, 2005).

The chapter describes the two-way causal relationship between good government and poverty; countries without adequate resources cannot afford the investments needed to support good government, while well-governed countries are more likely to be able to develop and implement the policies needed to reduce poverty. It recommends that every developing country's long-term MDG framework should include a strategy for strengthening governance. It distinguishes countries without the political will to improve their governance or to meet the MDGs, from those countries which have the will but lack the resources. For the first group there will be no real scope for long-term development policy until the current regime departs. For the second group it proposes investment and reforms in six main areas: public administration, rule of law, transparency and accountability, political and social rights, sound economic policies, and civil society. Surprisingly, given the significance of land ownership in many rural societies, property rights do not figure in this list.

The issues of monitoring achievements and dealing with the obstacles to success remain unresolved. The decisions in July 2005 to cancel some of the outstanding debt owed by developing nations to the international institutions, even if fully implemented, will take time to produce results. The need for radical improvements in the standard of government in many developing countries has now received more attention than ever before. But it is not apparent that the legitimate desire to see better-run and more stable governments is informed by a realistic appreciation of the effort, problems and time involved in making substantial progress.

THE ROLE OF DONORS

The flow of information and advice in the government field is essentially one way – North–South. Much of this derives from the practices of government in the major donor countries and the major Western powers. This is overlaid with the experience gathered by experts and consultants who have worked in a range of developing countries on government projects. This experience is often factored into project plans, but local experience and customs of governance are seldom built into the planning process. A classic example of how little attention is paid to relevant local experience emerged at the start of the Iraq war when offers by the Arab States to assist in Iraq were reportedly brushed aside by the US during the preparation for war; this at a time when 'building a coalition' was said to be a major US objective.

The government industry is donor-driven; almost all its projects are complex processes in their inception, planning and operation. They involve a range of people with very different objectives and widely varying motivation: contract officers, host governments, contractors, local officials, donor governments, politicians and electorates. The interplay between these different groups determines the planning of reforms to parts of governments and whole governments: the defining, advertising and letting of contracts, the process of contracting, its impact on the host government and the outcome at the end.

The key to understanding what goes on is to remember that the mainspring of the whole process is competition. Donors compete for 'local resources that will help validate their activities; good projects to fund; the assistance of local politicians and bureaucrats in expediting their programmes; and the secondment of the best local public servants to manage their programmes' (Moore, 2001). There is also competition between recipients and donors for observation of their priorities, and between potential subcontractors for contracts – new or renewed. The pressures of competition tend to force most of those involved to carry on doing things in the ways that they know best; the result is that much of the rhetoric, about the failure of traditional approaches and resolutions to do better, is not reflected in practice.

Government projects and programmes, like other forms of aid, take shape within the framework of the donor's current aid strategy for the country – in the UK case, embodied in Country Assistance Plans. Most of the major donors have offices in the capital cities of the principal recipient countries. In the case of the bilateral donors these are often physically located in their country's embassy. Local representatives are not always experts in the government field. The initial responsibility for working up proposals for projects rests with these locally based officials. They are described as experts, but 'experts' may be a relative term; one experienced consultant commented that DfID's experts might spend two years in post without initially knowing the region or speaking the language, and with only such expertise as they picked up doing the job. However, DfID's 'governance advisers' in general have a good reputation among consultants. Some of these problems are avoided by recruiting advisers locally. First-hand experience of reforming governments and assessing proposals for their realism and effectiveness is a scarce but essential skill at the early stages of project design. Relatively thorough arrangements were set up by the UK for the Know How Fund in Central and Eastern Europe in the 1990s, when there was a dedicated adviser in each embassy involved. However even these were, significantly, specialists in the procedures of the Know How Fund, rather than in government; in general, and probably inevitably, organizational skills to manage the donor's role take precedence over relevant expertise in the recipient's needs.

A flavour of how projects are identified by donors is given in the account of DfID practice in a recent National Audit Office report:

> Country staff ... told us that many projects followed-on from previous projects in the same geographical or sectoral areas, extending the project's life or deepening or broadening its scope, as new challenges emerged. Some resulted directly from requests for assistance from local communities or non-governmental organisations with specific projects already in mind. Others from consideration with the host nation of its development plan – which included some projects, such as those in the governance area, which reflected DfID analysis of development needs. Country staff said that finding good development projects, capable of being justified by research or experience, compliant with development strategies and likely to lead to sustainable improvements, was no easy task. (NAO, 2002)

To establish a programme or project, 'governance' advisers, or their equivalent, talk in varying degrees of detail and depth to representatives of recipient governments about needs and priorities as seen locally. This activity is normally undertaken by a series of visits from the local or main office. At best there will be several meetings to discuss proposals; at worst, one meeting supplemented by written papers and proposals. In some cases relatively junior staff discuss issues of government of which they have little direct knowledge, other than from reading papers, with senior officials and ministers whose agenda is very different and who are often attempting to engage the donor in their area of work in general, rather than seeking to promote any specific project. Some programmes of reform are better structured. They may have been based on previous in-depth exchanges, such as a series of seminars, visits and discussions which have provided a recipient country with a clear programme of their own and ideas on the advice and support they might need which they have been able to specify in precise terms. Thus, part of the modernization programme in Brazil of the Cardoso administration, during its first term, was based on a decision to set up new federal agencies after extensive investigation of different models. The Brazilian minister concerned knew exactly what he wanted.

In Russia, by the late 1990s the government had developed its own thinking and its own extensive networks of local experts, often very well informed about developments in other developed states. It needed neither to borrow funds to finance its civil service reform programme, nor to employ overseas advisers, as had been the case at the beginning of the decade. The World Bank, interested in participating in the programme, was required to produce a summary paper about the current situation; this was scrutinized by the Russians before Bank participation was approved.

In many cases project proposals emerge as a result of many months of discussion and debate. Some are more serendipitous. A friendly call by a senior ambassador on a newly elected minister or president has been known to result in a request for assistance in some area of concern. Ministers need all the help they can get and international interest would be a bonus; the ambassador can demonstrate how close he or she is to the senior levels of government; and the donor agency gets another project.

Problems can arise where the recipient, having ceded the initiative to the donor or even their subcontractors, has a change of mind, and tries to modify the nature of an activity. 'While the recipient may argue that national development priorities necessitate such a change, the [providers] strongly resist any brief that is not donor-sanctioned or approved' (Banerjee et al., 2002). In a Latin American case, extensive preliminary work and visits were followed by seminars given by visiting experts; the donor thought the seminar format useful and wanted to continue the successful model that had been used. The recipient government simply wanted continued contact with advisors who could help them, and agreed to the donor's proposal apparently as a way of maintaining the contact. A formal technical cooperation agreement was drawn up and duly signed and a contract for seminars was awarded after competitive tendering.

What was not explained – or understood – was that if the official documents specified seminars, seminars would be provided. By the time the expert arrived, ready to set up the seminars and recruit the expert lecturers, the recipient government no longer wanted seminars, but one-to-one advice over the whole area of the central departments of government. The donor had its process to follow and was irritated at a change to a formal intergovernmental agreement; the expert had to try to explain the position to each side and broker a modification of the contract. What should have been a good working relationship became difficult and unrewarding for both sides. In this case, poor project preparation and a failure on both sides to understand the implications of the agreement was made worse by the length of the process of arriving at the formal agreements and letting the contract (private information).

Some flexibility in the interpretation of contracts is essential. Activities in the governance field are inherently unlikely to proceed on precisely the lines originally proposed and planned. Governments change, individuals change, the background politics change. If projects, once approved, are not to become completely irrelevant they are bound to need some opportunistic modification. But in practice, once the terms of reference have been approved and the contract for a piece of work has been let, little variation is likely. The official responsible may be too inexperienced to grasp the need for any modification in how the work is done, and too junior to authorize this. Treating contract management, in this way, as a routine low-grade administrative task, has further consequences. It greatly inhibits the donor's ability to learn from the process, since the work done no longer corresponds to the specification on the record. On the other hand, it may encourage the contractor to play safe and to stick to the letter of the terms of reference whether or not these seem still to make sense in the changed context.

The donors, having established the need for and content of a programme, may then contract out project design to a consultancy or use one of their in-house advisers. As for the recipients, in an ideal world governments would have their own strategic framework, or at least a list of priorities, against which offers of assistance from donors, multilateral and bilateral, would be assessed and into which these would be fitted in an orderly and mutually complementary way. Different agencies within each government would be careful to ensure that their projects were consistent with the overall strategy. Donors would be fully aware of past, current and planned activities funded not only by themselves, but also by other donors, and would take full account of these in making their own proposals.

In practice several factors affect the way the participants behave when donors and recipients are considering new governance programmes and projects. For much of the history of these activities they have been 'owned' not by the notional clients – the governments of the countries being assisted – but by the donors. For many consultants it is far from clear whose view should prevail in a dispute – a demanding minister in the recipient country or the desk officer back at the donor agency. In one case an enthusiastic and determined reform minister was thunderstruck to discover that the consultant's report on progress was sent to the donor agency. He considered the project as his, and the consultant as a member of his staff; no one had indicated that the donor might take a different view. There was a serious issue of confidential government information going to the donor agency; the recipient government was quite unprepared for this to happen (private information).

In another more recent example, differences of view developed between the recipient's reform management unit and some donors about the publication of a report of a multi-donor financed study. The recipients said that the report touched on such politically sensitive matters that they should choose the timing of publication. Some donors tried to insist that the report should be published without delay as evidence – to be used by them – that the funds had been spent as budgeted. Others argued that the report was, morally and legally, the property of the recipient government for whom it had been written. One participant observed that there seemed to be 'a certain haziness' about donors' expectations on such matters (private information).

Most new projects are planned and implemented competitively. Despite the growing significance of the international financial institutions and other multilateral donors, most aid is still provided bilaterally. This is true even within the European Union and its member states.

Many donors do not deal with recipient governments collectively, but with separate sections or agencies within them that may have their own interests and development programmes – ministries of finance, education, health and so on. One result of these relationships, between donors and individual ministries and agencies, is that the financial implications of new proposals are frequently not integrated into a wider aid budget – or indeed into the government's budget as a whole. Unless there is a fairly sophisticated government-wide system for moderating aid bids and balancing the overall aid budget and the diplomatic balance between donors, such 'off-budget' activities can take place without any reference to the availability or suitability of resources of any kind, or to the longer-term implications. To some extent this tendency to fragmentation can be offset where a government has a central unit responsible for managing and coordinating the activities and funds of donors, as in the Foreign Ministry in Brazil, or in Chile. In Tanzania the government has devised an 'assistance strategy'; this provides a framework for the interaction of donor activities, which are in turn defined by 'agreed notes' negotiated with donors. This process helps to align donor resources more closely with the government's priorities (Mulley et al., 2005). This kind of coordination is uncommon. Coordination units can, on the other hand, act as a filter or bottleneck between donors and isolated enthusiasts for change scattered around the government.

Responsibility for planning and implementing projects is shared between three different types of actors, whose purposes, timescales, perceptions and interests may – and usually do – vary. The donor, which normally controls the timetable and the processes, tends to be driven by its own internal agendas, responding to pressures which may reflect domestic politics or multilateral policy rather than the direct interests of the recipient government. One pressure is the 'pressure to spend' – to ensure that legislators can see that budgets voted are fully disbursed. This can lead to unrealistically short timescales for complex pieces of work. The consultants under contract have their own problems and priorities; delays can mean a change in personnel, conflicts with other contracts or increases in costs. The most significant participant in the process should be, though often is not, the recipient government. The recipient may have instigated and planned the reform plan of which the project or programme is a component, but its role in the planning of the donor contribution may be as a relatively passive participant from the sidelines.

Chapter 7 discusses the interaction between reform programmes and local politics, and the problems created when programmes are derailed, when support for them ebbs away or opposition becomes uncontrollable. In principle such possibilities are taken fully into account in planning projects. Contractors are asked to set out the 'assumptions' which underlie their plans in the 'logical frameworks', known as 'logframes', which they complete at the start of a project. (Logframes are discussed below.) Such assumptions can include, for example, 'continuing political commitment to change' or 'stability of government' or of 'key staff'. In practice donors are reluctant to abort or suspend projects once begun – at least partly because this immediately endangers their objective of spending their budget within the budget period. As a result, they will often fail to take action even if assumptions are falsified by events.

CONTRACTS AND CONTRACTORS

Recipient governments may negotiate the content of any activity with the donor. This may be done in broad outline; or it may be done in terms of mutual agreement on the detailed terms of reference for consultants to design and implement specific projects – although the latter has been unusual. If the process is within Europe it must conform to EU requirements for public sector contracts, covering issues such as notification, elapsed time and advertising. The invitation to tender and the detailed terms of reference are then published, sometimes only to a shortlist of possible contractors, again with a time limit within which tenders must be submitted. Firms shortlisted by DfID are usually informed of their competitors on the list, a helpful device when they come to emphasize their relevant strength and competitive advantages.

The details of the process vary with the size of project. It can be lengthy. Much takes place out of sight of the recipient governments. Problems can arise when too much time has elapsed between the initial visit to define the project and the letting of the contract; in the case of the EU two years is not uncommon, and on one occasion in Africa the interval was as long as seven years. If the contractor has found it necessary to recruit expert subcontractors, they may be unavailable by the time the contract is actually let. Any government determined to proceed with reform would find delays of this kind unhelpful, to put it no more strongly. The time taken to get to final agreement can easily take up the major part of the term of office of the politicians concerned. Conversely, it is not unusual for a new minister to be informed that an expert will be arriving from Washington or Paris to undertake a project suggested or agreed to by his or her predecessor or by a different government.

DfID has recently taken to informing bidders of the weight that will be attached to several characteristics sought. These vary between contracts. A typical recent list, in order of priority, was as follows:

Table 5.1

Characteristic	per cent
Quality of personnel	20
Experience of similar work and track record	20
Experience in particular country/region	20
Methodology	10
Adherence to terms of reference and job specification	10
Commercial evaluation (cost, fee levels, etc)	20

The European Commission has a similar approach. Its categories are:

Table 5.2

Characteristic	per cent
Organization and methodology	
Rationale	20
Strategy	20
Timetable	10

And then a further 50 points divided among each of the experts sought according to qualifications and skills, general and specific professional experience.

In the first case, experience of the country concerned counts for 20 per cent of the marks, in the second it is apparently not considered at all.

Finally, the task of implementing the agreed activity falls to the firm – or individuals – awarded the contract. Specialists such as governance advisers apart, most first-hand experience and, up to a point, expertise in the field of government rests with the army of firms and individuals who bid for and secure the contracts for designing, implementing and evaluating activities of the kind outlined in the terms of reference. The most conspicuous are the major international consultancy and accounting firms, and especially the 'Big Five.[1] With offices all over the world, globally mobile experts and locally employed staff, they are a formidable competitive force. Between 1997 and 2002 DfID awarded contracts, largely in the general area of governance, to the Big Five worth over £118 million (War on Want, 2004). The 'consultancy industry' of OECD member countries is estimated to be worth $4 billion a year in sub-Saharan Africa – equivalent to 30 per cent of total aid to Africa (World Bank, 2004a). In 2005 about 5 per cent of DfID's budget was spent on consultants, down from 10 per cent a decade earlier (Hencke, 2005).

Beyond the really big consultants are a range of smaller though still significant firms: in Britain, Adam Smith International, Oxford Policy Management, Bannock Consulting and many others. The scale of their activities is considerable; thus between 1998 and 2003 DfID awarded Adam Smith new contracts worth over £34 million. Not all members of this group are private sector concerns; one of the most active players is the Civil Service College. The roles of both donor and contractor are played by the British Council, which may find itself in competition with other public and private institutions for contracts.

Below such firms come many smaller organizations, such as Public Administration International, formed from the former overseas consultancy wing of the now-defunct Royal Institute of Public Administration. Though these smaller organizations, like the larger firms, have permanent staff of their own, they also make much use of the army of individual consultants, many of them former public officials, operating on their own account. These individuals are also employed directly for specific contracts by donors such as DfID or the World Bank. Donor organizations keep lists of registered individual consultants. With the business of government reform booming, there is a global need for experts with the right experience and qualifications. Thus, for example, one finds the Washington-based firm AMEX International advertising for 'Democracy and Governance Specialists' to work on a worldwide USAID-funded project. Specialisms sought include experience in one or more of such areas as parliamentary development, electoral systems and processes, post-conflict support, conflict management, decentralization and local governance.

The jobs for which these contractors bid are scattered all over the world and, within individual countries, over all parts of the public sector. They are often advertised in official journals and, increasingly, on the internet. Sometimes they are advertised by word of mouth or to preselected shortlists. We have chosen a selection of the introductions to terms of reference from different donors to different recipients. What is striking is how similar and how vague the terminology is. It conveys little of the reality of the situation in recipient countries. The list of reforms for Uzbekistan appears almost hopelessly optimistic in the early years of the twenty-first century. For Russia and Pakistan the donors appear to be considering support for a process which is decades away:

> [Uzbekistan] The project aims to assist the Republic of Uzbekistan in the advancement of democratic reform to reinforce the development of civil society based on the supremacy of law, principles of human rights and freedom, generally recognised values of democracy and pluralism ... (2001)
>
> [Iraq] DfID is seeking expressions of interest from experienced service providers to provide technical assistance to new key institutions that have been established at the centre of Iraq's Government ... (2004)
>
> [Russia] Lot 1 [of this EU project] is aimed at strengthening the principles of mid-term performance-oriented budgeting in the [Russian] Ministry of Finance and the line ministries ...
>
> Lot 2 focuses on capacity building of Russian civil servants. It foresees the organisation of training programmes for about 140 Russian civil servants in European training institutions to transfer knowledge in the area of public administration ... (2003)
>
> [Pakistan] This [CIDA] program will support Pakistan's transition to democracy, and in particular the processes leading to the devolution of power, the devolution of governance, the decentralization of administration, and the participation of citizens in local governance. (2001)

These are, of course only the introductory paragraphs for much longer documents but, as many contractors have found, donors have both relatively little knowledge of the local political situation and also little understanding of the detail of the technicalities of reforming a state or its public administration. In this situation contractors can, on the one hand, find themselves with a surprisingly free hand. On the other, they may find themselves pressed to deliver results in timescales or in forms which they find completely unrealistic.

Consultants in general are hired as experts – but typically experts in reforming the civil service or public expenditure management, rather than in specific countries or regions. Their competitive advantage may indeed derive from their expertise in current fads and dogmas, such as PRSPs (Banerjee et al., 2002). Their task has been seen as offering advice on the discrete issues defined in the terms of reference for the projects in hand. The larger firms, working simultaneously or successively all over the world, inevitably develop their own approaches to problems and are liable to apply these almost regardless of local context. Particularly in the specialist companies there is a natural tendency to resort to off-the-shelf solutions. Contractors rarely have the time, skills or experience needed to work up proposals specifically tailored to local conditions; consequently they draw on accepted 'best practice' or on what is happening in other countries. The donor officials responsible for contract letting rarely know enough to be able to challenge what is being offered. The authors have sat beside training experts in a bar in a Latin American country, watching them hastily reformating training courses before catching the evening plane to repeat the same performance 2000 miles away. One of the authors was a member of a team working on a project in Moscow, the leader of which was simultaneously engaged on an assignment in Kenya.

The teams actually employed on projects may know little or nothing of the history, culture or politics of the country in which they are to work. They may include no local citizens. They may not speak the language of their clients. Some of the concepts with which they are dealing are quite hard to explain in any language, let alone when mediated through an often only partly competent interpreter. One experienced consultant commented on the difficulty in the 1990s of working in Russia and other ex-Communist countries 'where there is no tradition of, for example, western concepts in accounting and audit, payment by results, performance measurement, etc; one had to teach the interpreter basic accounting first' (private information). As DfID in letting some contracts gives as little as 20 per cent of available points for 'experience of particular country or region', that experience may be very general. However, today donors increasingly stipulate in terms of reference that expatriate firms must work with one or more local partners. This can be very valuable, provided that enough potential partners, of adequate quality, are available. But this is by no means always the case; the absence of suitable local partners may not be understood by donor contract staff remote from the scene. There is another side to this coin. The best-qualified local staff will often be serving or potential civil servants. The more they are poached to help overseas consultants by working on aid-funded projects, the less their skills are available where they are desperately needed.

More significant is the nature of the existing skills base in the consultancy field. This is dominated by the discipline of economics, and by the professional skill of management consultancy. The range of skills available within aid agencies and consultancies has not expanded to keep pace with the evolving discourse on development.

On the other hand, in some cases consultants or their subcontracted experts may know more about the subject matter than do the fund managers in the donor agencies – especially in the case of the EU, where managers' case-loads are at least twice those of their equivalents in other donors such as the World Bank. Consultants inevitably have more general understanding of the processes of implementing contracts than do contract staff, who may never have worked outside their own country – or may never have had to implement a contract. Some consultants will also acquire an understanding of the problems of implementing particular contracts in particular local circumstances. This can lead to tension between consultants and contract staff where the latter insist on implementation timetables which the former feel are unrealistic. An experienced consultant may try to vary the terms of a contract, particularly when it does not specify appropriate activities. But donors do not like variations to their projects or to the agreed plans. For example, there have been cases where verbal agreements to vary a contract have not been transferred to the monitoring system. Turnover of staff and inadequate recording systems pose difficulties when project reviews are based on objectives and targets which have been overtaken by events.

Less conscientious consultants may supply what they were contracted to supply, or may do what they think is interesting whether it is relevant to the needs of the recipient country or not. This is the area where the ambiguity of the roles of donor, expert and client becomes particularly acute. The development of programme-based projects can leave flexibility in the detail, but using this flexibility constructively depends on both knowledge of what is happening in the recipient country and, significantly, on continuity in the donor agency. It can be more difficult to do a thorough job for the recipient than to do a job which meets a donor specification. In the mid-1990s, when detail specification was popular, the government of Ecuador had a reform project funded by the World Bank. The project specification was 2 inches thick and set out detailed activity day by day and week by week. Two years into the project timetable, the Bank's project manager admitted that he had no idea whether what was happening reflected what was in his specification, and had no idea whether the people responsible for implementation had ever seen a copy of the specification. He was ticking off the weeks, not the activities (private information).

That is an extreme case; most donors are now unlikely to prescribe in such detail the work that has to be done. This is because in many cases they simply do not understand the detail. They have to lean heavily on the experiences and preferences of their contractors. In some cases they may of necessity relinquish control over the content of what is done in their name. To take a minor example, in Mexico a DfID contract for public service reform in Mexico was constructed around a series of seminars with supporting advice. The contract did not specify subject matter, handling or scope. It would have been perfectly possible and within the contract for the contractors to have covered subjects which the donor would have preferred to avoid, and indeed to have made recommendations directly contrary to the donor's policy.

More significantly, the contractor's skills and knowledge may or may not be relevant to particular local circumstances. A considerable amount of technical cooperation, quite legitimately, involves explaining new approaches which have been tried elsewhere, particularly in Western European countries. This can be a useful way of encouraging debate and opening up institutions to new ideas. Both authors travelled widely, discussing the changes to the UK public services during the 1980s and 1990s with governments considering reform and trying to identify areas where changes might be feasible. Widening debate and understanding is a valid and important part of international support. But both donors and experts can become too attached to a single solution or to the latest fashions at home and urge uncertain recipients to adopt whatever is popular back at the Bank or in Whitehall.

This can happen where projects are designed to spread similar methods and processes. The World Bank once described itself as having a 'toolkit' of models to fit all kinds of situations. That the toolkit contained models based on developments in complex advanced governments implied that in their eyes the similarities between countries are greater than the differences. Approaches and systems which seemed relevant in one should therefore be equally relevant in another. This led to problems as donors attempted to persuade governments to introduce the latest management fashion. In the early 1990s the World Bank and the British government enthusiastically peddled 'executive agencies' as the answer to management and delivery problems. But the structure for executive agencies was devised to deal with a particular British problem caused by the structure of government departments and the skills, or lack of skills, of senior officials; it was unlikely to suit anywhere else without substantial adaptation. Despite these limitations, executive agencies were described by a senior World Bank official to one of the authors as 'an essential part of our toolkit for reform'.

Consultants insensitive to the context in which they are working can confuse more than they illuminate. 'The cultural naiveté of expatriate consultants is often pointed out. Inability to grasp the logic of why things work the way they do, cultural nuances, work ethics and other unfamiliar features add up to mismatched prescriptions in fields like governance and institutional reform' (Banerjee et al., 2002). In a contract in Central America to provide a costing system which would mesh in with the public administration finance system, the British consultants gave, as an example, a detailed prescription for costing a Western European cheese sandwich, a confection never seen in the hospital concerned – which had no catering arrangements anyway. At a seminar in Warsaw organized for Polish civil servants by an American team, a case-study was presented of the functioning of the Massachusetts Department of Motor Vehicle Licensing. The bewilderment of the Poles was palpable.

Mutual understanding and trust between consultant and clients is essential. This requires both sensitivity by the consultant to the peculiarities of the local situation, and well-managed personal contacts. The latter take time to build up. Unhelpful discontinuity is sometimes deliberately programmed in. The rules governing EU contracts prohibited the same contractor from bidding for successive phases of the same project. One of the authors was a member of a multinational team employed for a three-year project, funded by the EU under the TACIS programme, working on aspects of the President's office in Moscow. Developing mutual trust and collaborative working relationships was a slow and laborious process. By the end of the three years much had been learned by both sides about how to manage the relationship – for the ultimate benefit, of course, of the Russian client. However, the rules required that the original team should stand down. The second phase of the contract was awarded to a completely different team, which started on the whole process from scratch, and without contact with their predecessors.

Insensitivity to context can lead to more serious misunderstandings between consultants and recipients. This was seen in the early days of programmes of assistance for Russia after 1989. 'PHARE got into trouble at the beginning because they employed old Africa hands and African-style technical assistance', recalled an experienced administrator at OECD. 'It went down very badly with the Russian clients.' Other experts attribute the Russian reaction, echoed in some Eastern European countries, to endemic racism. Greater care in selecting the relevant skills and in managing expectations could have helped to offset these kinds of difficulty.

In this context a major contribution can be made to the effectiveness of consultants working for bilateral donors by the local embassy or office of the aid agency. In neither case are activities focused on government necessarily of great interest; hospitals, schools, libraries or motor vehicles are more tangible, more comprehensible and make for better photographs in the local press. Some ambassadors are not interested in any aspect of aid, and prefer to focus on issues of security or commerce. But the interest and the involvement of the local post can make a major contribution to the effectiveness of consultancy activities. Embassy staff can identify key players in the client government, can brief visiting consultants on the politics of the local situation and, where relevant, of the current reform programme. Depending on the extent of their own contacts, they can help to open doors and smooth paths. They can also extend their own network. The authors' task in developing relationships with senior members of the Mexican government during the reform efforts of the Zedillo administration was greatly helped by the efforts of the British ambassador, Adrian Beamish; he supplemented and paved the way to the more formal discussions by organizing informal social occasions, including a working breakfast with ministers and senior officials.[2]

The benefits of such collaboration accrue to the post, too. Activities in the governance field often involve contacts at senior levels in the client government, sometimes with people not well known to embassy staff. Visiting consultants can thus help to open doors in their turn. In the Mexican case, contacts with the President's office helped to reinforce the Embassy's links there; a photograph of the ambassador and the President sharing a platform with the experts at one of the seminars hung in the hall of the Embassy offices. To the extent that the objectives of aid programmes are at least partly foreign policy objectives, the involvement of diplomatic staff can be a worthwhile investment.

ACTIVITIES

The range of activities funded under 'governance' programmes varies widely, taking account of local needs but primarily determined by the money and resources available. In the early stages of the growth in the market, seminars and lectures were a popular form of opening up discussion and widening understanding of the different routes to better government being used in other countries. These were easy to set up and cheap to run. An academic or an experienced public servant could be recruited and sent to a recipient country in a matter of days. Many donors kept databases of people who were happy to respond quickly to this kind of request.

Long-term expatriate expert support has a long history. From the 1950s the British government was sending to former and current colonial countries people with experience of the UK government system or, significantly, of other similar colonial systems. The task of the expatriate expert was to provide support in running the administration or to add specialist skills which could not be supplied locally. Thus judges, parliamentary draftsmen, tax experts, health experts or policemen could make a satisfactory living in considerable comfort, with the privileges of diplomats in many parts of the old Empire. France's overseas postings were particularly popular, as the allowances for being away from France were fixed at a rate where the multiplier was the distance of the posting from Paris; a job in the condominium of Vanuatu in the South Pacific was particularly sought after.

By the 1990s governance support comprised much more than simply modest expert advice. The British Customs Service has an elaborate overseas consultancy operation and was for some time responsible for much of South Africa's customs operation. The suburbs of many African capitals are home to long-term advisers who supply a crucial role in many governments. But much support is also given in short bursts. An expatriate expert may visit the same resident team at regular intervals, perhaps every two or three months, to monitor what was happening and give some help where there were problems. This can be valuable to both sides – it saves expert and expensive expatriate time, and it keeps both donor and recipient in touch with what is happening.

Experience suggests that one of the most successful forms of conveying understanding about the working of government is the study visit – though often resisted by donor officials on the grounds that it is simply a form of externally financed shopping trip. The visitor has the chance to interact with politicians or senior officials and to observe them in the context of their workplace. Where the visitor comes with both interest and an open mind, and where the host is willing frankly to acknowledge the existence of problems and even failures, visits can be used to demonstrate the multidimensional complexity of working relationships in a complex organization, and perhaps even that what might have seemed too difficult or unthinkable is actually possible.

Visits also enable visitors to see for themselves working practices about which they might not have thought of asking. For example, a feature of ministerial life in the newly independent countries of Central and Eastern Europe in the 1990s, which struck any visitor familiar with Western governments, was the minister's office. Here would be two or three low-grade secretaries, typing and telephoning and entertaining others present, and periodically putting their heads round the minister's door to check whether he was on the telephone. There would be several officials of various ranks, who had dropped in while passing to chat to the secretaries or to talk to each other. Sometimes they had come to see the minister, and would go in to see him unannounced. There would be the minister's driver, if he had one. The air was full of tobacco smoke and background noise provided by a radio. In his own office the minister sat behind a desk occupied largely by four or five telephones of different colours, one or other of which would be ringing at any moment and would eventually be answered by the minister himself. All this was normal and familiar, and accepted as such. Much the simplest and most direct way of conveying to those involved that there were other ways of managing was to show them a British minister's office with its elaborate arrangements for filtering and gatekeeping and thus ensuring the minister the time and space to deal only with the issues that he thought important. The visitors may, of course, decide that they prefer their own way of doing things.

The study visit is essentially a private affair which can make possible some frank one-to-one exchanges. The extreme contrast is with multinational, semi-public conferences where government representatives can rarely resist the chance to boast about the success of their own reforms, regardless of the reality, and where the audience, waiting their turn to make similar boasts, are reluctant to challenge the accounts given. In the 1990s the authors organized, with British Council support, two seminars for senior ministers and officials involved in their own reform programmes, at which the terms of reference required those present – to put it simply – to tell the truth. The result was a series of exchanges in which experience was shared about the difficulties of introducing certain sorts of change, and about failures as well as successes. Given that in this field the proportion of failures or partial failures far exceeds that of successes, this made for a much richer field of case material on which to draw. As one of those present said, 'This has been more useful than any meeting with the World Bank – we can learn far more that is valuable from each other.'

To be fully effective an incoming consultant should be aware, as a minimum, of the current political situation, including the imminence or otherwise of elections or governmental change, the strengths and weaknesses of the organizations to which the contract is directed, the identity and relative significance of individuals and factions likely to support or resist any reforms, the value which might be added by meeting specific people or people in specific posts, and the history of current and past activities funded by the employing and other donors. There is also advantage in providing, however subjective, some feel for the local 'climate' both politically and in relation to local reaction to former projects. 'Consultant fatigue' on the part of the recipient can damage the most well-planned project. A donor, anxious to send the best-prepared team, should want to make sure that their staff have been systematically briefed on these and other relevant issues, not left to pick up information at random from other sources.

The authors of this book have completed 50 or 60 assignments in some 30 different countries, working for for DfID, the Foreign and Commonwealth Office, the World Bank, UNDP, USAID, the EU, the British Council, OECD, and the Commonwealth Secretariat. They have never been briefed in this manner for any of them. In the 1990s, in the early years of assistance to Russia, the most effective way of learning what other projects were in hand was to look out for other consultants in the waiting room at Moscow's international airport and to interrogate them. That was only an extreme version of a situation which remains common. A genuine sign of progress is that terms of reference increasingly include descriptions of other projects and the activities of other donors, and sometimes require collaboration with the latter. Reciprocally, the authors have never been 'debriefed', either by the donor which had been employing them or by other consultants working in the same general area, unless they themselves made a specific request for a meeting.

Other consultants interviewed for this book confirmed that both situations are common.

This lack of interest in the lessons of experience is all the more significant when institutional experience is, for whatever reason, discontinuous. Although, as mentioned above, some donors such as DfID do now in evaluating bids give positive weight to earlier experience in the same country or region, it is far from uncommon for several different firms to work, in sequence or in parallel, on major projects without knowing what the others are doing. The pressures of competition militate against information-sharing, to the disadvantage of all concerned.

While attempts are now being made to share some information, this can be very one-way. One of the authors, on a visit to Chile, was asked by the representative of an American agency what had happened at a meeting with a senior member of the government. 'We can't get that kind of access', he said. In another country an ambassador asked to accompany one of the authors to a meeting with a vice-president; startlingly, he said 'I can't get in to see him in the ordinary way.' In a third country the representative of the World Bank, at a meeting set up by one of the authors, said: 'We can't get the kind of general view of what is going on that you get. It's really helpful to hear your views.' The response had to be careful and limited; no one would have spoken as freely as they did if they had thought everything was going back to the major donors. But what was surprising was how inadequate the links and the information systems were between international representatives who lived permanently in the country concerned and were supposed to be building up local contacts.

Another reason for discontinuity is the lack of institutional memory, or at least a reluctance to draw on it, on the part of donors. A striking, if minor, example in the authors' experience is provided by two British Council projects in Israel. In 1998 the authors were asked by the Council to arrange a high-level study visit to Britain by a group of Israeli director-generals (a very senior post roughly equivalent to Permanent Secretary, though more politically influenced). After an extensive fact-finding and briefing visit to Israel by one of the authors, the study visit was planned and arranged, and took place over the best part of a week in September. The D-Gs seemed well satisfied with their programme, as did the British Council. Three and a half years later, an academic was asked by another part of the Council to undertake a project which involved interviewing some 15 D-Gs. He too visited Israel for briefing on the project. He was unaware of the previous project, and was told nothing about it or about who had worked on it. He commented that some information of this kind would indeed have been useful.

At least as striking a gap in the learning process occurs between consultant and completed project. The minimum condition that must be satisfied for lessons to be learnt is that the potential learner should be aware of what happened, or did not happen, as the result of his or her activities. In the case of consultancy advice on questions of government, this means knowing in the first place whether or not recommendations were accepted, and, if they were not, the reasons for rejection. If the recommendations were accepted and implemented, it is at least interesting to know what the outcome was. For example, in a review of the workings of a Cabinet which had recommended better pay rates for the Cabinet Secretariat the first question would be, were rates increased? Did this lead to an improvement in the quality of Secretariat staff? Did the improvement, in turn, enhance the effectiveness of the Cabinet?

As discussed in a later chapter, one of the problems with evaluation in this field is that questions about outcomes are too rarely asked, partly because of the inherent difficulty of relating inputs to outcomes, and partly for reasons to do with the internal dynamics of the consultancy business and with the professional caution of donors and consultants. Contractors themselves are concerned mainly to be paid for the current project and to move on to the next one; medium- or long-term results are not of great concern to them. But at least the facts should be made available, should they wish to learn from these. It is a melancholy truth, and one of the several reasons why learning in this field is so slow and so defective, that such facts, if known to anyone, are rarely conveyed to those who carried out the contract. In only a handful of the present authors' 50 or 60 assignments have they ever had any feedback about any aspect of a completed assignment. In all the cases where feedback was given, it was only as the result of a direct question; the response was brief and clearly informal without any systematic content. The loop is very seldom closed. Experts therefore have no reliable basis for reviewing their analysis or for developing or modifying their advice. The assumption seems to be that neither they nor the donors have any interest in doing so.

LOCAL REPRESENTATION, COORDINATION AND COMPETITION

Donors' local representatives can play an important role in relationships both with recipients and with each other. They can have a significant impact on the process of negotiating a loan or a reform programme. Poor interpersonal skills can damage the relationship between donor and recipient for far longer than the duration of one individual's time in the country, and affect directly how that donor is regarded. In one country with endemic financial problems one of the authors listened to a tirade about an international donor. The local representative had been a bully, programmes were being forced on the government which they all knew would not work, and which the donor knew would not work but which was made a condition of hard currency support. Not only were the government's arguments ignored, but also everyone knew that the outcome was a foregone conclusion which would damage the economy in the long run. There was a serious discussion about the feasibility of asking the donor to leave the country, something which would have appalled the donor's headquarters. The damage done by one person was considerable to both the country and its longer-term relationships with the donor. It also had an impact on relationships with all donors, whose activities were regarded with more suspicion than before.

Inside the donor institutions memories tend to be very short, staff move on and sensitivities to local conditions are cushioned by distance and other pressures. Until recently it has been unusual, in the authors' experience, for even a contracting donor to provide information to its own visiting experts about earlier missions or about the reaction to earlier projects. On what other donors are doing, the silence can be almost total. The World Bank might be mentioned, if only because it is so often present and is such a dominant influence. The activities of other donors – even in the same area of work – seem to be regarded as irrelevant.

Lack of coordination among donors can exacerbate fragmentation on the recipient side. Bilateral relationships established in the past between individual donors and particular sectors – health, education – or agencies will endure despite formal commitments to multilateralism. All too often it suits both parties – donors and recipients – to continue in the same bilateral ways as in the past. One statement from a recent OECD report sums up the position:

> Although there are examples of effective coordination between donors, coordination is generally considered weak ... This is a result of many features including a common belief that donor coordination should be the government's responsibility rather than [that of] donors themselves, the need for agencies to deliver a readily identifiable product; and governments' preference of dealing with donors on an individual basis. Moreover, the evaluations also show that in several instances donors are not able to coordinate their support successfully with the partner government's policies, implementation plans and capacity building programmes. (OECD, 2004a)

One factor inhibiting coordination is the competitive nature of the aid business. Donors are in competition with each other – basically, because bilateral aid programmes are as competitive as the foreign policies of which they are important components, while the international institutions want to achieve their own objectives and to justify their continued existence. Donors compete for the ear of the recipient government, for good project and programme ideas and for openings which would give them influence and a role in a recipient government; recipients rarely appeal for help in vain. Most countries, if their objectives fit those of the donors and if they are prepared to accept donor conditions, however informal, can get support for their projects. Donors sometimes find it harder to find 'customers' for their projects. The World Bank is in an especially difficult position because it has only loans to offer; Bank projects tend therefore to be bigger and include dazzling sums of money.

Competition can incline the donors to secrecy about their activities, which is in the interests neither of the recipient country nor of the management of the reform process. It can also distort the nature of the projects that are finally accepted by the recipient. An evaluation of the Australian aid programme's response to the Asian economic crisis of the late 1990s noted that problems of donor coordination had arisen because 'donors do not want to fully disclose their pipeline projects' (Australian Agency for International Development, 2003).

Both authors were involved on behalf of DfID in a visit to Ghana some years ago, a country with as long a history as any other of constant donor involvement in government. The literature refers to effective donor coordination there, led by the World Bank, going as far back as the 1980s (Devarajan et al., 2001). But in the mid-1990s there was no trace of such arrangements. No one could describe the totality of donor involvement currently or over time. The authors arranged a meeting of the main donors to try to establish what was going on so that a view could be taken of where British help might be most usefully added. The donor representatives then in Accra, from both international and bilateral agencies, said that they had never previously met together to discuss their activities or the impact of these.

Lack of coordination is particularly significant because of the impact of any project or programme on other parts of the system, the inevitable interconnections between changes in governance – and the difficulty of anticipating their consequences. This is important within the structures of a recipient government. It is also important on the donor side; consultants working in a particular field, and unaware of other projects completed, in train or proposed in the same or related fields, will be unaware of information important for their own success. It is not unusual to find similar projects going on side by side and in ignorance of each other. The recipient may be too embarrassed to admit that two similar projects are under way; there may be complicated arrangements to hide the overlap. Sometimes one branch of the recipient government simply does not know that advice on budgetary reform is being provided simultaneously to two different agencies, or even to the same one, by two different donors. The recipient government may gain considerably from receiving different views and different experiences but it seldom gains from secrecy about it.

Things are starting to improve in this respect. Terms of reference for DfID projects now outline the relevant local activities of other donors. Regular meetings of the main donors are held in many centres. Such information, and such meetings, cannot guarantee that any donor will modify their planned or current activities, but they are at least a step towards making such modification possible.

SEQUENCING

Lack of contact between donors has a direct impact on one of the most tricky yet neglected aspects of governance reform – the most effective sequence in which to change interconnecting parts of the system. In most cases proposed activities seem to be treated as stand-alone; they are planned and implemented without reference either to other donors or to the crucial question of whether other steps, which could be seen as creating the essential conditions for their success, have been taken or not. Joseph Stiglitz noted in his polemic on the IMF:

> Perhaps of all the IMF's blunders, it is the mistakes in sequencing and pacing … that have received the most attention – forcing liberalisation before safety nets were put in place, before there was an adequate regulatory framework, before the countries could understand the adverse consequences of the sudden changes in market sentiment that are part and parcel of modern capitalism … Many of the sequencing mistakes reflected fundamental misunderstandings of both economic and political processes … (Stiglitz, 2002)

The World Bank's Operations Evaluation Division (OED) found in 1999 that the Bank often supported training activities in circumstances where civil services were incapable of making effective use of those trained. The result, OED pointed out, was that newly trained staff simply migrated to better-paid jobs in the private sector, and to the donors (Girishankar, 2001). Five years later the Bank acknowledged that in its support to transition economies, 'it is clear that the sequencing of reforms was often wrong. The Bank, along with other donors, should have tried harder to persuade borrowers to devote greater attention to improving the institutional framework for business and investment in parallel with promoting privatization' (World Bank, 2004a).

Projects and programmes are too often proposed and launched with little reference to what is, or what should be, already in place. It is impossible to do everything at once; the corollary is that some things must be done first. But there is no point in making changes which are so completely dependent on other conditions which as yet do not exist, that they are bound to fail and possibly to discredit the reform programme. Trying to do things differently can greatly complicate the tasks of those who prefer to focus on a limited number of issues at any one time. The rule of law, for example, assumes the existence of a non-corrupt and reasonably efficient legal system, a security system to enforce it, government respect for the rules operated by the legal system and public understanding of the social concordat embodied in a state supported by a legal system. It also presupposes lawyers who also understand and, most significantly, wish to uphold a legal system based on equality, human rights and consent. Further, it assumes an executive which does not meddle or intervene in the operation of the legal system or override its decisions when personal or political interests are affected.

Citizens' charters, popular worldwide in the 1990s in imitation of the British versions, are pointless in the absence of service performance standards or reliable measurements. Proposals for a high-status, authoritative Cabinet Secretariat will come to nothing if the pay offered is too low to attract the most able staff. Efforts to set up central arrangements to monitor the effectiveness of public spending programmes are a waste of time if there is no data even about whether budgeted funds have been spent or not.

There is, however, another aspect to sequencing which has to be watched with care: arguments for 'proper' sequencing can be used to justify delay. Waiting for the right moment or for when all the other problems have been solved – and some of them may never be solved – can push action, at least, into the hands of the next government, if not into the next decade. This tactic is said to have been used by some advisers in the 'transition' countries as a means of avoiding market-orientated changes (private information).

One of the problems here, as elsewhere, is that donors and their agents prefer to do what they know best, in the sequence with which they are familiar. Even the OECD's Development Assistance Committee, normally very cautious in criticisms of its members' activities, commented that:

> legal system strengthening is not necessarily the best place to begin a [rule of law] program. If the prior steps are not in place, legal system strengthening will almost certainly be unproductive, as was the case in Argentina and the Philippines ... This may not be a palatable lesson for USAID or other international donors to digest, with their long experience in institution building. (OECDDAC, 1997)

Recipients as well as donors are to blame here. 'Countries enamoured with a particular foreign model may be inclined to apply it without careful attention to the prerequisite conditions and capacity for doing so' (Nunberg, 1997). A Latin American government in the 1990s decided to improve the quality of senior officials by introducing management training based on the British Top Management Programme, and asked for advice. They were dismayed to be told that, without a human resources management system, which could ensure that graduates of the programme secured appropriate posts, staff would have no incentive to take part in the programme and it would fail to achieve its objectives. Another Latin American government wanted a citizens' charter, publicized its interest in this and received immediate interest from the police – a military-run operation with a reputation for violence and illegal shootings. The senior police commissioner was surprised to be told that a formal declaration that the police were the citizens' friend was not sufficient; they had to change their behaviour as well – which would mean a ten-year programme of recruiting and training. Parallel changes would also be needed in the courts, the legal system and the prisons.

It is only recently that sequencing has been recognized as an issue. A comment on reforms to the health system in Ghana noted that sequencing problems had been among defects in the implementation strategy. 'Structural changes preceded changes in processes and procedures. Legal and institutional frameworks have been slow to change to catch up with the creation of decentralised management structures and the introduction of new management structures' (Larbi, 1998). The World Bank acknowledged in 2001 that 'the ways in which complex interventions are sequenced and implemented have a distinct and potentially far-reaching impact on the way public management systems respond' (Girishankar, 2001). A few years later the IMF and the Bank were prepared to identify some specific examples:

> [In Lesotho] better sequencing and a more appropriate pace of reforms could have enhanced ownership and strengthened performance ... Some reforms should have come earlier in the reform process, such as civil service restructuring, measures to improve governance, regulatory and judiciary reforms, and reform of land and property rights. (IMF, 2000)

> Privatization and civil service reforms in Peru are threatened by opposition from the middle class. Their opposition could have been lessened by a different sequencing of reforms and social protection measures to mitigate the adverse consequences of privatization and civil service reform. (World Bank, 2004a)

Even more sweeping comments about the Bank's almost haphazard approach to institutional development were made in a review of its activities in Central and Eastern Europe and Central Asia:

> This review found no case in [Europe and Central Asia] where a comprehensive country institutional development and public sector reform strategy has been formulated. Such a strategy would have recognised the interconnectedness of the various components and not, for example, have proposed launching a legal reform without also proposing judicial reform, and not proposed launching judicial reform without also addressing civil service reform, nor without taking account of the financial implications of such reform, and so on. (World Bank, 2004b)

The most hostile critics of outside attempts at government reform could hardly have put the argument more strongly.

Insouciance about sequencing is linked to a general insensitivity to local conditions and local history. One of the authors was talking to a junior official in a donor agency who had authority to release badly needed funds. She pointed out that 'the senior ministers in Cabinet don't work with an agenda and papers and minutes like ours do – they have a different way of working'. 'Well', the official responded briskly, 'they had better learn to change then, hadn't they?' Some academics, particularly perhaps social scientists, might have better insights, but most consultants are not social scientists; their favoured prescription may well be their own or their firm's current orthodoxy, trotted out regardless of its relevance or applicability.

Most officials are not social scientists, either. One potentially unhelpful source of advice is serving officials from a donor government. Their implicit job description seems to require them to prescribe the 'solutions' currently favoured by their own government; professional loyalty and lack of analytical skill both dispose them to believe that these solutions are the best and to commend them to others regardless of any differences in context. The same is broadly true of bilateral donors, and of consultants, of any kind, with a specific country background. The World Bank notes that 'Donors often are most comfortable with service delivery systems of the type operating in their own country' (World Bank, 2004d). By contrast, an absence of such an insular loyalty can be a major bonus for the client. One of the authors worked on an EU-funded project where the team had to include advisers of different nationalities – at different times British, French, German and Dutch. All but one were former or serving officials. The value of this mixture was that the team's collective experience embraced four very different systems of government and prevented it from uncritically making proposals based on any single one of these.

Similar problems arise where specific organizational changes seem to have been successful in specific country settings. In the 1980s the UK government set up a small unit responsible for improving the management of the central government machine in the UK. It had some modest success and for some countries was surrounded with the glamour of the Thatcher years. In spite of the warnings of those involved in the original work in the 1980s, the 1990s UK government marketed the idea abroad and to visitors. Several countries – notably Columbia – were persuaded, set up their own 'Efficiency Units' and waited for miracles to happen. 'Next Steps Agencies', part of the same 1980s changes, were an even more popular off-the-shelf solution, marketed and adopted worldwide by international agencies as much as by the British. No warnings from the experts involved in the UK in 1980s could deter the enthusiasts. Agencies were put in place all over the world. In health care, the pace of change in the British National Health Service during the 1990s and the first years of the next century was so rapid that nostrums fell out of favour almost before they had been generally introduced. Thus 'general practitioner fundholding' was already in effect obsolete in Britain by the time that British consultants were pressing it on amazed Brazilians, still more so when it was being promoted to a baffled Russian health service a decade later.

NEW APPROACHES

Many of the donors are conscious of the need to develop more flexible ways of providing assistance, and ways which give the recipients greater control over how resources are used. Over time assistance has moderated from projects to wider programmes, involving a developing series of projects. One model used for the Brazilian modernization programme involved a set budget and a series of topics to be covered; the precise form, timing and structure of the assistance was to be determined over a three-year period by the Brazilian team with the approval of the donor agency. This built in flexibility in both subject matter and timing – particularly important in a highly politically sensitive area.

A further broadening is represented by Sector Wide Approaches (SWAps), in which 'all significant funding for a sector supports a single sector policy and expenditure programme, under government leadership'. More radical still is 'budget support'. This is a form of programmatic aid in which funds are provided to support a government programme that focuses on growth and poverty reduction, and on transforming institutions, especially those involved in the budgetary process; the funds are paid directly into the budget of the recipient government to spend, using its own financial management and accountability systems. The aim of these new approaches is to produce a better response to need and support where there is enough institutional capacity to develop rapidly.

But there are tensions between the budgetary and policy constraints of the donors and the needs and cultural differences of the recipients. Donors may sincerely want to give control to the recipient governments, but they remain accountable at home to legislators and others for the use of the money. Corruption in developing countries is well publicized. So is corruption associated with aid programmes. In the field of governance any implications of corruption do more to undermine the principles of improving government than the benefits from any amount of institutional improvement. In a corrupt or even an inefficient system, the budget support approach increases the chance of leakage of aid funds away from any acceptable activity. So too will sudden large increases in levels of support; the apparent belief of the Make Poverty History campaigners in 2005 that the large increases in aid demanded would go directly to the poor reflected, in the opinion of one experienced consultant, 'a truly breathtaking victory of hope over experience'.

All non-project-based, 'hands-off' approaches to aid raise similar problems, and difficult questions about accountability. Donors are no longer funding discrete, identifiable projects for the success or failure of which they can be held accountable at home. Instead, they contribute to a budget for the sector as a whole, in parallel with other donors, and accept that the budget should be managed by the recipient government. The result is that there is no longer a direct and exclusive link between any individual donor and any individual project in the sector. The recipient is now obliged to ensure that its own management – 'governance' – of the sector is effective enough, in the first place, to reassure donors that their money will not be wasted, and in the second to ensure that it does use the resources provided to good effect.

It is not surprising that one experienced consultant interviewed for this study felt that these approaches could work only in a very small number of well-performing states. This is, of course, satisfactory up to a point – the point being the very limited number of beneficiaries who qualify for SWAps or budget support – if the only aim is to reduce poverty. If the aim is to improve the quality of government, the donors have relinquished the power to ensure that their funds are used in ways that might achieve this objective

The British House of Commons International Development Committee was uneasy about this approach, noting that, 'While there are potential benefits, there are also risks because the Department is not directly responsible for the actual use of funds after they have been disbursed into partner government budgets.' DfID's response to the International Development Committee's probing on this point implied some optimistic assumptions about the speed and thoroughness of the necessary changes in governance. It told the International Development Committee that it met its 'accountability requirements' in three ways. First, by insisting on an agreement with the recipient country that 'it is committed to the right policies and poverty reduction targets'. Second, systems and people were put in place to 'provide reasonable assurance over the use of funds'. Third, DfID itself would monitor the government's ongoing commitment to poverty issues (Select Committee on International Development, 2002).

One innovation aimed at improving understanding of the possibilities of change is the so-called 'drivers of change' approach being developed in DfID. This, for the first time, tries to identify all the factors in a country context – historical, social, economic and political – which are relevant to its ability and willingness to develop 'pro-poor' policies. Reports have been completed for a dozen countries, including Bangladesh, Cambodia, Kyrgystan and Zambia. All are published. The teams working on the reports have included economists – no surprise here – but also historians and political scientists.

The reports focus on the situation on the ground, on the various groups and interests likely to support or to resist changes aimed at helping the poor, and on the actions that might be taken in relation to both categories. Reports are frank about the capabilities of local interests: in Zambia, 'among the thousands of registered NGOs there are probably only a relatively small number of good ones', while 'the civil service has become a central element of patronage systems that have led to a decline of professionalism'. Reports try to identify gaps in existing knowledge: in Zambia, again, 'the incentives that affect the behaviour of public officials ... need to be understood, and development agencies may have to develop the skills to undertake such analysis' (Duncan et al., 2003b). In Kyrgystan, 'institutions such as parliament, political parties and competitive elections are seen as exogenous and ill-suited to local conditions' (DfID, n.d.a).

This approach may help the donors to achieve pro-poor policies. But the examples cited contain some remarkably broad and imprecise judgements ('probably only a relatively small number of good ones'). The question remains, as always, how much weight will be given to them in day-to-day project planning and management, and how this will be done. Confidence in the judgements made in some reports must be affected by the speed with which they were reached; the Drivers of Change (DoC) study of India took precisely two weeks (Warrener, 2004). The DoC approach also implies a striking breadth, depth and detail of intervention in the recipient countries' affairs; what are donors to do about the implicitly regrettable Kyrgyz attitudes to political institutions? More basically, adopting this approach now must raise questions about how donors were proceeding in its absence: had they really given no systematic thought to identifying likely supporters or opponents of the changes they were trying to bring about, or to how they might strengthen the former and neutralize the latter? If they had not, it is hardly surprising that earlier efforts to reform government have been so unsuccessful – and, for the many countries for which such reports have still not been completed, are likely to continue to be so.

The next chapter looks at the management systems used by the donors, the results of the donors' own evaluations of the processes which have been discussed here, and the use made of the reports produced by the evaluation teams.

NOTES

1. Accenture, Deloitte Touche Kohmatsu, CapGemini Ernst & Young, PriceWaterhouseCoopers, KPMG.
2. Briefing can also be provided by others with experience of the country in question. One of the authors, about to visit Moscow for the first time, asked a former British Ambassador there for suggestions as to what to read to increase his understanding of Russian government. 'Gogol' was the one-word answer.

6. Evaluation and outcome

As we have seen, the donors spend billions of dollars intervening in government. Much of the work for which they pay is done at arm's length and thousands of miles from head office. Many hundreds of subcontractors are involved. Relationships are three-way, involving donor, client and contractor, with scope for misunderstandings of language, culture and objectives. Most donors are spending public money. They need to have a means of managing what happens and of assessing that they get what they pay for. In theory the process of evaluation should help recipients and donors keep track of what is happening and assess the outcomes. OECD's Development Assistance Committee, regarded by many as the overseer of the development process, has defined evaluation as 'systematic and objective measurement of an ongoing or completed project, programme or policy, its design, implementation and results' (OECD, 2001a). Evaluation and management are intertwined.

Donors have, in principle, taken the need for evaluation seriously. They recognize that they need to know whether or not their interventions are justified or useful. They need to know whether, on balance, their activities are doing more good than harm and that the benefits are proportional to the resource costs, both for donors and recipients. Donors also need to know, given that they are likely to fund many similar programmes in future, whether the same kind of intervention should be attempted in similar situations, and whether they can generalize from a particular experience.

EVALUATION AND CONTRACT MANAGEMENT

The management of a contract and the evaluation of what happens both need to be based on a similar structure: defined objectives for the task, knowledge of the state of affairs before any action was taken, an agreed language in which to analyse and measure the task, details of the specific actions taken, details of the position after the action was completed, and some means of demonstrating a causal relationship between the actions and the later state. To be of any use, the information has to be relevant to the subject, not merely technically elegant.

Logically the planning and construction of a government project or programme should start with the identification of a problem or issue in the country concerned. In the early 2000s most donors were focusing their activities on poverty. This meant that the problem was expressed as an aspect of poverty or its symptoms – levels of income, child mortality or educational achievement. The next step would be to determine that this problem was in some way caused by weaknesses in government – the incompetence of the civil service, the ineffectiveness of the Ministry of Finance. The third step would be to plan an activity, or a series of activities, aimed at correcting the weakness in government – for the civil service, a new pay and grading system or an attack on patronage, for the Ministry of Finance, a reorganization and new budgetary arrangements. When, if ever, the time came for the project or programme to be evaluated, the evaluator could work back up this sequence in reverse order: did the activity take place, did it correct the weakness diagnosed, and did that correction help to ameliorate the original problem?

LOGICAL FRAMEWORKS

The first logical step in evaluation is to have a prior set of evaluable intentions. Most donor institutions now use a methodology called a 'logical framework', or 'logframe' to establish the key elements of a project or programme and to set milestones against which to manage performance. In essence this is a process which involves putting as much as possible of the expected process and outcomes of a project into a series of defined boxes against which performance and achievement can be measured. This system, after the manner of ideas born of models for strategic planning and management by objectives, attempts to fit the planning and outcomes of a project into a structure. It has been drawn in part from the lessons of managing infrastructure projects where a succession of interconnected actions can be identified as necessary to a successful outcome. It is used to help establish the relationship of objectives to each other, to indicate progress and to clarify the critical assumptions that have been made in the planning of the project. Most logframes are based on a matrix; its vertical axis lists goal, purpose, outputs and activities – respectively the overarching objective to which the project contributes, its impact, the deliverables (as specified in the terms of reference), and the activities to be undertaken. On the horizontal axis are a description of the objective, verifiable indicators, means of verification, and assumptions. USAID and CIDA introduced the 'logframe' in the early 1970s, ODA – as it then was – in 1985 and the other major donors – the World Bank, the EU and the Swedes – did so subsequently.

MEASURING IMPROVEMENTS

It is relatively easy to determine whether or not the planned and funded activities took place – visits by consultants and others, seminars and workshops, studies, reports and recommendations, purchases of hardware. There should be a straightforward trail of activity and expenditure, managed and monitored by contract officers and reported on by the contractors at specified points in the contract. Problems begin at the next stage – the implementation of the initial findings. Many second-stage activities, however clearly defined at the previous stage and however firmly, perhaps even enthusiastically agreed, often turn out not to take the clear and unambiguous form originally envisaged. Were civil service manpower ceilings introduced? Drafts were agreed but not formally ratified. Was a staff appraisal system introduced? Only partially and behind schedule. Did the training programme take place? Yes, but it did not attract many high-level participants. Was a director appointed for the new public sector management programme? Yes, but only after a long delay and he resigned after 18 months and was not replaced. Did the President agree the new arrangements for organizing Cabinet? Yes, but nothing had been done by the time of the next presidential elections and the new President appears not to be interested in the matter.

This type of assessment deals with what might be called questions of record. They are essential, but even they are only preliminary to other questions which get closer to the heart of the matter – that is, those which touch on the issue of whether any of these activities helped to improve the quality of government. Here the earlier questions of fact and historical record intersect with those of definition. These questions may or may not have been posed when the project or programme was being planned. But if they were not considered and did not form part of the planning for a project, the project itself will probably have failed in its objectives. Unless the purpose of a project has been well defined and has been taken into account both in planning and in implementation, it is unlikely to fit the cause of the problem.

This does not require an elaborate analysis for a modest project, but awareness of what is happening can point to better forms of assistance. In Ghana in the early 1990s there were elaborate and expensive plans for new courthouses which were stalled because of all the other interests involved in planning and construction. What the courts really needed was recording machines or shorthand writers. The delay in access to the legal system was caused not by the inadequacy of the buildings but by the necessity, for the judges, of writing out all the evidence in longhand. That had a quick and simple solution, but one that had been missed by the project planners.

It is relatively simple to describe good government in general terms. It is harder to go to the next stage, and to define performance for any specific characteristic, organization or process in ways which would indicate the impact of the programme's activities. Is a well-functioning legislature one which passes a great deal of legislation in a short space of time? Or does the scale of legislation indicate excessive control of the timetable by the executive, and might a better indicator be the number of hours spent in discussing drafts – the more hours the better? On the other hand, a high figure for the latter might be due not so much to the zeal and intelligence of the legislators as to the incompetence of the legal draftsmen.

One of the authors was asked to review the working of the Council of Ministers in a sub-Saharan African country where it was clear that this body had lost authority and was playing no effective part in planning government strategy. One symptom of malaise, frequently cited at the outset of the project, was that Council meetings often lasted from nine in the morning till late in the evening. Something was clearly wrong. But at the other extreme, many argued that something was equally wrong in the post-2001 Blair administration in Britain, where the weakness of Cabinet was signalled by the fact that it met once a week for a maximum of an hour and a half.

The complexity of problems varies. It is not too hard to develop plausible hypotheses to explain why Cabinet meetings last all day or why decisions taken there are never implemented by individual ministers. Perhaps there are no formal agendas for the meetings or the chairman consistently ignores them. A consultant would need to develop a hypothesis as the basis for analysis and for later action. Nonetheless, few problems in government are likely to have only a single cause. In complex systems such as governments, it is hard to disentangle the many potentially relevant causal relationships. As a Bank expert has written, 'a low score on a rule of law index implicates multiple policy and institutional causes so that one cannot suggest what the solution might be or even who should implement it' (Manning, 2001).

Solutions may need to incorporate several different actions. If any of the causal relationships were initially misunderstood, and the actions taken were inappropriate, the solutions are likely to fail and to cause frustration to those carrying out the project or managing its implementation. The evaluator may not find it too hard to determine that the project has largely or wholly failed. It is much harder either to identify the precise reasons for the failure or to recommend different actions next time. It is also possible that in finding apparent failure to achieve the formal objectives of a project, an evaluator may miss gains which, while not part of the overt objectives, may be of greater long-term benefit. The hours of discussions, a different way of working and the opening of new ideas may not have produced a visible institutional change, but the approach of the client and the ideas of its officials may be radically different from those of the external experts. The result may be a better solution to the original problem.

It would be unfair to expect answers to evaluators' questions to be simple and clear-cut. Most discussions about aid evaluation tend to be focused on relatively concrete and visible outputs such as hospitals, schools or roads, or on health care, education or communications. Government is a relatively small sector of any aid budget in financial terms. It is also one where established evaluation techniques are difficult to employ. The problems of evaluating the effectiveness of interventions aimed at improving government are, indeed, so great that some experts prefer not to discuss them at all. In the course of a 350-page book on the evaluation of development aid (Cracknell, 2000), government is mentioned a few times – but only to discuss the uncertain influence of its quality on economic performance and the difficulty of defining it. The author has nothing to say about how one might evaluate the impact of development aid on the quality of government.

Approaches such as the logframe are based on a structured methodology. In nearly every case in the field of government they have to be adapted to ensure that they are relevant. The underlying assumption is that there is a predictable process, that most critical factors are accounted for and under an assessable form of control. It does not allow for any destabilizing events or for the analysis to be wrong. Difficulties can be caused by attempting to build in the capacity to respond flexibly to the needs of recipients. Contract officers need to be able to follow what is happening and to be sufficiently in touch to authorize legitimate variations and question uncertain ones. Technically funds are authorized for specific purposes and, however flexible the drafting may be, evaluators have to be able to follow a coherent trail of action and expenditure.

Difficulties can also be caused by lack of flexibility. In one Latin American project aimed at developing 'agencies', a neat and tidy logframe took no account of the prior need for a constitutional amendment before any further steps could be taken – inevitably a lengthy and chancy business that had to take its place among the government's other priorities. The logframe section on risk could allow for problems, and new areas within the programme could be created, but constitutional change was not under the control of the Reform Ministry, much less that of the expatriate contractor. It can be argued that 'blueprint approaches' of this kind are inappropriate for activities focused on institutional and even more on constitutional change – where objectives are diffuse, the relationships between inputs and outcomes less well understood, the outcomes less easily measurable and the timescales far less predictable, than in classic infrastructure projects.

THE DONORS AND EVALUATION

There are two main reasons for evaluation. First, accountability: to provide information as a basis for holding donors and their agents to account for the success of their policies and actions and their expenditure of public funds. Second, improvement and development: to enable the donors to learn from their successes and their failures, to improve the quality of future policies and practice and to gain insights to inform future development. For both reasons answers are needed as swiftly as possible without, in the case of big projects, necessarily waiting for the project to be fully completed. Formal evaluations, as defined – 'a systematic and objective measurement' – may take years to set up and complete. They are time-consuming for the staff involved and generally poorly regarded. Rapid or early evaluations are likely to be dismissed by operating staff as premature unless they are part of an internal management process of review to check that the project is going according to plan. Where there has been a thorough retrospective assessment of outcomes, by the time the report is delivered the context within which both donors and recipients operate will have changed. If the conclusions of the assessment are negative, elapsed time provides a convenient excuse for ignoring them.

OECD: DAC

Despite its problems, the donors engage in a great deal of evaluation. The Development Assistance Committee (DAC) of OECD acts as a focus for and disseminator of good practice in evaluation. It has published a study of the evaluation of governance (OECDDAC, 1997). There have been OECD workshops to study methods and recommend best practice. The aid activities of each OECD member state are peer-reviewed every four years or so, and the reports published. The report of an international conference, published in 2001, reported on the difficulty of conveying the results of evaluations to those who need to know them, and the obstacles to ensuring that the latter acted on what they had been told (OECD, 2001a).

WORLD BANK: OED

At the World Bank the Operations Evaluation Department (OED) was set up by Robert Macnamara in 1971. It began as a programme within the budgeting department; by 1973 it was a full department and in 1975 it acquired its own director-general, reporting directly to the board. In the late 1990s it adopted the mission statement, 'Enhancing development through excellence and independence in evaluation'. By 2003 OED had some 100 employees.

DfID

A major bilateral donor, the British government has given serious attention to the evaluation of its development work. In the 1980s the Overseas Development Administration started to take an interest in how it should introduce evaluation techniques. The existing Evaluation Unit became a full department within ODA, the existing Projects Committee was expanded to become a Projects and Evaluation Committee, and the logical framework methodology was adopted for all substantial projects, following the experience of other international donors.

The Evaluation Department carries out a programme of studies agreed annually by the DfID management team. The process is systematized and based on a system which sets out the purposes and use of evaluation. Projects are evaluated against an overall success rating within which performance is assessed against a range of criteria. The findings and lessons from each evaluation are published. The department is now moving away from detailed project evaluation to cover wide themes and topics of 'general interest' (National Audit Office, 2002).

The British National Audit Office summarized DfID's project monitoring and review process:

- A Project Memorandum describes how the project will be implemented and monitored;
- a logical framework sets out 'objectively verifiable indicators' against which progress will be measured;
- monitoring reports produced at regular intervals during implementation show progress against the logframe and explain where things are not proceeding as planned;
- all projects costing above £1 million must be 'scored' (an interim evaluation) at least once a year;
- at the mid-point of a project 'output to purpose reviews' are undertaken with the recipient to assess progress against objectives and check whether the initial assumptions are still valid. (National Audit Office, 2002).

The process of project monitoring described here would be perfectly acceptable for a project between two parties where both sides are in contact and can observe progress. But DfID's projects, like those of most donors, are three-way and geographically very distant. Once the project is running, the main actors are the recipient government and the contractors; the donor is unlikely to do more than glance at a quarterly report, visit the project perhaps once or twice in its life and authorize the payment of invoices if they are compatible with what is expected. In most donor organizations the people responsible for running contracts have little time or expertise to do more.

Evaluations are frequently carried out for DfID by former officials or by academics based in UK universities. Evaluations often rely heavily on information provided by DfID itself. For example, the 2004 review of the Know How Fund was undertaken by a former DfID official who had been responsible for the programme. The review was based on a large number of interviews, but only with DfID and FCO staff, EC officials and consultants. The only overseas trip was to Brussels. A Birmingham University review of a group of projects in a dozen accession countries was conducted as a desk study. By contrast, the UNDP team assessing UNDP's role in the public sector reform process visited Azerbaijan, Bolivia, Ethiopia, Mali, Pakistan, Tanzania and Vietnam. In general, DfID spends a much lower proportion of its budget on independent evaluations, and evaluates a much lower proportion of its own activities, than do some other agencies (Flint et al., 2002).

USING EVALUATION TO IMPROVE MANAGEMENT

Evaluation is not an easy task. After over a decade of work on evaluating governance, the World Bank was still acknowledging that it had some way to go before it fully understands how to measure the effectiveness of its activities in this area. In 2002 it admitted that: 'this area of work is relatively new and we all have a tremendous amount to learn … we need to continue to deepen our efforts to understand and measure governance realities on the ground; to monitor the impact of World Bank programs' (World Bank, 2002).

There are difficulties of definition, and consequential difficulties with the processes of evaluation which have to rest on these definitions. Many projects are tightly defined, but in terms primarily of activities. This is particularly the case with the advisory work coming under the heading of technical cooperation. Evaluations, too, therefore tend to focus on activities. They often say little about the quality or the outcome of the activity or about whether judgements may be needed about the contractor, the process or any possible follow-up.

In the reports of evaluations, and in other reports on governance activities, it is striking how often the admission occurs that those responsible for the projects could not, or at any rate did not, define what they were trying to do in terms which would enable them to manage the projects to a successful conclusion or others subsequently to determine whether they had succeeded in doing so. The World Bank, which has put proportionately more resources into evaluating its own activities in this area as in others, is frank about its own shortcomings: '[Operations Evaluation Department] projects … focused largely on whether projects met their stated objectives rather than capturing the intended and unintended impact on the sector or county as a whole' (Girishankar, 2001).

The British government is optimistic about the scope for systematic measurement. In a 2001 DfID paper, the concluding section was headed 'Measuring progress against objectives'. On the one hand this paper dismissed 'international development targets specific to the quality of government against which progress can be modelled and measured ... [and] government indicators which could be used to measure progress at the global level'. On the other it concluded robustly that:

> At the country level, assessment of state capabilities and human rights is possible and desirable. Assessing the status of government is a necessary step towards identifying areas which require improvement ... DfID developed a set of questions which it used in order to produce a more objective analysis of government systems in countries to which it provided support. (DfID, 2001b)

The National Audit Office were less convinced. In 2002 the NAO looked at how performance management was used within DfID. The report made uncomfortable reading. It commented on country strategies. These, it said:

> ... were often so generally worded that almost any intrinsically worthwhile development project would fit somewhere in the strategy. There was often little sense of the prioritisation between, or the cost implications of, different objectives ... There is little discussion or analysis of the relation between resources committed and impacts or outcomes resulting. (National Audit Office, 2002)

A commissioned paper annexed to the report noted that International Development targets, which DfID had actively supported and had made substantial steps to internalize, were in large measure outcome-orientated but that little effort was put into deciding how they were to be achieved:

> It is extremely difficult to say anything sensible to attribute changes in target indicators to the actions of the development community. To put it bluntly, the targets are not suitable for judging the performance of individual development agencies ... One must wonder on what data DfID management do base their decisions. (National Audit Office, 2002)

In 2001 USAID stopped using indicators related to its strategic goals on the grounds that 'in many cases one cannot reasonably attribute overall country progress to USAID programmes'.

The doubts of the donors sit oddly beside the enthusiasm of OECD. The 2001 report suggested several areas where 'donor evaluation units may play an active role'. The implication is that there is an effective, professional and influential community of evaluation and monitoring experts in the donor organizations.

The UK's National Audit Office had a valid point. Despite the efforts going into performance management and evaluation they had found it difficult to establish what the basis for decision-taking was. What appeared to be lacking was clarity about objectives and processes at the start of projects. This had the technical disadvantage that the material was not there for evaluators – and we shall see later in this chapter how widespread that lack of clarity is – but a more serious aspect of it was that the donors appeared not to know how to specify what they were trying to achieve or how to manage the process of getting there.

The quality and relevance of evaluation will be affected by the skills and understanding of the evaluators. One of the main themes of this book is that government, in any country, is deeply influenced by local values, relationships, history and culture – among other things. As mentioned elsewhere in this study, for most of the history of intervention in government, the dominant academic discipline has been economics. The dominant profession has been management consultancy. Like other expert groups, management consultants work with and provide the kinds of data with which they feel comfortable. But it is not to them that one would look for insights into the legacy of empire, attitudes to rulers, the significance of caste, tribe or hierarchy. There have been relatively few contributions from the historians, sociologists, anthropologists and social psychologists whose insights should be indispensable for understanding the background culture of any country.

It is therefore unsurprising that an official of one of the major international development banks has remarked:

> Genuine evaluation of reforms using social science techniques is rare ... greater investment is needed in more rigorous research on how to achieve high performance by the public sector in Asia-Pacific. Such research would lead to better prescriptions, and a better return on the considerable investment in reform by governments and international agencies. (Westcott, 2004)

EVALUATING DEMOCRACY ASSISTANCE

The problems that arise in managing and evaluating aid projects and programmes, and in identifying their intended objectives, arise in a particularly severe form in the field of 'democracy assistance'. Here project activities concentrate on the institutions of democratic government – parliaments, direct elections, the development of electoral lists and the establishment of political parties. The projects demonstrate the difficulties of defining outcomes and of relating activities to outcomes. Many commentators are critical of the evaluation processes used to assess democracy projects. This is partly because the data is so soft and causal connections so hard to demonstrate, partly because of what might be called the emotional or ideological character of the enterprise.

'The democracy aid community has not risen to the challenge of evaluating its own work ... Missionary zeal pervades the field, bringing with it a disinclination for self-doubt and a reflexive belief in the value of the enterprise' (Carothers, 1999). Describing the activities of USAID, this commentator points out that democracy is assumed to be desirable by definition; for those who share this view, evaluation as carried out elsewhere is unnecessary. Evaluations which suggest that, for example, the holding of free elections has had no apparent effect on the legitimacy of the government in power, let alone on its effectiveness, are so counter-intuitive to enthusiasts that they will simply be set aside. Evaluations have too often failed either to find useful criteria for success or to establish causal links between activities and results. The focus still tends to be on outputs – numbers trained or conferences held – rather than on outcomes. Significantly, evaluators of USAID-funded projects are often from organizations which are themselves dependent on USAID contracts and are therefore reluctant or unable to question assumptions about the design or the implementation of projects. Much of the evaluation is based on talking to those involved in implementing the projects and to beneficiaries who have an interest in favourable conclusions (Carothers, 1999).

Another observer makes very similar comments. He notes that evaluations of 'democracy and governance assistance', whether by USAID, the European Community or the Danish aid agency (DANIDA), have suffered from the same defects. They aimed to meet the donors' needs by demonstrating success and usefulness; all evaluations were donor-led, where 'external consultants make judgements concerning the relative efficacy and impact of donor programs, with limited input from local actors'. The opportunity for critical thinking was lost in 'mere corroboration and affirmation of donor efforts by those relatively dependent on their funds, both consultant evaluators and beneficiary organisations' (Crawford, 2003).

It is hard to find practical definitions of 'democracy' that will satisfy all observers. Many critics of the British, US or other advanced systems of government will argue, convincingly, that in several of these countries some of the necessary conditions of democracy are permanently, or intermittently, unsatisfied. If, as some opponents of the Blair administration in Britain would argue, this was a government uniquely impervious to public opinion on issues on which the Prime Minister's mind had been made up, could this be measured and demonstrated? And how would a future administration show that it was doing better on this score? The problems of measurement differ only in degree from those that arise in, say, Georgia or Egypt.

But some argue that even in the most difficult circumstances some form of evaluation is not impossible. The report of an independent evaluation, commissioned by the Swedish aid agency (SIDA) in 1997, of SIDA's activities in the 'democracy and human rights' field, quoted an earlier policy document. This had noted that evaluation initiatives were hampered by fundamental design deficiencies, such as 'vague and over-optimistic objectives'. The later evaluation selected 28 projects in four countries. It concluded that even projects in this notoriously difficult area were susceptible of being planned and evaluated – and recommended the logframe approach (Poate et al., 2000).

ACTING ON EVALUATIONS

There is clearly a temptation to reject the conclusions of evaluations because of weaknesses in the available data and in the project design. Evaluations are unlikely to be effective in demonstrating outcomes if there are defects in the planning and management processes of the projects. But the important message is therefore that projects are still being badly designed and managed. Better design of projects should as a consequence mean that the right data is available for more useful evaluations. For both project planner and evaluator, the priority has to be to get the projects properly constructed in the first place and then properly managed against a clear set of objectives.

The difficulties of using evaluation reports as a basis to improve the management of projects are exacerbated by the length of time between project and report. Over quite short periods of time the context changes, and so do development fashions and priorities. DfID itself prefaces its own studies with disclaimers such as: 'it should be borne in mind that the projects concerned [relating to policing in Uganda] were inevitably the product of their time, and that the policies they reflected and the procedures they followed may, in many cases, have since changed in the light of changing DfID knowledge' (Biddle et al., 1999), or, 'the most obvious common factor in [these] evaluations was the changing policies, priorities and practices of DfID over the period since 1997 [to 2004]' (Flint, 2004). By the time that the Uganda police study appeared, the British government's earlier emphasis on economic stability and growth had given place to the single-minded focus on poverty. All that the evaluation report could say on this point was that poverty was not among the issues that the project had set out to address – and that there were no 'easily verifiable means' of showing that it had reduced poverty.

Reviewing the World Bank's own evaluations of its civil service reform projects, one experienced practitioner noted that:

> ... flaws in the evaluation methodology and the narrow 'project' orientation of the analysis suggest that these evaluations were not helpful in answering the fundamental question 'does civil service reform make a critical difference in

helping governments develop the capacity to achieve sustainable performance improvements? (Nunberg, 1997)

The temptation is hard to resist – and is often not resisted – to report in terms which, in practice, do not set out verifiable achievements but simply express aspirations. Thus a recent annual report by USAID, focusing on work to promote democracy, contains such inconclusive items as:

In Rwanda, USAID successfully strengthened the capacity of 11 district government boards to develop, implement and monitor 32 community development projects … In Mali, after 4 years of USAID assistance, 100 per cent of targeted community organizations had developed the capacity to govern themselves democratically … (USAID, 2004)

The message of the SIDA 'democracy and human rights' evaluation was basically positive. Despite this, the evaluation touched on other problems symptomatic of widespread weaknesses in governance activities and thus in evaluations of these. The report suggested that there were two critical elements of the project design, improvements to which would increase the 'evaluability' of many projects. First, projects' purposes were often confused with their goals and therefore tended to be unrealistic; second, outputs were not always well specified and thus did not provide a clear and logical link between activities and purpose (Poate, 2000). In this case there was clearly not just a problem of 'evaluability' but of management as well.

These comments were echoed by a later OECD report, which noted that 'many donors have not systematically developed systems of indicators or benchmarks (quantitative or qualitative) in order to control quality outcomes or assess program performance' (OECD, 2004a).

As these comments suggest, the problems often start at the outset of projects. Too often the basic structure for reviews is never devised. In September 2004 DfID published an evaluation of its country programmes for Brazil, Cambodia and Romania. Its conclusions included the insight that there was:

… [a] need for … an adequate framework of objectives, targets and indicators for the country programme as a whole and recognition that the absence of precise, monitorable indicators of achievement at the initiative, outcome and objective level, means that it is not possible to make a meaningful assessment of progress or performance at the country programme level. (Flint et al., 2004)

An evaluation of DfID's work with the Indonesian police similarly concluded that:

… monitoring and evaluation work paid insufficient attention to the project's overall impact in bringing about change within the Indonesian National Police and

> improving police performance. No baseline was established on which clear judgments on outcomes can now be based. (Biddle et al., 1999)

Similar comments are made about the activities of virtually all donors. Evaluators reviewing Swedish project work in Armenia, Georgia and Moldova had a difficult task. The data for the indicators appearing in the project document were unavailable:

> This made the task of assessing impact much more difficult. …
>
> The logic of the projects in terms of the definition of objectives, results and activities were weak and limited the ability of partners to monitor the progress being made as well as the achievement of results. …
>
> It was more difficult to assess the socio-economic impacts of the projects, [partly] because no clear indicators for measuring this had been defined and no base line studies conducted. (SIDA, 2004)

A report on USAID projects aimed at developing democratic practices in legal institutions noted that the findings often focused on outputs – for example, the implementation of proposed activities – as opposed to the impact or achievement of desired results – for example, the spread of democratic practices, or greater respect for human rights (Mason, 1990). 'Stories of successful civil service reform initiatives told by consultants and government officials have tended to concentrate on inputs and processes' (Kiggundu, 1998).

There are understandable reasons for the difficulties of identifying plausible indicators of outcomes and of perceiving any measurable results in a timescale likely to be acceptable to legislators. It is also difficult to attribute improvements in outcomes to the specific programme or project under review. How would one measure differences in the treatment given by police or courts to members of unpopular minorities as compared with wealthy and well-connected tribal chiefs? How long might it take for institutions to change their practices and to provide more equitable treatment? Could any such change be unambiguously attributed to a specific aid project? One problem underlying these difficulties is that the most, indeed the only, reliable evidence for such changes would be the views of those who would be affected by them: the citizens, who are harder and more expensive to survey.

As elsewhere in the public policy field, programme managers seem often to have felt that any indicator is better than none. What is striking is the comparison with the domestic context, where understanding of these issues has evolved greatly over the past 20 years. In the development field, what might politely be called a relaxed attitude to performance measurement is not simply a phenomenon of the past – of the 1980s or 1990s; it appears to continue into the present time. Evaluations sometimes give the impression that these difficulties are not worthy of comment. An assessment of a training programme in Nigeria aimed at easing the transition from military to civilian rule concluded that training had 'stimulated an enabling environment of democratic governance' and had 'helped stimulate a process to aid the transfer of governance'. No evidence was produced to show that either of these desirable states of affairs had occurred. Indeed, questions are bound to be raised about the reliability of the assessment when one comes across statements such as: 'Although the electorate was not included in our sample [interviews and focus groups], which made it difficult to validate most of the claims made by the elected officials, most participants said that their constituents like the work they are doing' (Mason et al., 2000).

EVALUATION AND IMPLEMENTATION

Evaluations may have their weaknesses but many of them demonstrate with startling clarity what the real problem is. In working in a difficult and sensitive area – the government of nation-states – many, if not virtually all, projects are devised, planned and managed on the basis of inadequately defined objectives and desired outcomes by which projects could be managed and measured. This leads inevitably to poor implementation, exacerbated by a surprising lack of concern on the part of the donors about the mess they are in. Vagueness about aims, objectives and targets, lack of information about progress in achieving them, and incomplete achievement, are all bound up together. Reviewing attempts at public administration reform in a dozen countries, a World Bank report in 2003 said:

> Many of the reform programmes apparently have delivered only small parts of what their designers actually intended. Clear evidence as to the outcomes actually achieved is generally lacking. There has been very limited formal evaluation, either internally or externally, of the system in question. In many cases, there is a continuing controversy as to the outcomes of the reform programmes. (Manning and Parison, 2003)

The cumulative evidence is telling. Report after report makes the same points about the activities of agencies around the world. Consultants often have little to say about implementation, and projects terminate with the presentation of advice to the client. 'Many recent studies of public management reforms in developing countries ... do not pay enough attention to the real-world factors which intervene between the undesirable problem and the untidy solution' (Minogue, 1998).

The World Bank presented a case-study of non-implementation in

Bangladesh. It reported that a Bank study on public sector reform, completed in 1996, was circulated by the minister of finance to the Cabinet and to Parliament, and that several political priority measures were endorsed by Cabinet. However, none of the measures had been implemented during the next three years (World Bank, 2000). A survey of the transition from Communism in Central and Eastern Europe noted that in the 1990s consultants made 90 recommendations for reforms in the Romanian Ministry of Finance. Most of these were ignored, partly because no priorities were indicated, partly because no guidelines were provided on how to implement them. In Central and Eastern Europe in general, the provision of foreign experts under the PHARE programme had been most useful when recommendations 'were tailored to political realities and were supported by follow-up assistance: lamentably, this was all too often not the case' (Nunberg, 1998). A study of a failed project in Kenya noted that, 'It was never clear who was meant to supervise implementation' (Bevan, 2002).

At present, when poverty reduction is the overarching objective of reform programmes, the links between programmes and outcomes are based more on rhetoric than on analysis. There is a distinct similarity with the Alliance for Progress of 40 years ago (Chapter 2, page 21). A recent account notes that:

> The [European] agencies now see political reform, multi-party elections, pluralism, better central administration and decentralisation as essential for more effective poverty reduction. Yet they are seldom explicit about how these reforms will promote greater responsiveness to the needs of the poor or will counter gender discrimination and increase popular participation … [T]here is as yet no systematic evidence that even successful decentralisation of responsibilities is favouring the poor. (Healey et al., 2000)

In the absence of prior definition of outcomes, or subsequent evidence about their achievement, organizational changes are often presented, by donors and recipients alike, as adequate substitutes for real changes in the quality or quantity of services. Thus reports of action taken to improve public services so as to increase their efficiency, or to increase their effectiveness in reducing poverty or in achieving other desirable goals, tend to list improvements in processes for budgeting (such as introducing medium-term expenditure frameworks), in civil service recruitment (such as strengthening public service commissions or equivalents), or for regulation and audit (such as giving greater autonomy to audit authorities), without specifying whether or not such changes were actually seen through to completion, let alone whether they had the desired effects.

Such developments are not trivial or worthless. They may well be essential first steps in a reform process. The point is that the only real tests of any proposed change of this kind is whether the policies envisaged are in fact implemented – and, of course, that when implemented they had some effect.

It is hard to exaggerate the importance of this point. When the issue is improving institutions or policies, scepticism is needed about even the most emphatic public declarations of intent. Not because they are necessarily insincere, but because all experience, in rich countries as in poor ones, shows that what really matters is implementation. Promises to prioritize poverty reduction have to be followed by appropriate action that produces results; reforms agreed in principle have to be carried out; legislation has to be observed.

Ministers, including heads of state, often exchange statements and undertakings about government reform in public multilateral meetings. But senior politicians, of all people, should know better than to accept at face value undertakings given by their peers under pressure – especially if these relate to activities so difficult, unpredictable and protracted, so likely to meet with opposition or lethargy, and of so little direct benefit to politicians, as public sector reform. It is too easy for one political leader to accept the promises of another and to move on to other things: the crucial, though impolite, question should be asked repeatedly one, two or five years down the road: 'That's what you said, but what is actually happening on the ground?' A study of two African countries showed that two-thirds of Cabinet decisions were never implemented (Holmgren et al., 1999). When one of the authors was asked to make proposals for increasing the effectiveness of the Council of Ministers, the central problem was summarized by a Council member in the form of a question: 'Why does nothing happen when we make decisions?'

However, if there has been no prior definition of what should happen on the ground, it is not easy to tell whether anything is happening or not. There is no effective basis for judgements about the implementation of programmes, nor for corrective action where it becomes necessary. As a recent SIDA report said:

> Systematic and logical project planning and design would *have been beneficial to the implementation of the projects*: without this there are no clear links between different project components nor are there the possibilities to monitor the progress that is being made throughout the implementation of the projects. (emphasis added) (SIDA, 2004)

The World Bank, analysing the effectiveness of its capacity-building activities in Africa, concluded that much of this was ineffective:

> The Bank does not apply the same rigorous business practices to its capacity work that it applied in other areas … [M]ost activities lack standard quality assurance processes at the design stage, and capacity building interventions are not routinely tracked, monitored and evaluated. (World Bank, 2005).

There are some contexts in which outcomes are defined in terms which do make judgements possible. One such is the budgetary process, where – provided that the information is available – actual spending can be compared with forecasts. Budgets can illustrate a government's priorities. But budgets are valuable tools only if their predictions of spending outcomes are realistic. In Uganda in 2002 when the President wished to make an unbudgeted increase in the allocation for defence spending, the result was across-the-board cuts of up to 23 per cent in a wide range of domestic programmes (Garnett and Plowden, 2004). An independent report shortly afterwards noted that: 'The government's commitments to poverty eradication stated in the budget speeches and Poverty Reduction Strategy Papers do not seem to correspond with the adequacy of committed resources for the same critical area' (Uganda Debt Network, 2003). Merely creating an organization, or giving it legal powers, may have no impact at all on the real world. In Malawi, an analysis of the current slow progress of democratization there noted that 'many constitutional provisions are not being respected by the executive or enforced by other branches' (Brown, 2004).

THE FINDINGS OF EVALUATION

At an aggregated level the conclusions of evaluations about the outcomes of attempted reforms are unambiguous. These conclusions, with their largely unrelieved catalogue of failed initiatives and disappointed expectations, are the starting point for this study. They relate to every aspect of efforts to reform the institutions of government.

Over ten years ago a report for UNDP observed that, 'almost everybody acknowledges the ineffectiveness of technical cooperation … despite 30 years of a heavy technical assistance presence and much training, local institutions remain weak' (Berg, 1993).

In 2000 the World Bank acknowledged that:

> … until recently, (internal) evaluations consistently indicated weak performance in the Bank's portfolio of public sector management projects and in the institution building components of projects in other sectors … Bank and other donor efforts at technical assistance have been criticised for over a decade … (World Bank, 2000)

In 2002, OECD commented that structural public sector reform programmes (PSRPs) have had little positive impact on delivery of public services in Africa: on the contrary, they have often severely constrained both capacity-building and service delivery. Moreover, many of the gains of public sector reform programmes have not been sustained. For example in Ghana a

1992 wage rise more than cancelled any gain in controlling the public service wage bill, which doubled as a percentage of GDP. By 1996 the public service was 25 per cent bigger than in the late 1980s. Ugandan public service numbers have been rising since 1998 (OECD, 2002).

Some observers suggest that aid is sometimes not merely ineffective; it makes things worse. A Swedish report on their own aid activities in Kenya, Tanzania and Uganda (three of the more developed African states) noted: 'From our in-country evaluations we conclude that there are circumstances in which more development assistance, especially more in the absence of implementation capacity, can make matters worse. Uganda has probably reached that point' (SIDA, 2002).

The picture should not be an entirely gloomy one. The World Bank claims that a third of its projects are successful. The Commission for Africa reflects a measured view that things are getting better: 'the evidence suggests that there have been some improvements … in Africa, governance overall is getting better and the situation across the continent is markedly different from a decade ago' (Commission for Africa, 2005).

There are also reports of genuine and sustained improvements in the structure and operations of regional and local government in parts of India and in the pattern of elections, however frail, in the Middle East and Southern Asia.

One significant recent example of substantial change in government, albeit still far from complete, is in the new accession countries in the EU. There the pressure of time, the benefits expected to accrue from EU membership, regular reviews of progress and the temporary disqualification of countries failing to make progress all appear to have helped a process strongly supported by both politicians and the general public. Detailed 'assessment reports' published under the SIGMA programme analysed the competence and the outcome of the process. Progress has varied from time to time and from country to country; Slovakia under the Meciar regime between 1994 and 1998 was widely regarded as unlikely ever to qualify for membership of a club of democracies. Assessment reports even of countries generally considered to be credible candidates have been frank and uncompromising. Thus the 2004 report on the Bulgarian public service and administrative framework: 'The legal administrative system does not guarantee the rule of law and the full application of the principle of legality in the administration; it therefore remains unsuitable for a democratic state' (OECD, 2004c).

Or the equivalent 2003 report on Estonia:

> One very important fault is that recruitment through merit and competition is obligatory solely for higher civil servants …
>
> A strong central capability in charge of making and coordinating policies is lacking …

> Administrative reform is likely to stagnate unless the necessary instruments to carry out effective reforms are put in place … (OECD, 2003)

Progress made in the accession states emphasizes the contrast with the gloomy picture almost everywhere else. This, the only case of improvement on any substantial scale, relates to the desire of a group of small European states for accession to the European Union – a situation most unlikely to be repeatable. Otherwise, it is difficult to find supported evidence of major, sustained improvements. People working in the field with experience of what is happening, interviewed for this study, have not been able to produce a substantiated example of a major donor-led project which can be regarded as completely successful. Successful projects seem have been mainly small scale, almost invariably to have emerged from local demands and to be run by local project managers.

Evaluations have discussed weaknesses in the reform process at length – weaknesses which may be contributory causes of the unsuccessful outcomes described in the reports. The World Bank has been frank about its own failings. In 2000 its report reflected that there had been 'systemic shortcomings' in past Bank work:

- The Bank has sometimes taken a narrow and technocratic view of what is needed for public sector reform, interacting exclusively with government interlocutors and funding consulting services, computers and other inputs in the absence of deep and sustainable demand for institutional reform on the part of the borrower and society …
- It has sometimes relied on models of 'best practice' that have not been feasible in the particular country setting, given variations in human and institutional capacity;
- Traditional applications of Bank's lending instruments … have not always allowed the long-term commitment and systemic viewpoint needed to achieve lasting results …
- … [S]hortage of staff skills in certain specialised areas related to governance, institutional reform, and capacity building, in part reflecting the lower demand for these skills in the past given the limited emphasis placed on institution-building goals. (World Bank, 2000)

An academic assessment written at much the same time was even blunter:

> The litany of deficiencies [in technical assistance] is all too familiar: hasty and poor design of TA projects, defects in implementation such as recruitment delays, selection of unsuitable consultants, perfunctory attention to training components, sparse supervision, poor coordination between donors, lack of good local counterparts, weak local ownership and management. Perhaps more basic is excessive reliance on the resident expatriate–local counterpart model, long recognized as being a highly imperfect instrument for transfer of know-how. Many other weaknesses are cited – among them, the high cost of TA personnel, lack of

> cost-consciousness on the recipient side, acceptance of personnel in order to get access to vehicles, equipment, supplies.
>
> Most of these weaknesses have been known for twenty years or more. A report on the World Bank's TA in 1982 catalogues most of them. (Berg, 2000a)

The UNDP has made very similar comments:

> Technical cooperation [TC} has been accompanied by numerous dysfunctionalities. Despite the recognition that supply and demand of TC must be more balanced, donors continue to overwhelm local capacities with their projects and activities. Rather than coordinating activities, donors continue to litter developing countries with a bewildering array of independent projects – each one demanding administrative capacity, time and other resources. Many of the projects continue to be quite inflexible, with timetable and agendas set by the donors regardless of whether or not they are appropriate in the local context. Furthermore, TC continues to be a short-term endeavour, led by expatriate consultants who are paid – in local terms – enormously high salaries. Their projects lure away local expertise …
>
> Perhaps the most noticeable and important failing of TC is that for all the commitments made to local ownership, it is almost non-existent in many countries. Ownership in practice has come to mean 'the extent to which there is a coincidence of interest and ideas between aid agencies and the political leadership regarding the design and implementation of certain programmes and policies favoured by the aid agencies.' In the absence of local recipient ownership, TC remains fundamentally donor-driven and donor-implemented. (UNDP, 2001)

This was the theme of an evaluation of one of ODA's largest and longest-running public sector reform activities, the Ghana Civil Service Reform Programme. In its review of this over the years 1987 to 1992, the evaluation concluded: 'In general, the project proceeded according to plan with its diagnostic/design work, but implementation has been considerably less impressive, possibly owing to lack of commitment on the part of the officials responsible' (DfID, 1997).

The World Bank acknowledged that it had failed to grapple with the complexity of the local situation in its initial work in the former Soviet Union in the early 1990s:

> … early external policy advice appears … to have been simplistic: it concentrated too heavily on improving policies, and too little on building institutions. Furthermore, early expectations concerning the time it would take to complete the transition process turned out to have been highly optimistic … (Goldin et al., 2002)

FAILING TO LEARN FROM EVALUATION

Many evaluations contain salutary lessons about weaknesses in project planning, management and implementation. Learning from these could do much to improve, if not to eradicate, the poor performance of government reform programmes. It could certainly help to ensure that expectations are realistic. But it does not matter how well or badly evaluations are carried out if their findings are ignored or not, in practice, applied. A large proportion of evaluation work is almost valueless because its findings are not taken seriously by practitioners. The lessons of evaluations are all too rarely applied. On the one hand are the *mea culpas* of many of the aid agencies, and the comments of observers, about the ineffectiveness of many approaches and about the failure, or near-failure, of many programmes; on the other is the continuation of many of the same approaches and of programmes which appear to follow in a straight line of descent from those of the past.

One reason for this mismatch is the quality of evaluation. If evaluators do not have the information which would allow them to assess programmes' effectiveness, it is hardly surprising if their evaluations carry little weight – and that the status of evaluation, as a component in the aid process, is so low. But other factors are also relevant. If the lessons of experience are not conveyed to those who need to learn them and act on them, failed approaches will not be eliminated; good approaches will not be consolidated and built on. There was certainly little effective learning during the years when 'reform' meant mainly downsizing the public sector as part of the structural adjustment programmes developed by the IMF. As the World Bank admitted in 1994:

> How to manage the transition from an overstaffed, underskilled, and poorly motivated civil service to a smaller, realistically paid, and professional one in a way that does not provoke resistance to change is not yet adequately understood. (World Bank, 1994)

The World Bank conducts a great deal of scrutiny of its own technical assistance activities – some 10 per cent of the total – and its evaluations are sophisticated and accessible. But one observer suggests that, even when the quality is high, there is little evidence of any impact on subsequent projects (Lancaster, 1999). OED's rise in scale and status did not bring with it automatic influence. By the mid-1990s OED reports were being submitted eight years after projects had been appraised, by which time most of the staff who had been involved would have moved on and the underlying policies might have changed for other reasons. In 1995 the Bank's executive directors noted the slow pace at which lessons from experience were being reflected in new operations.

This is confirmed by some frank remarks made more recently by OED's director-general:

> Much of our reporting is perceived to be too abstract, too process oriented, and too far removed from the concerns of shareholders and civil society ... We still face a

> challenge in persuading our staff and our managers about the value added by our evaluation work …

He continued that, despite there being a wide consensus about the importance of evaluation, practice had lagged behind: 'Lessons drawn are not necessarily lessons learned' (Grasso et al., 2003).

Berg reached similarly negative conclusions about the effects of evaluation activities. He suggested that the main reasons are that too many evaluations are carried out, that few people read them and that they are often not distributed to the beneficiaries, the media, researchers or universities. There are very few impact studies, looking three, five or ten years down the line (Berg, 2000a).

USAID's projects may be subjected to impact evaluation by the department's Centre for Information and Evaluation, but the effect of these studies on the design and management of subsequent projects and programmes seems limited. Much the same is true in Britain. The NAO report already cited said that although DfID had a recognized track record in analysing and evaluating the performance of their projects, evaluation coverage was 'patchy and unsystematic'. Furthermore, the report said, 'there are indications that formal evaluation reports are not read by country teams … Those staff we spoke to in country teams told us that they made more use of their informal learning networks to identify good practice and lessons learnt than of formal evaluation reports.'

Remarks by DfID staff were quoted in support of this point. These included: 'It's very unclear what [the Evaluation Department's] role is at the moment', and 'I've always been very sceptical about the worth of evaluation in DfID … because as an organisation we rarely take much notice of it' (National Audit Office, 2002). A DfID staff member interviewed for this study said that evaluation reports appeared so belatedly that they were a tool of record, not of management. He added that the lack of impact of evaluations was not surprising given that the Evaluation Department was based 400 miles from headquarters, in East Kilbride. This issue was noted by OECD's DAC. Discussing the relatively low status of evaluation as an activity and of evaluation units as locations for staff, it noted that these factors could be affected by physical location: '[units] that are located at the centre of the organisation are more likely to be taken seriously than those situated in remote offices' (OECD, 2001a).

Despite this background donors have consistently urged evaluation on recipient states. OECD has an ongoing programme entitled Evaluation Capacity Building. There is plenty of evidence of the difficulties the donors have faced in trying to persuade recipient governments of the value of evaluation. One OECD study of evaluation capacity building noted that 'in spite of more than two decades of support there has been limited systematic assessment of the effect and sustainability of the assistance. It is therefore difficult to draw very specific conclusions about lessons learned.' The World Bank carried out a review of the links between monitoring and evaluation capacity development (M and ECD) and governance in sub-Saharan Africa – a similar review to that undertaken at OECD. The report concluded that:

> … substantial [monitoring and evaluation] achievements on the ground are rare in sub-Saharan Africa. The binding constraint would appear to be insufficient demand for M and ECD … Few leading bureaucrats and politicians … accept the value of an evaluation culture that supports fact-based administrative and political accountability. Demand for M and ECD does not flourish in a dysfunctional governance environment, in which the public administration is seen as a vehicle to achieve personal gain and nurture patrimonial patron–client networks. (Schacter, 2000a)

This report discusses the lack of effective demand for monitoring and evaluation in sub-Saharan Africa almost as though this were peculiar to the developing world or to Africa in particular, rather than an example of a weakness that has, from the start, undermined the impact of aid in general and aid on government in particular. The OECD report already mentioned was addressed to the same basic issue: why are evaluation systems so ineffective in practice? And why is so little learning applied to the practices of international interventions in governance? One might add a further question: why do donors urge evaluation on their clients when they make so little use of it themselves?

The picture is confused: the donors all appear committed to the importance of evaluation – and its significance is reiterated by the Commission for Africa (2005). But the evidence of the donors taking advantage of the lessons provided by their own evaluations – or even those of their colleagues – is less clear-cut. Repeatedly over the past few decades the reports have spoken of weak project planning, poor performance and unsatisfactory outcomes. It is indeed difficult to find evidence of satisfactory outcomes on which donor or recipient could congratulate themselves.

On the other side of the coin there is plenty of evidence of the desire of those involved to do better. Techniques for better evaluation are discussed, workshops held, and evaluations appear technically competent. But the crucial read-across from evaluation to policy and practice does not appear to happen. At the least one could argue that if it did happen, the same story would not be so often repeated over the years. There is evidence that the donors themselves recognize this weakness but appear helpless to deal with it successfully. Indeed if this degree of criticism were directed at their clients – the recipients of donor advice and money – commissions would be set up, workshops convened and swarms of experts dispatched to sort out the problem. Instead, virtually no operational attention appears to be given to the issue of how to absorb the lessons of evaluations into the activities of the donors and the recipients.

The phenomenon here might be described in terms of the concept, familiar in physics, and in science fiction, of a 'parallel universe'. That is, evaluators on the one side, donors' contract officers and contractors on the other, seem to pursue separate existences in worlds between which there is no connection. Evaluators have for years been accumulating the evidence that many, indeed most, projects in the governance field were not planned in ways likely to produce the results intended in the timescales planned, their objectives were vague and their goals, based on inadequate analyses of local conditions, unrealistic. In their universe the contract officers of the donors continue to plan and manage projects and programmes with the same basic faults – with the same lack of success. The evidence on the record has no impact on activities in the field.

REASONS FOR LACK OF LEARNING

Why should this be so? A great deal is now known and has been published about many of these difficulties, about past failures and about the reasons for these. A decade ago Robert Cassen and collaborators concluded regretfully that '[Donor] agencies are not all that good at learning from their own mistakes; they are even worse at learning from each other's mistakes, since there is insufficient information exchange among agencies of project experience' (Cassen, 1994). In spite of extensive evaluation by donors and others there is very little learning from experience; evaluation findings are ignored or not fed back into the operational processes, and have had little effect on the world of practice.

At first sight this is one of the most puzzling aspects of work in the field of governance. It seems irrational that donors should continue to spend taxpayers' money, charitable funds or moneys loaned to the recipient countries, on activities that are known to be likely to produce few positive results. Judgements that past activities have not produced the results envisaged in the time-schedules stipulated seem to have influenced subsequent activities hardly at all. Donors continue to seek contractors to help 'the Republic of Uzbekistan in the advancement of democratic reform to reinforce the development of civil society based on the supremacy of law, principles of human rights and freedom, generally recognised values of democracy and pluralism', or to support Pakistan's transition to democracy, and the contractors continue to fail to deliver the goods.

There are both institutional and political reasons for such failures. It is striking how outspoken even OECD, as an organization comprising the principal donors, has been about these reasons. The DAC has declared simply that 'the institutional characteristics of most donor agencies are not conducive to learning'. Those characteristics are said to include rapid rotation of staff and thus limited institutional memory, internal bureaucratic imperatives and external political pressures (including pressures to spend) which militate against learning and flexibility, dependence on external resources (such as consultants) resulting in fragmentation of responsibility (OECD 2000). An OECD conference the same year added 'organisational culture', noting that in some organizations accountability tends to be associated with blame, and 'lack of incentives to learn', exacerbated when staff or consultants frequently move jobs and have often moved long before the consequences of failure to learn are felt (OECD, 2001a).

Another in-depth analysis, by an independent expert, of aid organizations' failure to learn from experience in public sector management programmes suggests several other factors: the diversity of the 'market' and of activities in it, which makes comparisons and the transfer of experience very difficult; changes of staff in donor and recipient agencies; the excessive volume of projects, project money and competing donors in many recipient countries; the large number but inadequate circulation of evaluation reports (which one speaker at the OECD conference, cited above, felt generated 'lesson overload'); a lack of interest, in organizations such as the World Bank, in process issues; the intrinsic difficulty, whatever the theoretical case for doing so, of 'customizing' interventions to fit specific circumstances (Berg, 2000a).

In fact little detailed analysis is needed to show that the failure of many of those involved to change their practices, though regrettable, is wholly rational. The reasons suggested by OECD for the failure of capacity development activities included:

- weak and inconsistent political and administrative leadership of reform programmes;
- poor retention or ineffective use of professional and technical staff;
- capacity overload, inadequate donor coordination and recipients' unfamiliarity with donor procedures;
- corruption in both public and private sectors.

These judgements are doubtless fair. But if these are important reasons for failures, it is not hard to understand the second-order reasons why little action may have been taken to correct the faults. Few donors, or the leaders whom they have supported, are likely to acknowledge publicly that they were 'weak and inconsistent' or that there was 'capacity overload' and 'inadequate coordination', or ineffective use of staff. As for corruption, its ubiquity, deep roots and pernicious effects have become increasingly familiar, but mentioning it merely indicates the massive scale of the problem to be dealt with before 'learning' becomes normal.

More generally, and unsurprisingly, inertia is endemic in all parts of the system. Any large organization develops its own procedures and working relationships and – as enthusiasts for change too rarely recognize – there are real costs to disrupting these. Where relationships have been built up with partners outside the organization both parties have an interest in proclaiming the success of these; they will often be treated as a valuable achievement in themselves, regardless of what results they produce. UNDP country case-studies of technical cooperation (TC) for capacity development found that in some donor–recipient relationships, 'there were strong strategic or political reasons for the donor to be involved, suggesting that there was an incentive to keep the aid flowing but less incentive to worry about how much real contribution its TC made to capacity development' (Browne, 2002).

There is also inertia on the recipient side. A SIDA study analysed the reasons for excessive optimism on the part of donors about recipients' capabilities to assume ownership of projects. The study noted that optimism was 'inherent in the donor–recipient relationship. Few governments or communities decline development assistance; nor would it be rational for them to do so in SIDA's case, with the funding coming as grants' (SIDA, 2002). A UNDP study of the Kyrgyz Republic summarized the many rewards available to those involved in TC programmes there – overseas trips, allowances, vehicles, and so on. 'Clearly, people who benefit in these ways from TC are not going to have an interest in upsetting the cozy relationship … and will be likely to drag their feet if asked to make changes' (Browne, 2002).

Many of these issues are well understood by people involved in the governance business. A former senior official with long experience of governance programmes contrasted those working in the field with their superiors at headquarters. The former have continuing direct experience both of programmes and of the specific contexts in which these are being planned and implemented; they are often acutely aware that at least some of the activities in which they are involved have been shown to be misconceived; they would want to do things differently. Those at the top of the organization are equally aware of the general findings of evaluations. But, given their position, the 'macro-politics' of aid bear much more directly on them; they feel under much more pressure to ensure that their agencies' budgets are fully spent and to justify current programmes by reference to the success of past ones. Aid agencies are competing for funds to spend overseas. Given their continual competition for funds with domestic spending programmes with much greater electoral appeal – health, education, transport, pensions – it is a high-risk strategy for top people to acknowledge publicly that funds spent on government reform have been or may still be wasted.

There is the additional difficulty that evaluations in this field are almost bound to be inconclusive. Every project or programme differs from every other on so many dimensions that 'controlled' comparisons, and thus systematic learning, are impossible. The main differences are not in the nature, aims and processes of the projects themselves; one medium-term expenditure framework can, in principle, be identical to another. The differences are in the context in which the activities are taking place: topographical, historical, political, economic, anthropological and so on. The next chapter explores the impact of context, and the 'culture' which is linked to context, on attempts to improve government around the world.

7. Culture and context

MODELS AND REALITY

A speaker at a conference in Latin America over 40 years ago discussed the use of models in the reform of public administration. If his advice had been heeded a great deal of time, effort and resources might have been saved and disappointment avoided:

> The temptation is strong to copy from a model, especially if that model happens to be extant in a country which governmental officials or elected politicians happen to admire greatly, and if it is felt that the effectiveness of the civil service of that country is one of the major reasons why that country has achieved the modernization and development which it has. My advice is simply this, Do not do it! Follow the more painful way of careful research, of careful study, of suiting the remedy to the disease, the organization to the situation, and the policies to the needs of place and time. There is probably no common set of laws and institutions that can be adopted by any given country with the model of any other country as a basis. (Reining, 1965)

That temptation has not been resisted. Models have been peddled worldwide, 'best practice' has been advocated, with little sensitivity to context. Processes and organizational forms have been introduced, from Katmandu to Bogota, Bishkek to Maputo, regardless of their likely relevance to local circumstances.

'Our [public sector reform] programme is home-grown', the Permanent Secretary to the Cabinet Office of a sub-Saharan country told a receptive seminar of senior South African officials in 1996. 'The donors try to control you by bringing in something that has worked elsewhere. Sustainability is crucial' (private information).

The task of reformers of government has been complicated because 'good government' can mean widely different things in different contexts. As discussed above, to some people good government implies a democratic system, to others it merely implies efficient government. There is little international consensus not only about the precise meaning of 'good government', but also about the significance of individual features of specific governmental systems. To take one familiar example, what has been the long-term net value-added in Britain, of having a permanent, largely non-political, merit-based, high-status civil service? Its supporters argue that such a civil service is honest, objective, dedicated, hardworking, ensures continuity and is motivated by the 'public service principle'. Critics reply that it is expensive to maintain, exclusive in its make-up, poor at management, conservative, too often obstructive towards the elected politicians who form the government, and in general a brake on progress.

Commentators have argued that the economic success of countries in East Asia can be attributed to the relatively low level of political appointments in their bureaucracies. It is difficult to determine how high 'too high' would be. Those familiar with either Britain or the United States, which vary widely in the scale of political appointments, may have different views on the issue.

Again, comparisons do not conclusively show the relative effectiveness of a Cabinet system of government as compared with a presidential one; if generalizations are too difficult, do we even understand in which circumstances one form might have the advantage over the other? At the time of writing it was not yet clear whether Britain in the short or the longer term has been better or worse off as the result of Tony Blair's cavalier attitude to his Cabinet and to the principle of collective responsibility.

A study of the prospects for administrative reform in Russia, published by the World Bank, noted at the outset that:

> There is … a growing recognition that institutions are important for development, but it is not at all clear which institutions are the most crucial, and there is very little evidence that the specific details of government structure and accountability arrangements affect growth. (Manning and Parison, 2003)

At a much broader level, there has been an extensive but so far inconclusive debate about the relationship between democracy and political freedom on the one hand, and development and economic success on the other. As Meghnad Desai summarized the issue some years ago: 'Is there any causal link between capitalism and democracy; between freedom and development?' At that time his answer was inconclusive (Desai, 1994). Amartya Sen's view (Sen, 2000) that there is indeed a causal link is not unanimously endorsed (though it would be surprising if there was evidence in this debate which would make any proposition conclusive).

But there is still a practical question which can be asked – whether it is possible to analyse the activities of countries which seem to be doing relatively well, so as to be able to make a judgement about the contribution of their governance to their success. Most analysis tends to have been based on relatively short-term assessments. During the 1970s and 1980s when Japan, in the title of a popular book of the time, looked likely to become 'Number One', much was made of the ruthless sifting of the senior civil service and of the symbiotic relationship between the civil service and the Ministry of International Trade and Industry (one of the legacies of the American occupation after 1945). Much less has been heard of this since the Japanese economic collapse of the late 1990s. In France, one factor cited by observers contemplating the relative success of the country in the 1960s and 1970s was the dominance of the elite educated at the Ecole Nationale d'Administration, the *énarques*. After a series of scandals and a period of relative French decline in the 1990s, in the early 2000s a major virtue cited for the presidential contender Nicolas Sarkozy was precisely that he was not an *énarque* – and indeed, not a classic insider, given his non-French parentage.

GOVERNMENTS AS SYSTEMS

Governments are systems; it is in practice impossible to treat any single component – whether election procedures, courts, bureaucracies, local governments or Cabinets – in isolation either from the other components of the system or from the wider context in which they have developed and in which they must function. The impact of changes on any part of a system greatly complicates efforts to assess the impact of projects or programmes aimed at other parts, especially if the system as a whole is not in a steady state but is subject to the activities of several donors focusing on several different components simultaneously. The structure, the functioning and, often, the values of any single feature of a government are inseparably connected to other features and to the features of the society of which it is itself part.

Anyone dealing with public sector reform has to take into account many things: how particular processes or institutions interact with other features of the government systems of which they are part and with the wider social context in which they are set; on what conditions they depend for their effectiveness; and what preconditions may need to be satisfied for them to be effective. Well-meant attempts to graft on components copied from elsewhere, or to change the ways in which specific components function along lines which seem successful elsewhere, may well be defeated by the differences in the context in which they are to work. A commentator on the changes introduced by the colonial powers in the dying days of Empire observed that 'each institutional innovation … reordered the structure of power in ways that could not be easily foreseen or prevented' (Warrington, 1999).

COMPARISONS

Once the discussion turns to the transferability of governance processes across national borders the number of relevant variables increases enormously. In practice, those advising other states all too rarely consider the relative appropriateness of the various alternative institutions and processes that they might or could import. It is useful, to put it no higher, to have an idea of what are the most important dimensions on which to compare two countries when trying to decide whether they differ too greatly to enable successful transfers to be made. For example, what needs to be available within the system before there is any point in introducing the adoption of a new approach to recruiting civil servants, a 'citizens' charter', a reorganization of the revenue department, a medium-term budgetary framework, or a poverty strategy? What conditions need to be satisfied for any of these to have any chance of working successfully? What other changes should have taken place beforehand or should at least be planned to complement the new approach and to increase its chances of success? Behind these detailed questions, difficult enough in themselves to answer, are the broader questions about the general context: what kind of society is it and how much does it differ from other societies, and how important are those differences likely to be?

If such questions were asked, the answers would have to take into account some of the obvious dimensions on which recipient countries can be distinguished from each other. These were outlined in Chapter 4 above. One of the most basic is physical scale. In recent years the donors have been placing much emphasis on decentralization and delegation, whether this means developing local government systems, or empowering NGOs and trying to encourage the growth of 'civil society'. It is obvious that the constraints, implementation problems and likely consequences of any programme of this kind will differ greatly between, say, Mozambique, 1500 miles from north to south and with a communications system still suffering from the ravages of 20 years of destructive civil war, and Poland. One of the authors ran a workshop for Cabinet ministers and senior officials in a small island state. It was pointed out by one of the participants that the 'distance' which is often cited as fundamental to the working relationship between ministers and their permanent secretaries in many Westminster systems is in practice impossible in a very small society where not only do all senior people in government know each other, but many of them are related to each other as well.

Differences on another basic dimension discussed above – resources – will clearly affect the ability of a state to implement the advice funded by a donor, and indeed the relevance of such advice to the local situation. In some African states the layer of competent graduates in the public service is still alarmingly thin – and, in common with the rest of the society, being dangerously eroded by the spread of AIDS. In some Latin American countries the proportion of officials with second degrees is probably higher than in Britain. It is too easy for incoming foreigners to assume that certain physical resources will be easily available – telephones, computers and vehicles. As one senior official at the World Bank remarked to one of the authors a decade ago: 'We want to put

Africa at the forefront of the computer revolution now, every school will have a bank of them for the children to use.' 'But what about power, back-up, systems support?' 'Not a problem, that can all be fixed, this is going to transform Africa.'

Reform programmes often include optimistic and ambitious proposals for major systems changes. These are sometimes drawn from the current 'toolkit', and are advocated almost regardless of their relevance and indeed feasibility in local circumstances. Poverty Reduction Strategy Papers and Medium Term Economic Frameworks are contemporary examples. Too rarely is it asked whether these make sense in the context. Many schemes of this kind depend critically upon the availability of timely, comprehensive and reliable data. The proposals often assume that the data is available or can be provided. This is often not so. Many well-meant recommendations for improving central monitoring of budgetary outcomes ignore the fact that nothing is known about expenditure patterns, where the money actually goes or even whether it has been spent at all. It is worth noting the warning issued, in a slightly different context, by one of the developed world's more seasoned experts on budgetary reform – in an article whose title makes the point: 'Why most developing countries should not try New Zealand reforms':

> Politicians and officials must concentrate on the basic process of public management. They must be able to control inputs before they are called upon to control outputs; they must be able to account for cash before they are asked to account for cost; they must abide by uniform rules before they are authorized to make their own rules ... (Schick, 1999)

UNDERSTANDING THE DIFFERENCES

Superficial similarities, based on common experiences, can be helpful up to a point. Despite Britain's sometimes apologetic attitude towards its lost Empire, there remain strong links of language, custom and governance. Commonwealth countries have evolved differently but share common roots. Some procedures and customs have withered as independent countries have adapted their governments to their own needs. But legal systems, parliamentary procedures and some of the structures of government, at least in form, are very much the same as before. A Public Accounts Committee, or its equivalent, puts permanent secretaries through a thorough grilling in Kingston, Jamaica in much the same way as it does in London. In Delhi Permanent Secretaries meet to discuss how to handle forthcoming government business as they do in Honiara in the Solomon Islands. By contrast in Mozambique, which has joined the Commonwealth recently despite its history as a Portuguese colony, Permanent Secretaries never meet as a group with common interests. It can be argued that Commonwealth countries which have inherited similar structures of company law have an initial competitive advantage over other countries that have no tradition of, for example, abiding by a contract.

On the other hand, institutional labels and apparent similarities can be misleading. It has been argued that even in the Commonwealth:

> informal institutions are the critical determinants of whether imported public management ideas will work or not. It is not reasonable to expect, for instance, that the governance arrangements and controls which are effective against patronage in civil service appointments in a developed country, will necessarily work in a developing country where the relative attractiveness of a civil service job is vastly higher than in a developed country, and where clientelist and tribal structures may be integral to the deeper organisation of the society in question. Each society needs to calibrate its governance and controls to its own dynamics and risks. (Matheson, n.d.)

Institutions which appear similar function quite differently in different systems. In the United States, committees of the legislature have a key role in the policy-making process. In twenty-first century Britain, the Select Committees of the Houses of Parliament, although growing in status and professionalism, are still by comparison toothless tigers whose growling can be ignored by the executive with impunity. The government of Tanzania is formally 'Westminster-like' in assuming a mutually agreed division of tasks between officials and ministers. This does not in fact exist. 'A long-standing mutual distrust between Ministers and senior civil servants continues, exacerbated in recent times by the donor community which prefers negotiating with fellow-technocrats in the bureaucracy than with politicians' (Caulfield, 2002). In Mozambique, the post of Permanent Secretary was recently imported and inserted into a basically Napoleonic system. The principle that a permanent official should be involved in policy formation does not fit comfortably into a system where ministers are constitutionally responsible for policy and officials for administration. The roles of permanent secretaries are consequently very much more limited in Mozambique than in many other Commonwealth countries; the title of the post gives a completely false impression of its holders' authority.

Professor Dror too has observed these differences:

> One must guard against reading too much into superficial factor and surface processes. There is a world of difference between the formal structure of democratic institutions and the way they operate in practice. They may function quite differently, depending on the cultures and other specific characteristics of particular countries – mainly historical and cultural, but also related to the size and composition of populations, ethnic and religious structures, and traditional lifestyles. (Dror, 2001)

ATTITUDES TO ADVICE

Recent history can also influence how willingly and effectively a country accepts and uses advice from outsiders. Many recipient countries with years of experience of external advice, some of which has proved helpful and some less so, still welcome assistance and use it constructively. But for countries unused to listening to or learning from any outside view the process can be seen as threatening.

Consultants working on an EU contract in the Russian President's office in the mid-1990s had to grapple with intense suspicion from the officials with whom they were dealing day-to-day. The latter, all of whom had worked in the same posts under the Communist regime, were deeply unenthusiastic about a project whose aims were to modernize a system with which they had felt entirely at ease. They were cast in the role of 'clients', but in practice it was not they who had entered into the contract with the EU, one of whose secondary purposes was to release further funds available under the TACIS programme. But it was they whose style of administration and, potentially, whose jobs were under review. They were uncomfortable with this process, and made this clear. It was not until at least the third year of the project that the consultants could reasonably feel they had won the trust of their interlocutors and could proceed as though they had some interests in common.

RELEVANCE OF ADVICE

Superficial similarities between institutions may over-persuade donors and their contracted advisers that the advice on offer is relevant to the circumstances and needs of client governments. One of the authors helped to manage, in a small island state, a workshop on the finer points of working relationships at Cabinet level, between ministers and officials and among ministers themselves. The workshop appeared to be well received and its lessons to have been absorbed. It was disconcerting to read, in an English newspaper several months later, that two of the ministers present, apparently jealous of the greater opportunities for corrupt dealing offered by a colleague's portfolio, had conspired to hire an assassin – the son of one of them – to murder their colleague, and had succeeded in the task. More fundamental forces seem to have been at work which the civilities of the workshop did not touch.

CULTURE AND GOVERNANCE

The historical, social and political context are among the influences which determine the culture of a society – the combination of the complex of values, beliefs, assumptions and informal rules which shape the behaviour of people towards each other, a combination which is likely to be unique. Institutions can have their own cultures; the culture of different government agencies may differ in important respects even while they share some features that distinguish government as a whole from the wider community of which it is part. Within the UK central government, for example, the culture of the Home Office differs substantially from that of the Department of Trade and Industry. In Britain and the United States, as repeated court cases have shown, many financial institutions have a 'macho', intolerant culture which shocks even the easy-going British. Successive Commissioners have clearly been powerless to eliminate racism and sexism from the culture of the Metropolitan Police.

The culture of any institution, whether a village, a business corporation, a government department or a sovereign state, can be difficult for outsiders to understand; it is profoundly influential on the ways in which the formal institution functions and on attempts to change those ways. Klitgaard has suggested that 'the strength of program or policy effects may depend on aspects of the sociocultural context'. Citing Putnam, he draws an analogy between this context and the soil in which a gardener has to work (Putnam, 1993): 'Policies and projects may work better or worse, depending on the soil conditions; if we understood the soil conditions better, we might choose a different kind of policy or project' (Klitgaard, 1998b).

In Britain, the day-to-day working of institutions is influenced by factors which to outsiders may seem inconsistent with formal values or simply obscure – the acceptance of a monarchy and an aristocracy in an apparently fiercely proud democracy, a concept called 'public service' to which a great deal of lip-service is paid but which is nowhere defined or clarified, a civil service whose ability to defend its own sectional interests against governments of any party has been clearly demonstrated for decades. In the United States, overseas commentators were shocked by the glaring infringements of human rights that followed 11 September 2001; urban liberals were taken completely by surprise by the extent of popular support for George W. Bush in the 2004 presidential election, and by the significance of religious adherence to this support. A similar range of factors need to be taken into account in attempts at public sector reform anywhere. The culture of a society shapes the informal rules which, far more than the formal rules, determine both how institutions operate internally and how they relate to the wider social context: how society feels about government and behaves towards it, how people in government behave towards the rest of society, and how they behave within government.

ATTITUDES TO GOVERNMENT

Generations of external rule taught Filipinos to be wary of any government:

> Traditionally, Filipinos gave their loyalty more to the family than the state. This was the result of their attempt to mitigate the harshness – or neglect – of colonial occupation. When finally they gained independence, they continued to regard government with suspicion, as an instrument subject to exploitation for the benefit of families. (Romero, 1999)

In some formerly Communist countries the years of oppression have influenced the attitudes of citizens towards government. This can be expressed in a deep mistrust of the state and a disbelief in its capacity or willingness to help citizens. An experienced economic consultant working in Russia in the 1990s remarked: 'The Russian people have very little faith in the ability of politicians to do very much for them' (Layard, 1994).

A survey of civil service reform efforts in the Baltic states noted that:

> The Soviet nomenklatura system's unwelcome legacy to the Baltics is two-sided. On the 'supply' side it has saddled them with not only an outsize public management staff but also one steeped in an administrative culture, a set of norms, which is inimical to good administration generally but particularly to state administration in a democracy. On the 'demand' side, the Soviet state administration has made Baltic citizens … profoundly cynical about government and its officials. (Vanagunas, 1997)

Fifteen years after the demolition of the Wall, the citizens of the former German Democratic Republic were still much more pessimistic about the future than Western Germans, while younger people there were far more critical of democracy than Westerners (Beaumont, 2005).

Some attitudes have even deeper roots. In Russia, paradoxically, citizens have traditionally looked to their rulers to help them in their struggles with the government apparatus. One result has been what one expert has described as the 'petitioning culture' in Russian society, whereby individual citizens appeal direct to the President – as they appealed in the past to their Little Father, the Tsar – for redress of grievances often arising from actions in other parts of the system. The central 'Apparatus of Government' receives 80000 individual appeals each year (Parison, 2000). One writer notes the Polish belief that the character of the Polish central bureaucracy had been shaped by history, starting in the twelfth century (Nunberg, 1998).

There are striking contrasts between European and US attitudes to government as an institution. Fukuyama posits a caricatured contrast:

> … many countries, particularly in continental Europe, have always had a concept of the state as the guardian of the public interest standing above the particular interests

> of the state's citizens. This state, usually embodied in a professional permanent bureaucracy, at times has to lean against the popular will because it has a clearer view of the common interest of the nation. The Lockean liberal view of the state that prevails in the United States, by contrast, sees no public interest apart from the aggregated interests of the individuals who make up a society. (Fukuyama, 2004b)

One need not accept this crude comparison (in which the 'continental European' concept, as defined, seems closer to that of Lee Kuan Yew's Singapore) to see that the principle of such comparison is important and could have real explanatory value. In the history of the United States, history and topography have combined to generate a widespread suspicion of central, federal government and to preserve a system in which the powers of the executive are constrained to an extent that often amazes Europeans, with their very different traditions. Variations are concealed behind the convenient label of 'the Western democratic state'. There are significant differences of emphasis between the European and the US model, and between individual European states. One commentator has suggested that the lack of a feudal tradition in the USA, its abundant territory and material wealth, and its relatively homogeneous population distinguish it from most other societies and make its own model of democracy largely irrelevant to them (Hartz qu Hook in Schraeder, 2002).

An effect of the American tradition has been that US technical assistance has often advocated decentralized, 'balance-of-power' systems which client countries, struggling to develop effective and credible executives, have found completely inappropriate. The almost missionary zeal with which this has often been done reflects a deep American conviction in the value of US experience and of its lessons for the rest of the world.

This conviction is not always shared. The new post-apartheid government of South Africa, struggling to maintain control of a deeply divided society, had no interest at all in a constitution on the US model. By contrast, Japan's passive role in democracy promotion has been attributed to the fact that contemporary Japanese culture does not encourage the exportation of political values (Akaha, 2002).

The differences between the main European states remain virtually intact despite a quarter of a century of unified legislation, much of which assumes that the structure of all the states involved is similar. There are differences of structures and systems – legal systems, local government, levels of delegation, the ambit of state power, the extent and nature of patronage. There are notable differences of values and public attitudes: in France or Italy politicians can survive allegations of political and financial corruption or sexual behaviour which would have ended the careers of their British equivalents.

BEHAVIOUR IN GOVERNMENT

Behaviour within government, as in society at large, is also influenced by culturally determined, deeply entrenched attitudes in society at large towards the professions of politics and government. In many societies, at one time or another, public office has been recognized as a means to personal material gain and has been openly sought for this reason. This was so for centuries in Britain until the mid-nineteenth century reforms, and it remains the case in much of Africa, Asia, Latin America and large parts of the former Communist world.

Once in government, people's behaviour, and their attitude to changes in the ways in which government operates, are affected by the culture within government. In Britain, for example, the combination of a historically strong executive and a professional, permanent civil service leads ministers and officials to hold a profound, and largely disinterested, belief in the principle that 'the Queen's government must be carried on' at virtually all costs. This view, in spite of its advantages in maintaining the Queen's Peace and allowing the regular collection of taxes, also justifies resistance to any changes that might seem to weaken the power of government in almost any form – hence the unyielding resistance by many in the apparently liberal British establishment to attempts to increase freedom of information.

Within government, working relationships between permanent officials and elected politicians play a key part in determining the character and activities of government. Relationships, and the attitudes which underlie them, can vary greatly. Some years ago American researchers compared several civil services in terms of their attitudes to a range of issues. One of the most striking contrasts was in the responses to the proposition, 'The interference of politicians in affairs which are properly the business of civil servants is a disturbing feature of contemporary public life.' In Italy, 62 per cent of civil servants polled agreed with this; in Germany, 16 per cent; in Britain, a mere 1 per cent (Aberbach et al., 1981). In Britain the view may have changed since 1997.

Much of the thinking about government bureaucracies, and most attempts to reform them in less-developed countries, still implicitly embody a Weberian model of rules and hierarchy that should leave little space for the idiosyncratic exercise of personal authority or for the pursuit of personal gain. On the other hand, most modern organizations give themselves scope to handle the new and unexpected, and to change in changing circumstances, not by trying to anticipate every problem, and to regulate every detail of their members' behaviour by excessively detailed rules, but by prescribing acceptable behaviour in fairly broad terms and by trusting people's willingness to operate within these. The essential element here is trust, without which effective cooperation is virtually impossible (Misztal, 1996). In the 1990s one of the problems of Russian bureaucracy was the dual legacy that the dominant relationships were personal ones, and that anyone not included in these was treated with great mistrust. A similar model, which has been described as 'neo-patrimonial', is found in many African governments, where position still depends upon powerful individuals and where official behaviour is regulated by the personal rather than the institutional relationship (Erdmann, 2002).

Attempts to develop more structured systems of administration can founder on aspects of national culture which permeate government organizations and are invisible to the uninformed outsider. The principles and processes of rational policy-making, and efforts to strengthen them, may conflict with personal and social relationships. In the Solomon Islands bureaucracy, like traditional life, is highly personalized. 'A public servant may not be able to direct subordinate officers efficiently because of kinship relations or because they have higher village status than him – being older, for instance' (Turnbull, 2002). It has been suggested that in some Asian societies similar factors may inhibit modern methods of human resource management:

> Western conventions are not appropriate in industrialising countries such as China where the role of appraisal is quite different. In particular, the intrusiveness of typical western staff performance appraisal systems implies that senior managers have certain rights to invade the privacy and dignity of their staff, which would be wholly inappropriate in many cultures. China, compared to the UK, emphasises high power distance, collectivism and high levels of risk avoidance. (Rubienska and Bovaird, 1999).

Deference based on position within hierarchies may inhibit rational policy-making but is common to most organizations. Juniors who dare not question decisions taken by their superiors, who may be less well informed, are not unusual. On a recent UK-based training course for members of an African justice department, including not only officials but also the Attorney-General, free exchange of ideas was largely stifled by the fact that the officials would not even speak when the minister was present. The same pattern has been observed in British institutions, where policies encouraging open debate are powerless against an individual's rational sense of self-preservation. Collaboration within and between government organizations can be inhibited or prevented altogether by tribal and other divisions. In Vietnam, donors complain that their encouragement of innovative participatory processes involving government and civil society organizations has been resisted by officials brought up in a hierarchical society which emphasizes unquestioning respect for public officials (Lux and Straussman, 2004).

The pervasive influences of culture, and the difficulties of changing attitudes and values, are among the reasons for the almost inevitable time-lag between organizational changes and any consequent changes in behaviour. In

Britain, some of the former nationalized industries had been in private ownership for several years before they even started to develop the values and reflexes of genuinely competitive, customer-friendly enterprises. The World Bank made a belated discovery of these facts; OED remarks in its 2004 report on 'transition economies' that 'institutional reform goes beyond changing organisational structures and rules; it also involves discarding long-established habits and patterns of behaviour – a complicated and lengthy process' (World Bank, 2004b). By 2004 the Bank's insight should have seemed completely superfluous to anybody who had been involved in turning round organizations in developed economies.

8. The constraints on reform

The full significance of the contexts in which governance and public sector reform must operate, and the intrinsic complexity and difficulty of the processes, are not well understood by many of those involved. Part of what needs analysis and understanding is the relationships between organizations and their context. It is not a new discovery that how organizations work, and how people behave in organizational settings, are powerfully affected by the cultures both of the organizations themselves and of the wider social context in which the organizations are set.

This is all the more important when the organizations being subjected to change are part of the government sub-system. Governments have great influence on the distribution of all kinds of resources within a society. As a result, in most societies positions in government have been sought after either because they are valued for themselves or because they can improve their holders' access to resources of one kind or another including, in particular, money and power or influence. Changes which affect the ability of some individuals or groups to acquire positions in government, or to use those positions as they think best, will almost certainly be resisted by those who believe that they will lose from the changes.

RESISTANCE TO REFORM

A study of reforms in South-East Asia notes that to the extent that the civil service system in some Asian countries is built upon institutionalized patterns of patronage and corruption, coupled with low pay and undue discretion in levying charges and finding other means of income supplementation, 'civil service reform along lines of efficiency and merit is very often easier said than done' (Brewer, 2003). As a Mexican official remarked to one of the authors in the early stages of the planned Zedillo reforms of the civil service, the first question to ask anyone newly appointed to a key post in Mexico City was (and is) 'Whom do you know?' To shift the basis of recruitment from patronage to merit, and thus to make the question irrelevant, threatens not only established traditions but also the interests of both those who benefit from patronage and those who dispense it.

Proposals to reform the revenue or customs services and efforts to modify systems involving the issuing of licences or permits can have similar consequences. A recent report on Zambia notes that the reforms which have made least progress are precisely those which 'threaten the ability of the elite to maintain patron:client relationships', citing as examples privatization of the mines and civil service reform (Duncan et al., 2003b). Interests will also be threatened, less obviously, by apparently neutral changes such as budgetary reforms – which may increase the grip of the finance department over previously powerful spending departments or vice versa, and over those departments' often cosy relationships with representatives of the international donors who provide financial support.

These points are obvious enough, but have too often been ignored by those who have used aid programmes to try to reform governments and government processes. The result has been that their reforms have largely or partly failed. Reforms have been resisted, defeated, sidelined, ignored or reversed. The experience, particularly in the past 20 years, of attempted reform in the developed countries has also been ignored. There, most attempts at reform have been strikingly unsystematic; ideology has influenced both the shape they have taken and subsequent attempts to justify them. There has been far too little analysis of the reform process and how it should be planned and managed. Reform-minded governments are regrettably liable to launch second waves of change before the consequences of the first wave have been even mapped, let alone analysed. In consequence there have been few examples of learning from experience which might have increased the effectiveness of later attempts. In some cases, such as the British National Health Service, the sheer frequency of reform efforts, and the repeated failure to complete any specific phase of reform, has made it virtually impossible to evaluate reforms and to build on the experience in future.

Governments' official literature over the years has been replete with opinions on what should be done, but largely silent on how it should be done – especially when, as so often happens, early plans for change are derailed by events. Governments have been even more silent about what should not have been done. When reforms have been less than successful, governments do not discuss the reasons for this; they move on to implement the next idea, leaving the field littered with the unanalysed, unexplained wreckage of the earlier attempts. This is perhaps one good reason for the conspicuous failure of those advocating changes in the governance of less-developed countries to offer advice about the management of such changes.

UNDERSTANDING THE CONTEXT

Where reformers have targeted governmental systems in developing countries they have faced difficulties many times greater than those experienced at home. In the first place has been the difficulty of understanding the current political situation. Who, and which interests, are likely to support change (and why?) and who will be opposed? An evaluation report commissioned by the Swedish aid agency SIDA notes that 'a sophisticated and detailed understanding of the internal politics of a country is required for effective partnership and ownership' (SIDA, 2002).

Secondly, reformers need to understand the social dynamics of the organizations with which they are dealing, whatever the current political situation. The functioning of a government department will be affected by issues such as attitudes to hierarchy and seniority, to tribe and family, to 'political' and to 'appointed' staff , to political party and to personal gain and advantage as compared with any sense of the public interest. Other relevant issues include the significance of money as a motivator, or of formal rules, compared with the informal expectations and self-policing patterns of behaviour of those who work in the system and who have accepted its norms.

A recent report on pro-poor change in Zambia recognized the importance of such factors. It concluded that 'the incentives that affect the behaviour of public officials … need to be understood, and development agencies may have to develop the skills to undertake such analysis. In particular there is a need to understand the ways in which patrimonialism operates, and the impact this has on wider economic performance' (Duncan et al., 2003b). This poses a serious challenge to conventional consultants, advising on, for example, civil service reform in a country which they do not know in general. They are unlikely to have much grasp of these issues in particular. What they have learned elsewhere may be irrelevant in this new setting.

Many consultants, both within donor organizations and their subcontractors, simply lack the relevant background knowledge which would help them to understand the full complexity of the issues: the academic discipline of many, if not most, of them is not history, sociology, anthropology or any of the social sciences with a focus on behavioural issues, but economics. The World Bank, which over the years has gradually stumbled into recognizing that institutions matter, has only very slowly come to understand that economics, even development economics, will not help it to understand much of the motivation of the key people it is dealing with. In 1999 an official of another development bank said, somewhat despairingly, 'It is essential that donors stop appointing untrained people (usually economists) into public management reform, social impact assessment and community involvement jobs. The reverse would never be tolerated (say, asking social impact experts to do economic analysis …)' (Westcott, 1999).

This is a major reason for engaging local experts to complement expatriates. The benefits of doing so go far deeper than merely satisfying a local desire to be involved or providing a fig leaf of 'partnership' to the project. Local experts can bring both understanding of the system and knowledge of current realities. The team on which one of the authors worked in a major project in an ex-Communist state gained immeasurably from including a former local official. Faced with half a dozen senior officials round a table he could explain to his visiting colleagues which of them were unregenerate *apparatchiks* desperate to preserve the status quo, what was the pecking order among them and what was the deeper meaning of the remarks made by each.

Advisers are sometimes not professional consultants but former or serving officials from the donor government. In that case they may have some feel for politics and for bureaucracy and for the interactions between the two. One British consultancy is trying to recruit people with a background of experience in government to provide some of the essential background experience and wisdom that they feel to be lacking in bright young PhDs. But if, as a result of their professional background, officials have experience of only one government system they may find it very hard to translate concepts from that familiar setting to a very different one. It can be difficult to grasp the difference in the roles of a Permanent Secretary in the UK, an Israeli director-general or of a *chef de cabinet* in a Napoleonic system.

The reverse proposition applies. Consultants insensitive to context may use terms familiar to them, which may be misinterpreted by their clients. But 'these words have been used quite casually in the design of government initiatives, forgetting that the application of these terms in a new environment has to deal with the embedded values, history and the capacities of the system' (Carden et al., 1999).

In any case, a more important question is not what permanent secretaries, or director-generals, or *chefs de cabinet* actually do in current systems of government, but what needs to be done in any effective system and where, and by whom, it should be done in any particular circumstances. More generally, consultants without the necessary background knowledge and understanding are unlikely to be able to grasp what effects their proposals, if implemented, would have on the relative positions and powers of different groups within the civil service or on the relationships between the civil service and the wider society. They are therefore unlikely to understand how their proposals will be viewed and received by those affected.

Both the major donors and their principal subcontractors operate globally. If this is Tuesday this must be Cambodia, if Friday, Azerbaijan. Donors and their agents follow current fashions in reform, advocating agencies, citizens' charters, performance-related pay and so on. Contractors develop approaches of their own, with which they feel comfortable and which they will advocate in almost any context, largely regardless of local conditions. The World Bank, perhaps regretting its earlier pride in its portable 'toolkit' approach, observed in 2001 that in general donors had not discriminated effectively among different countries and different phases of the reform process. 'Donors tend to provide the same package of reform assistance everywhere and at all times.' (World Bank, 2001). Another critique of Bank activities noted that attempts at institution-building in Eastern and Central Europe and Central Asia had often been proposed by 'a technical sector specialist, who had little institution building experience and therefore simply replicated institutions that he or she knew of elsewhere' (World Bank, 2004b).

POLITICS AND REFORM

At issue in almost every case are far-reaching changes, not just in formal structures and rules, but in well-established and often deeply-rooted values and patterns of behaviour, as well as in privileges and access to resources of all kinds. One result is that the problems of implementation are often not fully anticipated. DfID's analysis of the Ghana civil service reform includes a melancholy list of ambitious proposals, many of which had no effective local partisans (DfID, 1993). The pace of change may be strongly influenced by deeply rooted cultural factors which donors are powerless to influence. Thus the World Bank commented that in Uruguay attempts at economic reform foundered despite initial enthusiasm on the part of the government, because 'the Bank's program was premised on a pace of reform more rapid than could be handled by the Uruguayan system, where a slow but steady pace of reform reflects a consensus style of policymaking in a traditionally democratic society'. Very much the same thing had happened earlier in Costa Rica (World, Bank, 2004a).

Any reformer has to be concerned with the extent and depth of political support for change. However strong may be the enthusiasm of the politicians currently in power, the depth of opposition is as significant; the timescale over which a project or programme may be expected to last and to need support will be longer than the interest span or indeed the political life of all but the most determined politician. This is the Achilles heel of governance reform. Public sector reform is a political activity. Any changes will affect the answer to the classic question defining politics: 'Who gets what, when, how?' A change that affects the distribution of access to power, influence and control over resources instantly raises political issues. Changes that disrupt familiar relationships and working practices are likely to generate opposition, particularly among the staff whose collaboration is essential if reforms are to be implemented and effective.

Even a basically technical administrative change, such as strengthening the rules controlling the submission of proposals to the Council of Ministers, may be threatening to some. Such a change can inconvenience those ministers who tend to smuggle oral items onto the agenda at the last minute so as to outmanoeuvre opposition, or a prime minister who prefers to take his ministerial colleagues by surprise. The deliberately informal, unstructured, un-collegiate style of the Blair administration in Britain between 1997 and the time of writing in 2005 was integral to the Prime Minister's particular style of autocratic government and his personal authority; he would have strongly resisted any attempts to reintroduce arrangements which would increase the influence of Cabinet members generally. One of the authors was working in an African state in the 1990s with a brief to extend the reach of Cabinet and to increase the number of issues that had to come to it for collective discussion. He was surprised by the apparently unreasoning reluctance of one ministry to have any of its proposals, however far-reaching, put on the Cabinet agenda. It was only from a chance meeting with the local representative of another donor that he learned that the Permanent Secretary involved was known to be involved in diverting aid-financed supplies and selling them on the private market for his personal benefit – hence his determination to keep other ministers out of his ministry's business, and to ignore the new procedures which had been agreed.

These insights are not new. In 1994 a British Council seminar bringing together senior officials and ministers responsible for managing their countries' reform programmes concluded that: 'Public sector reform is not merely a technical matter. It is an intensely political matter precisely because it threatens important interests' (Jenkins and Plowden, 1995). What is striking is how slow the major donors have been to recognize this basic fact. Optimistic would-be reformers tend to be confident that the sheer merit of their proposals will ensure that they are accepted, without doing the necessary background work which might materially affect the outcome. The need to take action seems so urgent, and it often is, and the pressure for results from all sides so heavy, that any issue which might derail activity is brushed aside.

A decade later two World Bank staff members could still write, thoughtfully but a little ruefully, that 'more careful up-front analysis of political and bureaucratic commitment to reform would enable reformers to be more discriminating about whether comprehensive programs of public sector reform are worth attempting in specific country settings' (Engberg-Pedersen and Levy, 2004). The same year, the Bank's OED noted, in italics to emphasize the importance of the truth on which they had belatedly stumbled, that: '*The design and implementation of reform initiatives should be based on an understanding of the underlying political and social processes at the core of government that determine the motivation and behaviour of stakeholders*' (World Bank, 2004b).

Recipients have no strong reasons for acknowledging these facts, let alone the possibility that reform activities may not be successful. There is a 'motherhood and apple pie' dimension to assistance on governance which makes it easy for governments to accept reform programmes in principle, particularly when assistance is seen as the passport to other benefits including other forms of aid. Few potential recipients of aid aimed at good government will be willing to argue publicly in favour of bad government. This applies equally to improving public services and to strengthening democratic institutions and processes. Recipients are well aware that if they appear to be committed to improving the institutions and processes of government, they will be more eligible for support under other programmes. Overt enthusiasm for reform can cloak a determination to preserve the status quo. It has been argued that in Vietnam:

> So deep-seated are the norms and conventions which the reform agendas challenge and so embedded are they in prevailing structures that it is tempting to conclude that public administration reform is a smokescreen, behind which jockeying for power and position carries on as usual. (Painter, 2003)

One observer of reform efforts in Africa has observed that the inclusion of public sector management reforms in structural adjustment programmes, as part of the attached conditionalities, has 'encouraged game playing rather than serious efforts at joint problem solving', because the important overriding objective is the financial one rather than the reform programmes, which have a much longer lead time (Berg, 2000b). Even when there seems to be support for good government programmes it is important to look behind the façade of what is said to establish whether anything is likely to happen. It would be hard on many countries, where officials and politicians have a genuine sense of public responsibility, to assume that this Macchiavellian approach to reform is universal. Nonetheless, it would be naive to take all ostensible support for change at face value.

The degree of local support can vary from the very beginning of a project. At one extreme in project design were the structural adjustment programmes of the 1980s, effectively forced by the international financial organizations on governments who had little spontaneous interest in the activity but had an urgent need to borrow and who often accepted the programme – reluctantly – as a condition for borrowing. At the other extreme are reform programmes launched by administrations determined to improve the processes of governance and sometimes elected on the basis of a promise to do so.

CHANGES IN SUPPORT

But politics imposes conflicting priorities and rapidly changing demands.

Even where the local input has initially been substantial, support may evaporate. More often than not, governments in power at the earlier stages of the process have lost office, or interest, well before its conclusion. They may have been forced to give priority to other issues. In Ghana the Rawlings administration was highly committed to economic reform until the mid-1990s, when democratization, a decline in Rawlings's personal authority and protests against the effects of earlier reforms largely derailed the programme. In Lesotho, one commentator has described the problems:

> World Bank [anti-poverty] strategies also underestimated the extent of political instability and did not adequately assess the effect of political upheavals on the Bank's program ... In particular, the Bank did not appear to understand policy decision making in the country and was too optimistic in assuming that democratization and stability could be accomplished soon after the May 1998 elections ... The Bank's assistance plan did not include contingency plans in the event the democratization process fell apart, as it did. (Hassan and Ojo, 2002)

In Mexico the initial enthusiasm of the Zedillo administration for civil service reform was expressed by Zedillo himself at a seminar in early 1996, managed by the authors of this study, which outlined the main issues on which action was needed. But by the end of the presidential term three years later, other pressures prevailed. While the reform agenda had included substantial changes to internal regulation and budget reform, political interest in administrative reform fell behind other priorities. In the succeeding presidency of Vicente Fox the issue of public administration reform was on the agenda for private discussions with the President Elect and was the subject of private papers written for him. A senior reform-minded official was put in charge of a major new initiative to deal with the endemic corruption within the public service. But by 2003 Mr Fox was doing badly in mid-term elections and his reform plans, too, had been shelved.

Much depends upon individuals. The arrival – and disappearance – of key people in the recipient's government system can be critical. One firm recently working in Eastern Europe dealt with three different governments in Romania, and on a project in Macedonia found itself having to work with five Secretary-Generals in as many years – and commented that only one of them even understood what the issues were (private information). In Brazil in the mid-1990s, the Brazilian team initially responsible for reform knew what the issues were and what assistance they needed to make progress. They brought in internal and external support but kept a very clear idea of what their objectives were. But politics intervened, within four years the reform minister was moved, control passed to the Department of Budget and the original team was dismantled.

LEARNING FROM EXPERIENCE CLOSER TO HOME

It is remarkable how optimistic advisers can be about the prospects for public sector reform in other countries, in the light of what they should know about experiences nearer home. In many countries including Britain, bureaucrats, like the German machine-gunners in the First World War, have simply gone to ground while the reform artillery have bombarded their entrenched positions with wave after wave of projects.

The history of British civil service reform is an object lesson in itself. The first wave of reform in the 1860s took nearly 50 years to implement fully. Throughout the twentieth century further bouts of reform occurred regularly every ten years or so. The pace of reform was even more hectic in the last two decades of the twentieth century. Mrs Thatcher in the 1980s was critical of the amateurish management skills of the civil service. She was foremost among those who regarded it as a source of obstruction and a brake on economic and social progress.

The Blair administration took up the cause of reform when it came to power in 1997. Despite all the previous attempts at change, some of which had produced substantial changes in structures and in processes, Blair and his senior colleagues continued to regard the civil service as both seriously in need of fundamental change and deeply resistant to it. In 1999 Whitehall's permanent secretaries were reported as beginning 'an unprecedented 48-hour think-in about Britain's permanent administration, under the implied threat that unless they come up with bright ideas, Tony Blair will impose reform on them' (Walker, 1999). But five years later the Prime Minister was still said to be demanding 'a major shake-up of Whitehall, where many practices have not changed since the Northcote Trevelyan report' of 1854. He proposed four-year contracts for senior officials to keep them on their toes. He declared that 'the talented amateur is simply not equipped for complex, specialised tasks' and demanded more recruitment from the private sector. Officials should no longer work in 'traditional departmental silos' (Watt, 2004).

The language and the proposals were much the same as those of the 1980s, 1970s, 1960s and earlier. In this case they were put forward by senior politicians with considerable leverage in the system they wished to reform, familiar with the British context, with the specific culture of the British bureaucracy and with the kinds of incentives that should be needed to persuade reluctant traditionalists to change their way. Down below ground the machine-gunners were leisurely overhauling their weapons and confidently anticipating a resumption of business as usual. The issue in the UK as anywhere else was the weakness of reformers when faced with well-entrenched, reform-resistant culture.

Even in the US in 2004, attempts to improve the management of the much criticized security services proved almost impossible. As one senior politician remarked grimly as legislation ground its way through Congress: 'the status quo always has an army'. Few bureaucracies would be quite as open and brutal in neutralizing reformers as were those in Russia who simply abolished the agency responsible for much of the reform activity, Roskadry, in 1993. But there are many other effective techniques. Anyone who has worked in a well-established organization, at any level, knows well how easy it is to learn and to use the rhetoric of change, and to install the window-dressing needed to satisfy one's superiors, while ensuring that everything important remains as before. How likely is it that proposals just as far-reaching in their aims, relating to an African, Latin American or Central Asian system of government, and made by eager proselytizers of good governance from the United States or Britain, will speedily bring about comparable changes in values and institutions in the recipient countries?

Change will be slow even when there is continuity at the top political levels, where support for change is crucial. Mrs Thatcher's unusually long period as Prime Minister between 1978 and 1990 made possible the consolidation of innovations begun in Britain during her administration. But very often there is discontinuity, whether among key individuals or parties in power or in the amount of attention that those in power can give to the change process. In Mexico the PRI government of Zedillo abandoned its ambitious civil service reform programme when other issues, particularly budgetary reform, largely crowded it off the agenda without any effective resistance from well-placed supporters (Philip, 2003). Zedillo's successor, Vicente Fox, was initially hailed as being equally determined to leave public administration reform as 'one of his most enduring legacies' (*The Economist*, 2002). But his reforms, too, stalled when his administration ran into difficulties on other fronts.

SUPPORTERS AND OPPONENTS

Even where those at the top genuinely want change, advisers can be unrealistic about institutional realities, and too easily take at face value assurances with little substance behind them. If in Britain today there was a repetition of the 1976 economic crisis and the Prime Minister was faced with demands from the IMF for major reforms, prime-ministerial promises of change might be made; but nobody, including the Prime Minister, could be confident that these promises could be kept. Exactly the same is true of a President or Prime Minister or minister of public sector reform in any country which is pressed to make changes by the World Bank, DfID or any other agency. It is often meaningless to boast of the support of 'the government': what matters is whether the PM's enthusiasm is backed up by senior colleagues and by powerful interests elsewhere in the system – or, sometimes, whether the PM's own reluctance to make changes is outweighed by the enthusiasm of his or her colleagues.

Individual ministers may be potential allies, or they may be opponents. The Prime Minister may have far less clout than the Cabinet Secretary or vice versa. Especially in patrimonial states, ministers feel threatened by poverty reduction programmes, because their constituents lose their jobs when spending programmes are cut back or public services are downsized. In one African country the only real enthusiasts for poverty reduction were said to be the President and the minister for the civil service (Caulfield, 2002). In general few people in recipient governments, as in donor governments, are likely to be disinterested when contemplating the possibility of change. Those who are principally in contact with donors, both ministers and senior officials, may well support reforms which strengthen their own positions – 'opportunistic [institutional development] interventions with immediate pay-offs rather than systemic reforms with long-term pay-offs' (Girishankar, 2001). Those at the top may not want change. In Congo in the 1980s, discussions between the World Bank and senior officials reached a gratifying consensus about the desirability of economic reform and the details of what needed to be done. However, these foundered completely on the determination of President Mobutu to resist any changes which might constrain his prerogatives and his freedom to manage the country as he chose (Kiakwama and Chevallier, 2001).

In any government the plans of reformers can be obstructed by bureaucratic jealousies and politics. In Mexico the authors were involved in arranging a senior-level seminar, with the patronage of the President, to discuss reform. The speakers were startled to be told the evening before the start that the whole programme would have to be changed from a two-day discussion into two one-day seminars because representatives from one of the major ministries would not discuss reform with their colleagues from other ministries since it might imply there was something wrong with how they worked, while the discussions might provide ammunition for future debates about policy. Only an elaborate process of bargaining succeeded in getting a reasonable number from both ministries to sit together. The seminars, chaired by the authors, took place in an atmosphere of elegant calm once the brokerage was over, overlooked by one of Mexico City's best-preserved pyramids where the blood of human sacrifices once ran, on the far side of a huge plate glass window.

Finally, it is easy to overlook both the interests and the potential importance of one of the major stakeholders in the whole reform process – citizens themselves. Public sector reform can be, and tends to be treated as, a highly technical affair of concern mainly to a handful of insiders and advisers who understand the issues and the techniques, and best left to them. This is a short-sighted view, for two main reasons. First, to repeat a point made above, because one purpose of reform is to provide citizens with the effective public services to which they are entitled and which they want, as in contemporary Afghanistan or Iraq. Second, because public apathy can only complicate the tasks of would-be reformers struggling with the inevitable resistance to change. If citizens are unconvinced that change would benefit them, they are potential supporters for anyone wanting to claim that reformers are threatening well-loved institutions and hallowed traditional practices. The Conservative government in 1980s and 1990s Britain made precisely this error with their ambitious attempts to change the structure and practices of the National Health Service.

TIMESCALES OF REFORM

If one axis on the would-be reformer's chart should show intensity of support, the other should show timescale. The donors' timescales, if they are governmental aid agencies, have to take account of the timescales of the legislatures which fund them – a maximum of five years in the British case, four years (for the presidency) in the US. Moreover, budgets are rolled forward annually and performance measured on the same timescale. These are the periods within which legislators, and ministries of finance, are likely to look for results and to assess performance.

In practice, whatever happens on the political front, most fundamental changes take far longer to implement than this, even if all goes smoothly; the relevant unit of measurement is not so much years, as generations. If there is resistance, results could take far longer. It is unlikely, to say the least, that any positive constellation of forces will survive unaltered for over five or six years.

One result of this is that, even when changes have been successfully introduced with the apparent support of the recipient government, at some point momentum and direction may well be lost. In one African country a robust and well-designed system of support for the Cabinet, funded by USAID, was put in place in the early 1990s. It was well written up in an account available on the internet. A World Bank publication in 2000 hailed it as 'a model for cabinet office reform in Sub-Saharan Africa' (Schacter, 2000a). In fact by the time these words were written many of the elements of the system had fallen into disuse and Cabinet-level decision-making was as chaotic as ever. Some of the original proposals had proved unworkable in all but the very short term; some had been accepted only in principle. A further USAID grant was made to review the situation; many of the original recommendations were repeated. These recommendations, too, appear to have been accepted by the client government. It was not clear at the time of writing whether or how far they had been put into practice (private information).

Changes of government and of key personnel can destabilize the best-planned project. Fluctuations in political support are unpredictable, but donors seem to conduct little risk analysis of the likelihood of political changes occurring. In the 1990s Brazil put considerable efforts into trying to modernize the structure of the federal government – since described at length by the minister concerned (Bresser Pereira, 1998; Gaetani, 2003). The reforms had political support; the necessary changes to the constitution were achieved. But the focus altered after the elections; the same President remained in power but radical changes were made to the ministerial team and to the reform programme.

The speed with which support for change can fluctuate can baffle even expert observers. The Russian case is instructive. In the 1990s help of all kinds, including advice on structures and systems of government, was provided to the Yeltsin presidency. In 1992–93 an outside consultancy team, funded under the TACIS programme and working closely with the central Apparatus of Government, made proposals for rationalizing the central decision-making structure. At about the same time further proposals, put together jointly with the government's personnel management agency Roskadry, outlined a sweeping programme of civil service reform – downsizing, re-certifying serving officials and purging the system of political appointees. The net result was nil. The first set of proposals were simply ignored. Roskadry was dissolved. In 1996–97 the then First Deputy Prime Minister announced his plans for streamlining the government machine. President Yeltsin intervened and nothing was done. In 1997 a group of Yeltsin's advisers worked up an outline for administrative reform. The principle of reform was accepted by its incorporation into the government's forward programme. Once again, nothing happened.

When Yeltsin's successor, Putin, was preparing his bid for the presidency he commissioned a major stocktaking. With financial support from Russian business, he established the Centre for Strategic Studies, to put together a programme for his first term – taking account of previous successes and failures. Some 500 Russian experts were commissioned to review the recent past. Their conclusions, very broadly, were that projected economic and social reforms had failed largely due to the failure to reform the state apparatus. When Putin came to power many of these experts moved into government with him. Guided by Dmitry Kozak, Putin's campaign manager, they were by now fully confident of their ability to plan and manage a reform programme, selecting from developments in G8 countries such as Britain and New Zealand, many of which they had themselves visited.

Mr Putin approved a comprehensive plan for civil service reform in August 2001. At least one experienced observer commented shortly afterwards that 'this reform does indeed seem to be for real. The president and government appear extremely serious about ensuring real implementation of civil service reform' (Parison, 2002b). But some observers were sceptical about his sincerity. An academic observer noted at the time that 'despite a substantial volume of legislation, real changes in the management of the civil service are hard to find' (Gray, 2003). In July 2003 Mr Putin set up a commission on the subject. A year later it was suggested that as long as oil prices remained high, Mr Putin would be unlikely to 'decide in favour of serious and bold steps' (Yudaeva, 2004). But the momentum of this programme was already diminishing – partly due to Kozak's move to another post, partly due to political crises such as the Beslan school massacre and the failure of Mr Putin's candidate in the Ukraine presidential election, and a consequent reluctance of the administration to make any changes which might rock the boat. But by 2005 the civil service reform process appeared to be under way again.

In trying to anticipate the future one may note the record of an OECD discussion, in the spring of 2004, following a presentation about administrative reform in Russia: 'Delegates found the presentation very interesting, and noted that the reforms were very ambitious, and would require a major cultural change in the Russian administration' (OECD, 2004b).

Sometimes fluctuations in support are more or less inevitable. This is so when a change of government is constitutionally required. In many countries the constitution prohibits a President from standing for a third or, in some cases, a second term. The maximum 'window' during which there may be some guarantee of consistent support for reform may thus be five or six years. An incoming President, even of the same party, may need to be persuaded from scratch that improvements in governance are a worthwhile area in which to expend his political capital. One of the authors was asked to conduct a workshop in one Latin American state for the staff of the presidency. It appeared to be well received. But at the conclusion one of the staff expressed regret that they had not had the benefit of this advice several years before; it was unfortunate that the President's term expired the next year and that they would have so little opportunity to put the advice into effect. The workshop had to be repeated for the successor administration the following year.

ASSESSING THE FEASIBILITY OF REFORM

More significant are the contexts in which lack of support can be predicted from the start. In 1995 the British Council funded a workshop in Swaziland which was intended to give some momentum to the local civil service reform programme and which was attended by senior officials from several other African countries. The brief given to the consultants said blandly, 'The Public

Sector Management Programme is a programme of the Government of Swaziland with a fundamental objective of improving the efficiency and effectiveness of, in particular, the civil service. It has been approved in principle by Cabinet' (private information). There was nothing in the brief even to hint at the background facts which later led one commentator to describe Swaziland as 'a veritable graveyard of reform attempts'. (McCourt, n.d.). The country is an absolute monarchy, where there has never been a general election, and where the King has executive, legislative and judicial powers; well-meant efforts to develop constitutional democracy are bound to seem irrelevant and have been treated as such.

Discussions in the workshop held in a lavish hotel showed enthusiasm for the principle of reform in Swaziland; senior speakers from the governments of Uganda and Zambia described in encouraging tones the progress made in those countries in reforming the public service. The conclusions of small-group sessions stated that the reasons why reform was now needed in Swaziland included 'unprofessional civil service', 'low morale and motivation leading to corruption', 'poor response to public needs' and 'lack of discipline'. The recommendations of the workshop included a proposal for the appointment of a national director to manage the reform programme (private information). But in the circumstances it is perhaps not surprising that it took 18 months to make the appointment, that the director resigned after only 18 months in post and no further action was taken (McCourt, n.d.).

The question in such a case is why any resources were expended on the workshop in the first place – or indeed on similar abortive ventures. A clue may be found in a comment made on another project in Swaziland: '[T]here was little effective pressure for change from anyone. The donor wanted to lend lots of money to Swaziland as it was one of the few African countries likely to reply' (Bevan, 2002). This comment, highly untypical of most discussions of attempts at reform, lifts the lid on an issue which is rarely confronted but which is absolutely basic to the success or failure of interventions: whether anyone involved is seriously interested in the outcome.

It is worth repeating the reasons why this might not be so. Donors – as in the example just given – want to spend or lend money. At the policy level, this may be related to commercial or political considerations. At the operational level, it may be because current incentives tend 'to encourage heads of country offices to spend the budget they have been allocated even when their judgement indicated that this may not be necessary' (Warrener, 2004). Spending patterns often owe as much to these factors as they do to any strong belief in the improvability of the recipient's government arrangements. Recipients want to show that they are making an effort. Contractors want contracts, and repeat contracts. And any of these may sincerely feel that something should be done to improve local arrangements, that it is better to be engaged in a dialogue of some kind with any regime, however contemptible, and that any activity is better than none. All of these wishes can be satisfied whatever the outcome of the activities to which they may give rise. Moreover, if the outcomes are unsatisfactory, nobody involved – donors, contractors, recipients – has anything to gain from drawing outside attention to this unfortunate fact.

There is a range of situations in which interventions are more than usually unlikely to succeed. At one extreme are the small minority of states which, at different times, have fallen into the hands of individuals or group regimes which are both completely impervious to world opinion and single-mindedly set on exploiting their country's resources for the sole advantage of themselves or their clan, combining corrupt and inept government with varying degrees of brutality – Mobuto's Zaire, Idi Amin's Uganda, Lukashenko's Belarus. Next are the states in which a semblance of good practice and constitutional government barely conceals degrees of corruption, undemocratic behaviour, infringement of human rights, and differing forms of patrimonialism. Fujimori's Peru, Arap Moi's Kenya, Musharraf's Pakistan are examples. Finally there are the regimes in which an amiable willingness to work with donors is offset by a complete lack of interest in the outcomes and a reluctance to invest human, political or other resources in the activity. Swaziland is a good example.

Donors are now sufficiently sophisticated and realistic to regard the first group as off-limits. Problems arise with regimes on the borderline between this and the second group, such as Karimov's Uzbekistan, especially where there are strong political reasons for maintaining a dialogue. But for much of the time the second and third groups are active recipients of aid for government, their inadequacies treated as justifying further assistance rather than disqualifying them for it. It is surprising how little published analysis even tries to make distinctions of this type, or to identify the characteristics which might distinguish promising candidates for assistance from the rest.

One recent article suggested some criteria for predicting the success of consultancies in this field, including the extent of political stability and control, levels of corruption, the quality of the donor's own organization, and coordination between donors. It was as refreshing as it is unusual to find, among the case-studies cited, one headed 'Consultancies highjacked by a corrupt government'. The basic situation in this case was portrayed as being the need of a regime, whose public support was declining, for new arrangements to extend its patronage. The problems listed included corruption among field officials, increasingly poor administration, lack of planning and monitoring, and the influence of a bureaucracy 'which saw rich pickings in sloppy donor funding arrangements' (Bevan, 2002).

In this last case the author's summary judgement on the consultancy activities was that they were 'a waste of effort'. This should in itself be a strong argument against the donors' use of scarce resources – their own and the recipients' – in cases where failure seems likely. Much more serious objections can be raised when donors embark on the elaborate charade of pretending that a country's system of government is susceptible of being brought into line with acceptable international standards – by launching aid-funded programmes aimed at introducing the merit principle into public service appointments, or at imbuing the police force with respect for human rights.

Projects with these ostensible aims can damage the credibility of 'governance' programmes in two ways. First, by concentrating on what are in practice cosmetic changes while ignoring the grosser underlying defects of the regime, they will almost certainly be ineffective. Second, and more important, by ignoring the defects they inevitably put the donors in the posture of condoning those defects and the undesirable behaviour which results from them. It should be unacceptable to hold workshops on modern methods of human resource management for senior officers in a security service which routinely tortures opponents of the regime – and all the more so given the high probability that any evaluation of a workshops project is likely to conclude that it was, in some sense, a success. For example the evaluation conclusions in a case like this might read: 'Attendance was high throughout the course. Participant satisfaction ratings ranged from 70 to 90 per cent. The head of the security service said that he would welcome a further course in the near future. The President himself came to the closing reception'.

UNDERSTANDING DIFFERENCES IN CONTEXT AND CULTURE

The values and habits which make up the cultural background to the institutions of any government are too important to be ignored by those who wish to have an impact on how that government is run – and often too complex for outsiders to understand. At the very least, outside advisers should be able to take full account of the context in which they are working. This requires in-depth understanding of the local society and how it works. That in turn calls for skills and knowledge of a kind not traditionally ranked very high either in managing the careers of donor staff or in selecting consultants. Practice in DfID, for example, has followed the pattern long familiar in British central government, whereby promising staff are rapidly cycled through a number of different posts so as to give them the breadth of experience thought necessary for the most senior jobs. This neither enables nor encourages them to specialize in the society and government of, say, South-East Asia or sub-Saharan Africa.

However well informed outside advisers may be, they still need to free themselves from some understandable but unhelpful preconceptions. Most of those involved in attempts to reform other people's governments assume that the desired end is some form of a modern, secular, democratic state. But George Kennan's wise words of half a century ago should be kept in mind. Judgements about the right form of governments are best made by those who have to manage and live with the changes. Afghanistan and Iraq may well, in due course, illustrate the unpredictability of institutional change in unfamiliar and imperfectly understood contexts. Ten or 15 years down the track, the character of the local society, the role of religion, attitudes to civil and human rights, are likely to combine to produce a state which will differ considerably from the model originally in the minds of the intervening powers.

These issues are beginning to be recognized, at an operational if not fully at a political level. Some of them are referred to by some of those developing the 'Drivers of Change' approach (Duncan et al., 2003a; Warrener, 2004). It remains to be seen how far donors' policies will be adapted to recognize the enormous importance of context and culture, and the barriers that these can generate to introducing apparently rational changes which seem to have been successful elsewhere.

9. Conclusions

Expectations of what can be achieved by outside interventions in 'governance' remain high. But expectations do not seem to have taken account of many years of disappointing experience. The quality of government in Africa, Latin America, and parts of Asia remains desperately low despite years of aid-funded efforts to improve it. Incompetence, corruption and autocratic behaviour are rife. So too, partly as a result, are poverty, low life expectancy, poor education and civil strife. In recent years interest in 'nationbuilding' has increased, and there have been a small number of high-profile episodes under this label. Nationbuilding raises many of the same issues as attempts to improve government, and has encountered similar disappointments. Throughout the world, the process of reforming government, as the experience of most countries demonstrates, is unpopular. The idea of reform is usually popular; it is the process of doing it which causes the trouble. This is also a task which can never be said to be complete. Few projects are completed as planned and many are never finished at all; the pressure of events is as likely to derail attempts to reform as internal opposition or simple incompetence.

In this book 'governance' has been interpreted quite narrowly, to cover the activities of governments and the public sector, rather than the total complex of institutions, processes and relationships through which societies manage their internal affairs. This book has therefore referred to 'government' or 'public sector' reform.

WHAT HAS GONE WRONG?

There are many reasons for the failure to achieve better results in government reform, some minor and specific to local circumstances, but three main reasons stand out from any analysis. First, there are external factors, notably linked to debt and trade which, by limiting the material resources available to countries which are already seriously deprived, severely constrain their ability to improve their own economic situation. Second, there are political, cultural and institutional problems in recipient countries which inhibit reform. Third, the activities of the donors, the ways in which they are managed, and the nature of the donors' relationships with recipients, have had a direct impact on the success of reform. This book has focused on the third reason, the activities of the donors, but it is important to acknowledge the significance of the external factors and of the condition of recipient countries.

The important external factors are mainly economic in nature. They include the trading environments of developing countries, and the degree of repayable debt which they have to service. It is easy to see that poor countries trying to compete with subsidized production in the richer countries, with the enormous economies of scale available to global corporations, and with debt burdens which overshadow their productive capacity, will often find it hard to mobilize the extra resources needed for public sector reform programmes. The key to progress is for the donor governments to accept the importance of these external factors and to acknowledge that they are, to a very large extent, under the donors' governments' own control.

The second main reason for failure is the condition of the recipient countries. At one end of the continuum there are countries which by any standard are not suitable candidates for external help, and where donor resources would inevitably be wasted: Mobutu's Zaire, today's Uzbekistan or Belarus. There are then the obviously 'failed states' such as Liberia or Haiti in which, though they may have escaped from the very worst style of regime, few features of the system of government and administration function effectively, and where culture, institutions and recent events combine to render a state virtually unable to manage its own affairs, let alone to plan and manage a reform process. Slightly less weak than these are countries with many of the attributes of statehood – for example Ecuador, Zambia or Bolivia; there a lack of resources, incompetence, corruption or a combination of these and other problems have meant in practice that any reforms made are frail, non-sustainable and alarmingly vulnerable to political crisis or economic downturn.

There is a further large group of countries with specific but not disabling weaknesses and problems – Peru, Zambia and Cambodia. In some cases the absence of any effective administrative infrastructure means that, apart from competent NGOs where these exist, there are no reliable means of delivering the public services optimistically envisaged in reform programmes and anti-poverty strategies. In some countries the problems have been intensified by donor activities, in particular where the multiplication of external consultancies, combined with well-intentioned efforts to employ skilled local people in aid projects, have deprived governments of scarce high-quality human resources that they desperately need. At the end of the continuum are countries such Brazil or Russia where resources are abundant, donor assistance is often regarded askance, and all that is intermittently lacking is the political will to make the necessary changes.

The third reason for disappointing outcomes is the activities of the donors – what they do and how they do it.

The process of reform has been almost entirely supply-driven, not demand-led. The donors have both defined the problems and devised the solutions. Often neither task has been well done, because many people on the donor side have failed to understand the intrinsic complexity and difficulty of what they are trying to do, and the full significance of recipient countries' history, politics and culture. In many cases ambitious programmes of reform have been conceived by the donors, worked up by paid contractors, and left to the local administrations to implement with little or no help on the most difficult issue of all – how to do it. In some cases the donors have ostensibly tried to improve the governance of states which are manifestly unready for reform – and whose rulers are uninterested in it. There the obstacles to change have been more severe, and the results even less successful.

Many years of experience in the developed countries have demonstrated the intrinsic difficulty of reforming well-established public sector organizations. But there has been little read-across from this experience of how to do it – or how not to do it – to reform activities in the development field. There are some well-known negative lessons to be learned about the obstacles to making changes. In particular, would-be reformers in both contexts have often been slow to understand the political dimension of what they are trying to do and to minimize the predictable resistance from those who fear that any change will be to their own disadvantage. Reformers have often failed to make the case for their proposals for changes, whether to those within the government system or to the general public; as a result, they have not mobilized support from those who might be expected to gain from the changes.

The shortage of people who have relevant expertise in analysing and changing the patterns of government institutions and behaviour reinforces the tendency on the part of donors and contractors alike to promote fashionable 'remedies' – poverty reduction strategy papers, medium-term expenditure frameworks – regardless of their relevance or indeed of their feasibility in local circumstances. The donors' experts are liable to recommend their favourite remedies without ensuring that the conditions necessary for success are present. Donors seem to prefer the big schemes to humdrum but essential projects – restructuring the civil service rather than developing reliable national statistics – without which the other schemes cannot function.

The timetables set for reform projects by donors and recipients are frequently complex and overoptimistic. Some of the ambitious changes envisaged in reform projects could take decades to work through; they are hard to programme, and heavily dependent on personalities and on often transient political support. It is often impossible to predict accurately how and in what sequence the several components of reform programmes will take shape in practice, or over what timescale. But those who plan projects are reluctant to accept this. The belief that projects will be 'completed', and results achieved, according to plan and according to some preordained timetable, is implicit in most of what is done; it is almost certain to lead to disappointment and disillusionment.

One of the weakest parts of any reform process is the implementation stage. It is difficult to exaggerate the importance of this, the source of so many apparent policy failures in government systems of all kinds, developed and undeveloped alike. Too often donors and contractors behave as though their responsibilities end when studies have been completed and reports delivered to the client. Reports often have little to say about the protracted and untidy business of turning proposals into actions, or who is responsible for ensuring that agreed changes are in fact implemented. When donors are involved in implementation their role is not sufficient to ensure success. The interests of those at the top or at the centre of a government are not necessarily shared by those lower down the hierarchy or outside government or beyond the capital in the provinces, especially if they do not understand why changes are being proposed or if they fear that change may be to their disadvantage. The lack of attention paid by donors to political analysis, and their incapacity for it, means that resistance to the proposed changes has often not been anticipated, and plans have not been made for managing opposition. Neither donors nor their contractors nor, often, recipient governments, have any strong interest in ensuring that proposals are followed up in practice or that objectives are realized in the medium to long term; promises and declarations are often taken as equivalent to actions by all the parties concerned – donors, contractors and recipients.

Failure to focus on implementation is compounded by donors' lack of interest in outcomes. Most evaluations of programme effectiveness focus on activities and on outputs. The result is that, despite extensive evaluation by donors and others, there is very little learning from experience; evaluation findings – which are often produced only long after projects have been completed – are ignored or not fed back into the operational processes. The widespread failure of donors to provide feedback on the operation of projects or to share with contractors any information about the outcomes of their work is symptomatic of the lack of interest in learning from experience. Contractors can go on giving their clients the same advice, year after year, with no reliable understanding of whether it is helpful or even relevant.

A great deal is now known and has been published about many of these difficulties, about past failures and about the reasons for them. Some of the most cogent critiques of past practice have come from the donors themselves, especially the World Bank. Much of the argument is accepted, at one level, by those professionally involved. It is, for example, well established in the current 'contemporary wisdom' that donors' activities should be shaped not by their own preferences but by the experience and needs of the recipient governments.

It is equally well established that lack of coordination among donors and their agents lessens their collective effectiveness and imposes unnecessary burdens on recipients.

But although there have been some moves towards encouraging local 'ownership' and better consultation among donors, and although lip-service is now widely paid to the importance of these, little progress has been made on either front. This is partly because over the years donors have developed their own professional skills and their own views about priorities, and partly because they are in competition with each other and willing to change their practices only if doing so does not put them at a competitive disadvantage. The internal dynamics of aid have the effect of reinforcing the status quo. All parties involved – donors, contractors and recipients – have powerful incentives to continue their current practices, and few incentives to pause to consider whether their practices are effective or not.

The overall effect is that analysis, understanding and acceptance of the need for change are largely confined to a 'parallel universe' of their own. Experts in places such as the Institute of Development Studies or the Overseas Development Institute publish their critiques of current practices, and the World Bank repeatedly acknowledges the inadequacies of its methods in the recent past. In another 'universe' practice continues essentially unchanged, and disappointments multiply.

Donors and contractors have, unfortunately, exaggerated their ability to transform the systems and processes of government, and to do so in short order, and they have allowed the world at large to believe this too. Those who are not directly involved in the business of aid for government, and whose support is vital for continued aid funding – citizens, legislators, journalists – find it difficult to follow what is happening. None of those who are involved – recipients, donors or contractors – has any interest in being entirely honest with them. All the participants have strong interests to defend and no wish to divert the aid flow to other countries, topics or competitors. As a result those outside the aid system can often be left with exaggerated expectations of the certainty and speed with which aid can improve the effectiveness of governments, and can thus pave the way to achieving other important objectives such as reducing poverty.

THE NEED FOR MORE EFFECTIVE ACTION

The evidence of the donors' past failures is so compelling that there is a strong temptation to argue for less, not more, intervention until ways of intervening more effectively have been devised. But there can be no doubt that without improvements in the competence of their governments many countries will be unable to absorb and utilize aid funds; without better-managed public services many aid programmes will fail to deliver and much of the money will be wasted. The World Bank belatedly addressed this issue in its *World Development Report 2004*, with its sub-title *Making Services Work for Poor People*. There is a strong practical case for action, however imperfect, aimed at helping to bring about improvements. Moreover, the climate for taking action is more favourable now than it has been in the past. The early twenty-first century has seen, even if only temporarily, increased political and emotional pressure to act and to be seen to be acting to tackle world poverty. Inevitably the kind of action that might be effective in improving the performance of governments is neither interesting for politicians nor emotionally satisfying for the public. Successful changes here will not change the television pictures overnight. The effects will be visible only when the new schools, roads and clinics can be seen in existence and operating over time to improve the living standards of citizens in general, including the very poor. The easy solutions represented by announcing projects or promising finance are no longer adequate. Television generates demands for visible outcomes, not merely for promises. But unless governments can perform better, results will continue to be poor. Effective solutions involve changes to established ways of working that are politically difficult, both for the aid agencies and for recipient governments – which is why those involved are reluctant to contemplate them.

MAIN TASKS

There are three main ways in which achievements could be brought more closely into line with expectations. The first is to work on the external factors. The second is to adjust expectations to correspond more closely with reality. The third is to make changes in the attitude and approach of the donors.

Some actions are already being tried under all three heads; others have been proposed but not yet implemented; yet others have long been acknowledged to be desirable, but their implementation has been obstructed by the internal dynamics and politics of the aid business. The fact that by now most feasible proposals are not original does not mean that they should be regarded as obsolete; as already pointed out, the task remains of getting some action taken to implement them.

External Factors

If donors were willing, exceptionally, to subordinate their commercial objectives to their aid objectives, they could transform the situation. While they were beginning to address the problems posed by the debts run up over many years, they should also take action to dismantle the serious imbalances in the terms of trade which they have formulated to protect their own economies, and which damage the economies their aid programmes are attempting to help.

The new willingness of the wealthy nations to cancel the indebtedness of many countries should be a powerful mechanism to improve the quality of international lending. It gives an opportunity for the lending banks to put in place a system which takes an informed view of the burden on the borrowers, the likelihood of a successful outcome and the realistic chance of getting the lenders' money back. There is a strong argument that lending for projects on government reform fulfils none of these simple criteria. Government reform is a lengthy, difficult and chancy business. It should not be the subject of loans – at the very least because the politics makes a nonsense of repayment. Impoverished countries have been required to repay debt lent to oppressive regimes, weak political parties or long-dead governments for schemes which have long since vanished into the sand. No competent commercial bank would have lent for such schemes and any other lender would have long since made adequate provision for bad debt and written it off. But because the borrower is a government and there remains a recognizable entity, the debt continues.

Adjusting Expectations

Expectations of the speed and effectiveness of reform in government are almost always unrealistic. Reform is far from being a straightforward activity: it will always be difficult, problematic and uncertain of outcome. The donors must acknowledge this and must convey it to their clients and to their funders. Nobody benefits from unrealistic expectations. In 2005 there was much public discussion of making improvements in the quality of government in Africa the principal condition of increased assistance. The implication that both of these could be achieved in the same timescale was bound to lead to disillusionment. The donors are rightly regarded as the experts in this field and must do more to control levels of expectation of what can be achieved.

As a start they should try to convey some understanding of the concept of risk. Several basic propositions should be kept in mind. First, that every project or programme is, to a large extent, unique, both in its priorities and over time. Civil service reform in Peru will raise different issues from those raised by civil service reform in Zambia. Civil service reform in Zambia in 2005 will raise issues different from those raised by civil service reform in Zambia in 1998. This being so, there can be few cast-iron certainties about the future of any specific project.

Second, it is hard to stick to timetables. There are several reasons for this.

Support for any project is likely to fluctuate over its lifetime and may well at times evaporate altogether. A great deal depends upon individuals, and on their availability. The dynamic head of the central reform unit may unexpectedly go into political exile with his or her patron or, conversely, may be promoted by him or her to be ambassador to the UN. One result of longer project lifetimes is that the local context may well change, so that the final outcomes differ from what was originally envisaged both in their nature and in how they are received by the client.

Third, aid agencies must be opportunistic, and agnostic. They may need to ignore some countries whose rulers would clearly be opposed to change, until changing circumstances present a window of opportunity; for example, the transition in Ukraine from Kuchma to Yevtushenko may prove to have offered such a window. Donors may need to support a strategy for reform in a particular country, or a reform-minded administration, without initially being able to specify the results anticipated. Some aspects of projects may be neglected while others flourish. Some projects may cease to make any progress at all, for months or even years at a time. There may be no results to show at a time when audit committees are demanding results. Reform is usually pursuing a moving goal; by the time the original objectives have been wholly or partly achieved, new needs will have been perceived and new objectives defined. For all these reasons it must be understood that projects and programmes, however well planned, and even if ultimately successful, will take a long time to complete – and often far longer than originally envisaged. This is all the more so in severely damaged states such as Sierra Leone or Liberia, or those emerging from generations of dictatorship in Central Asia, where there may for years be very little to show that real change is taking place.

Stops and starts do not necessarily mean that a project has 'failed', or that it will never lead to positive outcomes. But the possibility of such fluctuations does mean that aid agencies must be resolute in justifying their activities in this uncertain field. They need both the courage of their convictions and the analytical justification for what they wish to do. They must be capable of defending individual interventions in principle even when there is little to show in practice. They must accept that these activities are risky, in the strict sense that in individual cases there will always be a possibility of varying degrees of failure. They must be prepared to defend their policies even when there are failures, provided that they did not initially pretend that the outcomes were certain. Risk management is more important than risk avoidance. Donors might keep in mind the comment by a senior member of one development bank: 'Reforms take hold when they are important, and have a good potential to be carried out in a timely manner, and to be a catalyst for additional reforms. Selectivity means filling in the reform timetable in a pragmatic way, while supporting the long-term vision' (Westcott, 2004).

A consequence of more realistic expectations and a more realistic view of risk will be more selective intervention. Setting minimum standards for administrative competence or democratic behaviour as a precondition for help with government reform should focus the attention of both donors and recipients. The key to using resources more effectively in future will be to recognize the enormous variations in the suitability of different countries. There are some whose intrinsic weaknesses should rule them out altogether. This is not to propose an end to all forms of aid to such countries. It is important to recognize that some proportion of the motivation for overseas aid of all kinds has always been donor self-interest. This is unlikely to change. The politics of the Cold War against Communism have been replaced by the politics of the increasingly hot war against terrorism. Governments of the richer countries will, therefore, continue to see compelling political reasons for supporting particular countries – reasons which have nothing to do with merit or, indeed, with a country's ability to use assistance effectively. Aid funds will continue to be used to help a corrupt, brutal dictator by paying for a new airport, or even for a new fleet of armour-plated presidential Mercedes. Such gifts are recognized to be bribes aimed at keeping bribable rulers on side.

Help with reforming government is different. Transparency International and Amnesty International regularly produce evidence that demonstrates the links between corruption and human rights abuses and poor government and social decay. It has been argued above that activities purporting to improve the government of the worst states almost inevitably waste resources. In addition, they associate the donors with the government of regimes from which they should be distancing themselves. Attempts to secure the goodwill of a government by presenting it with hardware of various kinds can be deprecated and may be difficult to eradicate, but the donors can more easily control absurdities like running, in the same country, an elaborate seminar on government reform or a police training programme. Activities of this kind are almost certain to be ineffective, but the mere fact that they have taken place implies that in the donor's view only marginal changes are needed for the recipient's government and internal security arrangements to be internationally acceptable.

There are less dramatic cases which raise many of the same issues, where the recipients of aid and advice are demonstrably unlikely to be willing to act on the advice. These activities, once again, waste donor resources; they often act as a fig leaf behind which other activities more significant politically, whether commercial or diplomatic, can be carried on.

The conclusion should be, as far as the politics of overseas aid allow, that donors should recognize the existence of a category of potential recipients which are unsuitable for assistance because they are incapable of benefiting from it. This category ranges from Uzbekistan to Swaziland. Donors should not risk further damaging the credibility of activities related to government by offering help to such states.

Donors: a New Approach

Changes are needed in where donors work, and how they work. For a start, they should be much more discriminating in the nature, scope and depth of their intervention, case by case. There should be fewer interventions, more carefully planned. Donor resources should be concentrated on activities which are most likely to have a favourable cost–benefit ratio. This should mean that a higher proportion of programmes and projects would have some probability of a satisfactory outcome. It would also limit the demands on local skilled people, whether working in the recipient government or recruited by incoming consultants. In general, the donors need to accept that the priority given to different activities will vary from one country reform programme to another, and that the sequencing of projects can be planned only in relation to each country's own objectives for reform. Priority may be influenced by the urgency of the need, as perceived by the recipient and by the possibility of building on what is already there, so as to achieve some useful results as quickly as possible. An efficient refuse-collection service may be a priority in one context, speedier administration of justice in another. Available resources are always limited; they should be spent by the donors where there is the best chance of success.

For most recipient countries, success seems to be most likely when they plan and run their own reform programmes, accept relatively small amounts of external assistance linked to specific outcomes and develop at their own pace. There are severely damaged states in conditions of crisis, like Sierra Leone or Liberia, where the government may be in ruins and local capacity relatively limited, but even in these conditions assistance should be tailored to need and come from the most suitable source; it need not necessarily comprise big projects planned and managed by the big donors. When a recipient government has prepared its own reform programme that should form the framework within which the government plans its priorities and its timetable, taking into account political and social realities. Contributions from the donors should be considered where a government has neither the capacity nor the resources to manage parts of its programme itself and only where that contribution is consistent with the government's overall programme and priorities. Some countries – for example Tanzania – are now trying to use this kind of approach. Success will depend crucially on the donors' recognition of the government's role and its responsibility for its own programme, and on refusal to bypass it on the part of influential donors and influential interests in the recipient government.

Countries which are ready for reform will need to have a clear view of what needs to be done, in what order and how urgently, and what help they may need. Donors wishing to be involved should subordinate their priorities to those of the government as defined in its own strategy. They need to accept, in principle, that their activities are most likely to benefit the recipients when they are harmonized with those of other donors, and that 'freestanding' initiatives are unlikely to be cost-effective. They would have to recognize as a matter of practice that proposals for activities incompatible with the programme would be likely to be rejected and to be ineffective. The same would apply to activities which would simply duplicate those already being funded. An approach of this kind might also raise valuable questions about the relevance and feasibility, in many contexts, of fashionable and sometimes over-ambitious approaches such as Poverty Reduction Strategy Programmes (PRSPs) or Medium-Term Expenditure Frameworks (MTEFs). Modest improvements to hardware procurement arrangements might well be more useful and more welcome than elaborate strategies which may make no sense in local circumstances.

Leaving the initiative to the recipients would also help in selecting and prioritizing countries to be helped. Brazil and Russia are examples of countries in which many donors wish to play a role and to have a long-term stake; but these are sophisticated and relatively wealthy states who are quite capable of deciding for themselves how much real value would be added by donor-funded interventions. The same is true of the 'middle-income countries' where the British justification for intervention has included the view that their 'governance systems' had 'not responded *quickly enough* to [political] changes' (emphasis added). It is not clear that value judgements of this kind are an appropriate basis for using aid funds. The credibility of the government component of the aid programme can be compromised and damaged if it is used to achieve what are, in fact, foreign policy objectives; far better to focus on Sierra Leone or Bosnia, where much more needs to be done and where the outside expert can bring desperately needed skills and resources.

Working Relationships

A more selective approach would imply changes in working relationships between donors and recipients which would continue throughout the lifetimes of projects and programmes. Donors should not be indiscriminate or unconditional in their support. If they are waiting for a window of opportunity they should not try to show their good faith by pouring in funds regardless of what the recipients are doing. The point has already been made that donors should be extremely cautious in their dealings with corrupt or oppressive regimes; this applies just as much to a regime which starts to behave corruptly or oppressively in mid-project. If donors do not act in this way, they risk contradicting the principles which underlie their activities and their funding. There are few developed countries which would be happy to see their tax revenues being used openly to support oppressive or corrupt regimes. Donors would also face operational inconsistency; they may find themselves implicitly condoning bad practices in one country where they have an ongoing project, while insisting on changes in similar practices in another country as a condition for funding a new project there.

For the same reasons, where donors have, on whatever grounds, been withholding funds from particular states, they should try to ensure that real changes haves taken place before giving premature expression to their anxiety to intervene and to spend money. A change of ruler may herald a new era, but new rulers have to take over existing systems, and may in any case share many of the values of their predecessors. Kenya, Zambia and Ecuador are among many examples of countries where successive regimes have been welcomed as promising an end to the corruption, incompetence and excess of their predecessors, only to fall into very similar patterns of behaviour. It may be some time before it is clear whether Yevtushenko's Ukraine differs significantly from Kuchma's.

As so often, an important contrary principle needs to be observed, and a balance must be struck. Any large-scale donor involvement in the affairs of a recipient country creates expectations and dependency relationships. Abrupt changes in the flow and character of assistance can have serious destabilizing effects, especially where aid represents a large proportion of GDP. Unexpected termination of projects for financial or other reasons can cause disruption. The sudden transfer of British aid resources to Iraq led to cut-backs in aid to Latin America and other regions and, for example, to the abrupt closure of the DfID office in Peru-Honduras and of a local community capacity-building project, after only two and a half years. (Livingstone and Bowcott, 2003; Select Committee on International Development, 2003). Such actions can also cause local resentment disproportionate to any savings realized. Predictability is at least as important as the volume of aid. Donors who wish to change their level of support, whether because of domestic budgetary pressures or because they feel that recipients have failed to meet agreed conditions, should ensure that they have assessed the full costs, to the recipient, of doing so.

More broadly, donors should be realistic about the nature of any relationship in which an outside party is trying to assist in improving the workings of a government. Donors doing so are, inevitably, intervening in the internal affairs of sovereign states. This is a relationship which needs extremely careful handling. Donors' activities can too easily undermine the authority of the governments which they are trying to help. The issues of accountability are complex in any state, but particularly where large flows of money come from external sources. A government which has little accountability and less responsibility for the content or the financing of a reform programme is unlikely to feel committed to it, or to be willing to defend it against opposition. The World Bank is inextricably associated with reform programmes originated by itself rather than by the governments with which it is working and consequently is used, worldwide, as a convenient scapegoat when such programmes run into difficulties. The donors can actively damage the prospects for reform unless they recognize the role they play in the political dynamic of the countries they work in. In turn, a recipient government which is anxious to reform but needs external help to do so must balance the value of that help against the threat to their own accountability and responsibility for the outcome.

Two words recur in suggestions for solutions to this problem. The first is 'partnership'. But partnership is often not the right term to use to describe the relationship between donor and recipient government. Some donors have larger budgets than the governments they assist. It would be meaningless to describe their relationships with recipient governments as partnerships. The donors may assist, they may even support, but they are not partners. They are suppliers, and should be involved in reform within clear, contractual limits. When, as can happen, as an outcome of reforming the processes of government they become more closely involved in the development of policy and in the taking of decisions – on economic management or poverty reduction – the donors inevitably acquire some responsibility for changes in policy or expenditure levels for which the government should in principle be accountable to its electorate – and would be in a democracy. The term 'partnership' implies a degree of equality of status which is as unrealistic, on the one hand, as that between an international organization and a failing state as, on the other between a nation-state and a supplier of services under contract.

The second word is 'ownership'. But this term too can be misleading. The negative proposition, that reform proposals should not be 'owned' exclusively by a donor, is unexceptionable. Plans for change devised and supported only, or mainly, by a donor, an external agency, are unlikely to be sustainable or to be able to overcome any strong local resistance. It is harder to express the positive proposition in operational terms. Who exactly, in addition to a donor, should 'own' the proposals? One answer would seem to be all important stakeholders – that is, important in the sense that they stand to gain or lose substantially if the proposals are carried out, or that they have the power to derail or obstruct change programmes of which they disapprove.

Acting on this principle must mean, for a start, going beyond any simplistic collective formulation such as 'the government'. It requires an understanding of who are the key players in the government – President, Prime Minister, minister of finance, Cabinet Secretary, senior officials, *éminences grises* of different kinds. Beyond the government is the legislature, and beyond that major organized interests such as the principal NGOs, trade unions and so on. Beyond the organized interests lie the unorganized, most notably, at a time when the focus of all major aid programmes is on poverty relief, the poor.

The dilemma for donors is that if recipient governments request funding for programmes or projects which are not 'owned' by more than a few people in government, these may not be sustainable. If they are backed only by the government, a change of party in power or of key people may result in total loss of support, and the donors' money will be wasted. On the other hand, if proposals are to be truly owned by governments, it is not for donors to suggest who else should be involved or consulted, let alone to try to manage the process. The right approach should be for the donors to allow the recipient government to do its own thinking, to identify and to define both the problem it wants to solve and, perhaps with advice, how the problem should be tackled. The donor's responsibility is to satisfy itself that the recipient has done all that it can to ensure that the changes made will be sustainable.

Learning from Experience

Many of these new approaches would require new skills, new knowledge and new attitudes on the part of those involved. The donors need greater realism about what they can achieve, better processes for planning, more sophistication in their approach to intervention and more sensitive management of their relationships with recipient governments. The kinds of judgement that would be needed for planning and managing better-informed interventions in different countries must rest on in-depth understanding of all the relevant circumstances – social, political and economic. Donor staff, and the staff of consultants engaged as contractors, need clearer direction about their role and how to perform it, and more local and regional expertise, as well as understanding of government; donors should give greater weight to these factors in selecting and training their own staff and their contractors, while contractors hoping to work in specific countries or regions should select or develop individual team members on the same basis.

If there were to be large-scale changes in the ways in which aid on reform to government is planned and managed, it would be all the more important to ensure that real learning processes are put in place without delay. One need is for more and more rigorous, formal evaluations – carried out with emphasis on speed, independence and consultation with the recipients. The suggestion has been made of an 'independent evaluation fund', financed by at least four or five major donors to ensure its independence from any single agency. This would review the multilaterals in particular (Birdsall, 2004). This might simply add an additional layer of bureaucracy to the aid process. It would be more economical and more effective if the donors would pay more attention to the results of their own evaluations and the views put forward in their own publications, as well as improving their planning processes so that the conditions for more effective evaluation could develop.

It is important to distinguish between long-term evaluations, focusing as far as possible on outcomes, and the kind of learning of lessons which can be fed rapidly into the system. Both are important. But the first almost by definition must wait till an activity is complete, by which time it is beyond correction. The second is essential if projects and programmes are to be adapted to the inevitable changes in circumstances. This argues for more intensive informal consultative processes involving recipients as the 'owners' of the projects, donors and contractors. A review of progress should focus on processes and on outcomes and on the relationships between them. The same project or programme might be reviewed at different stages to ensure that the relevant facts could be ascertained, and also that most of those involved were still in post and so could be held accountable, however informally, for their actions. Donors could be questioned about the contract-letting process and about the preparation of terms of reference; contractors could be questioned about the resources which they had brought to the task and about the approaches used; recipients could be asked about their relationships with donors and contractors and about the significance of specific projects in their overall strategies. Questions about outcomes would normally be the final stage.

Implementation

Implementing earlier proposals is less glamorous, and secures far fewer headlines, than making new proposals. But it is crucial. Unless implementation is given far more attention, and more resources, than in the past, neither changes in relationships, nor in donor working practices, nor in public expectations, will be sufficient: outcomes will continue to be disappointing.

The keys to effective implementation of the reform programmes are twofold. First, the role and status of the person responsible for ensuring that the agreed action is actually taken must be understood and recognized. Second, a system of support from senior management and any donors involved must be in place to protect the implementers when, as will happen, the going gets difficult. Reform will be unpopular because it invariably affects vested interests. Few serious programmes of reform have worked in the absence of a single point of responsibility and constant pressure for action and results. Without support, projects will founder and people will be more reluctant to take on the responsibility for implementation next time.

It is at the implementation stage that donor experience ought to be most useful to recipient governments. Donors need to understand the problems of implementation and to define a role for themselves where they can provide genuine expertise and advice and support without detracting from the authority of the government politicians and officials directly involved.

Additionally, if more attention were given at the planning stage to the implementation of all projects and programmes, this would provide a much sounder basis for evaluations. This would require attempting some answers to the question, 'Who is to do what, by when – and with what expected results?' By identifying the several stages to be achieved on the way to the final goal, and the responsibilities in each case, it should be easier to identify deviations, to explain the reasons for these and, possibly, to take corrective action. This approach also slightly increases the chance that, at least at the earlier stages, some of those responsible will still be in post and capable of explaining what has happened. But evaluation must also be sensitive to changes in need and context. Evaluators as well as the people directly responsible for implementation must recognise that, in the medium to long term, the original project specification may cease to be wholly relevant and its objectives may need to be redefined. The implementation plan may need revision if it is not be become irrelevant.

CONCLUSIONS

Little of what is said above will be new to many people engaged in the business of trying to improve government through aid programmes, particularly those closest to the action working in recipient countries, or to those who have kept up with the substantial literature. Few of the facts are seriously contested. The need now is to recognize the gulf between what is promised and what is done. Failure, and the reasons for it, has been well documented. It is accepted by the donor organizations themselves.

Obstacles to Action

The obstacles to effective action derive partly from the political context of the aid business including, in particular, the multiple constraints which prevent the managers of any individual publicly funded programme from choosing their own objectives and the means of achieving them, without regard to corporate goals and ambitions. Aid ministers are members of Cabinets in which their colleagues from other spending departments are competitors for resources; in addition their colleague the minister of finance is always alert for evidence that they are either not spending the funds allocated to them or are not producing results. Their colleague the minister for foreign affairs is keen to ensure that all activities, including aid, are managed in ways that will achieve wider diplomatic objectives – unless they are one and the same person, in which case this pressure is internalized. Their colleague the minister for trade has similar commercial objectives. The tax-paying public can always be excited by stories of waste and corruption, but does not see the links between getting food to babies and improving the management of public services. The international donors, spending less than a third of total ODA, are influenced by similar pressures at one remove.

Other obstacles are internal to the agencies themselves. Aid agencies are conventional bureaucracies, and like any other bureaucracy will continue to do things in the ways they know unless forced to do things differently. More, perhaps, than other parts of government, they have a sense of mission which reinforces their belief in the rightness of their own professional approach. The current emphasis on local ownership of programmes, and of non-specific techniques such as budget support, directly challenges donor staff whose professionalism consists in knowing how to plan civil service reform or decentralization. They are reluctant to lose control of the activities which they fund. Their subcontractors the consultants, who comprise a multi-billion dollar business worldwide, have their own knowledge and skills and ways of doing things. They advise the donors on the shape of projects and compete for the resultant business. They are operating in a highly competitive market and can adapt their 'products' in response to changing demands; but they will see no reason to do so until the demand changes. Meanwhile they continue to contribute to the inertia in the system.

The Future

These obstacles to any changes are formidable and are clearly daunting to the management of the donor agencies. But the countries which look to the donors for help, expertise and support face problems which are of a different order of magnitude. It is precisely because their problems are so grave and the suffering caused by them so unacceptable that the donors have an obligation to make their role more effective.

We have suggested six main changes in the ways in which donors operate. They should be more selective in choosing where and how to intervene. They should be more realistic and more modest in their expectations about what, in any specific context, can be changed and how long change will take. They should also recognize that the process of change is usually unpredictable. They need to acquire much greater understanding of the local context in which they are intervening, and of the importance of this for the character of governmental processes and structures. They need to develop less prescriptive relationships with recipients, combined with more open and rigorous contractual relationships in which both parties are seen to have obligations. They must develop a much more systematic approach to implementation and a much clearer focus on outcomes, both as an end in itself and as a basis for evaluation.

Establishing the detail of how this might be done will not be easy. It will mean hard thinking about what changes will achieve these results, and determined management to make sure that they happen. But it is not an impossible task; many large organizations have been through similar upheavals successfully, and have emerged better organizations, better able to achieve their aims.

In doing all this the donor organizations will need the support of the many other interests which, in different ways, are concerned about aid to government. These include ministries of finance, who provide aid agencies with the funds needed; legislatures, who initially vote approval for the funds and, subsequently, scrutinize the use made of them; national audit offices, who review aid and other activities; journalists and academic commentators, who can play an important role in analysing and reporting activities in this as in other fields; and the taxpaying public, whose support for all aspects of the aid programme is ultimately critical in determining its scale and direction.

The time may in fact be ripe to start doing things differently. In 2005 public opinion and politicians in the developed countries seemed genuinely to want to do more to tackle poverty in developing countries. At the same time the aid agencies themselves seem to have realized that little can be done about poverty without improvements in the institutions and processes of government. They also seem to be starting to realize how long it takes to bring about change in this field, and how many different complementary changes are needed. Aid agencies must now do what they urge their clients to do – to reform fundamentally the way in which they work.

Bibliography

Aberbach, J.D., Putnam, R.D. and Rockman, B.A., 1981, *Bureaucrats and Politicians in Western Democracies*, Cambridge MA and London, Harvard University Press.

Ablo, E. and Ritva, R., 1998, *Do Budgets Really Matter? Evidence from Public Spending on Education and Health in Uganda*, June, Washington DC, World Bank.

Ahrens, J., 2001, 'Governance, conditionality and transformation in post-socialist countries', in Hoen, H.W. (ed.), *Good Governance in Central and Eastern Europe*, Cheltenham, UK and Northampton MA, USA, Edward Elgar, pp. 54–90.

Akaha, T., 2002, 'Japan: a passive partner in the promotion of democracy', in Schraeder, P.J. (ed.), *Exporting Democracy: Rhetoric vs Reality*, Boulder CO, Lynne Riener, pp. 89–108.

Arndt, C., 2000, 'Technical co-operation', in Tarp, F. (ed.), *Foreign Aid and Development: Lessons Learnt and Directions for the Future*, London, Routledge, pp. 154–77.

Australian Agency for International Development, 2003, 'Economic governance and the Asian Crisis', an evaluation of the Australian aid programme's response, www.developmentgateway.com.au.jahia/Jahia/cache/offonce/lang/en/pid/1941.

Bailey, P.J., 1996, *Postwar Japan: 1945 to the Present*, Oxford, Blackwells.

Baker, K.L., Dalton, R.J. and Hildebrandt, K., 1981, *Germany Transformed: Political Culture and the New Politics*, Cambridge MA, Harvard University Press.

Banerjee, N., Valdivia, L. and Mkandla, M., 2002, 'Is the development industry ready for change?', in *Development Policy Journal*, **2**, New York, UNDP, pp. 131–54.

Batley, R., 1999, 'The new public management in developing countries: implications for policy and organisational reform', *Journal of International Development*, **11**, 5, pp. 762–5.

BBC News, 2001, Asia-Pacific, 18 July.

Beaumont, P., 2005, 'Divided without a wall, Germans are now split by a rift of the mind', *Observer*, 3 April.

Bennett, J., 1995, *Meeting Needs, NGO Coordination in Practice*, London, Earthscan.

Berg, E.J. (ed.), 1993, *Rethinking Technical Cooperation: Reforms for Capacity-Building in Africa*, New York, UNDP.

Berg, E., 2000a, 'Why aren't aid organizations better learners?', Expert Group on Development Issues, www.spa-psa.org./index.

Berg, E., 2000b, 'Aid and failed reforms: the case of public sector management', in Tarp, F. (ed.), *Foreign Aid and Development: Lessons Learnt and Directions for the Future,* London, Routledge, pp. 290–311.

Bevan, P., 2002, 'The successful use of consultancies in aid-financed public sector management reform: a consultant's eye view of some things that matter', *Publlic Admininstration and Development*, **20**, 4, pp. 289–304.

Biddle, K., Clegg, I. and Whetton, J., 1999, *Evaluation of ODA/DFID Support to the Police in Developing Countries: a Synthesis Study*, Swansea, School of Social Sciences and International Development, University of Wales, Swansea.

Birdsall, N., 2004, *Seven Deadly Sins: Reflections on Donor Failings*, Washington DC, Center for Global Development.

Boehling, R.L., 1996, *A Question of Priorities: Democratic Reforms and Economic Recovery in Postwar Germany*, Providence RI, Berghahn Books.

Bose, S., 2002, *Bosnia after Dayton*, London, C. Hurst & Co.

Boyer, Peter J., 2004, 'The true believer', *New Yorker*, 1 November.

Brady, J.S., Crawford, B. and Wiliarty, S.E. (eds), 1999, *The Postwar Transformation of Germany: Democracy, Prosperity and Nationhood*, Michigan, University of Michigan.

Brautigam, D., 2000, *Aid Dependence and Governance*, EGDI Study 2000:1, Stockholm, Almkvist and Wiksell International.

Bresser Pereira, L.C., 1998, *Reforma do Estado para a Cidadania*, Brasilia, Brazil, ENAP.

Brewer, B., 2003, 'Thailand: building the foundations for structural and systemic transformation', in Cheung, A. and Scott, I. (eds), *Governance and Public Sector Reform in Asia: Paradigm Shifts or Business as Usual?*, London, RoutledgeCurzon, pp. 186–207.

British Embassy, Warsaw, 2002, 'From recipient to donor', proceedings of seminar From Recipient to Donor, at www.britishembassy.pl/en/.

Brown, S., 2001, 'Authoritarian leaders and multi-party elections in Africa: how foreign donors help to keep Kenya's Daniel arap Moi in power', *Third World Quarterly*, **22**, 5, pp. 725–39, October.

Brown, S., 2004, '"Born-Again Politicians Hijacked Our Revolution!" Reassessing Malawi's transitition to democracy', *Canadian Journal of African Studies*, **38**, 3, at aix1.uottawa.ca~brown/pages/Stephen_Brown_CJAS.doc.

Browne, S., 1990, *Foreign Aid in Practice*, London, Pinter.

Browne, S. (ed.), 2002, *Developing Capacity through Technical Cooperation: Country Experiences*, New York, UNDP/Earthscan.

Cabe, D.K., 2002, 'Nation building', in *Kennedy School Bulletin*, Cambridge MA, www.ksg.harvard.edu/ksgpress/bulletin/spring2002.

Carden, F., Baranyi, S., Smutylo, T. and Giulmette, J.H., 1999, 'Evaluating governance programmes', Report of a workshop, International Development Research Centre, Ottawa, Canada.

Carothers, T., 1999, *Aiding Democracy Abroad: the Learning Curve*, New York, Carnegie Endowment.

Carothers, T., 2002, 'The end of the transition paradigm', *Journal of Democracy*, **13**, 1, pp 5–21.

Carothers, T., 2003a, 'Is gradualism possible? Choosing a strategy for promoting democracy in the Middle East', Washington DC, Carnegie Endowment.

Carothers, T., 2003b, 'It's too soon for democracy', *Washington Post*, 20 July.

Carothers, T., 2003c, 'Promoting the rule of law abroad: the problem of knowledge', Washington DC, Carnegie Endowment.

Cassen, R., 1994, *Does Aid Work?*, Oxford, Oxford University Press.

Caulfield, J., 2002, 'Executive agencies in Tanzania: liberalization and Third World debt', *Public Administration and Development*, **22**, 3, pp. 209–20.

Centeno, M.A., 1994, *Democracy within Reason: Technocratic Revolution in Mexico*, University Park PA, Pennsylvania State University Press.

Centre for Democracy and Governance, 1998, 'Democracy and governance: a conceptual framework', Washington DC, USAID.

Chalker, L., 1991, 'Good government and the aid programme', speech at the Royal Institute of International Affairs, 25 June, London, Overseas Development Administration.

Chapman, W., 1991, *Inventing Japan: the Making of a Postwar Civilisation*, New York, Prentice Hall.

Cheung, A.B.L., 2003, 'Public service reform in Singapore: reinventing government in a global age', in Cheung, A.B.L. and Scott, I. (eds), *Governance and Public Service Reform in Asia: Paradigm Shifts or Business as Usual?*, London and New York, RoutledgeCurzon, pp. 138–62.

Cheung, A. and Scott, I. (eds), 2003, *Governance and Public Sector Reform in Asia: Paradigm Shifts or Business as Usual?*, London, RoutledgeCurzon.

Clarke, R., 1999, 'Institutions for training overseas admininstrators: the University of Manchester's contribution', *Public Administration and Development*, **1**, 9, pp. 521–33.

Commission for Africa, 2005, *Our Common Interest: Report of the Commission for Africa*, London, DfID.

Conradt, D.P., 1996, *The German Polity*, White Plains, NY, Longman.

CorpWatch, 2003, 'US blocking World Bank, IMF governance reforms', www.corpwatch.org.article.php?id=7348.

Courtney, M., Riddell, H., Ewers, J., Linder, R. and Cohen, C., 2005, *In the Balance: Measuring Progress in Afghanistan*, Washington DC, Center for Strategic and International Studies.

Cracknell, B.E., 2000, *Evaluating Development Aid: Issues, Problems and Solutions*, London, SAGE.

Crawford, G., 1995, *Promoting Democracy, Human Rights and Good Governance through Development Aid: a Comparative Study of the Policies of Four Northern Donors*, Leeds, University of Leeds, Centre for Democratization.

Crawford, G., 2000, 'Promoting democratic governance in the South', *European Journal of Development Research*, **12**, 1, pp. 23–57.

Crawford, G., 2003, 'Promoting democracy from without: learning from within, Part I', *Democratization*, **10**, 1 (spring), pp. 77–98.

Das, S.K., 1998, *Civil Service Reform and Structural Adjustment*, Delhi, India, Oxford University Press.

Degnbol-Martinussen, J., 2002, 'Development goals, governance and capacity building', *Development and Change*, **33**, 2, pp. 269–80.

Dempsey, G., 2004, *The Folly of Nation-Building in Afghanistan*, Washington DC, Cato Institute, 11 May.

Denny, C., 2000, 'A mercenary for democracy', *Guardian*, 9 September.

Desai, M., 1994, *Measuring Political Freedom,* London, London School of Economics, Centre for the Study of Global Governance.

Devarajan, S., Dollar, D. and Holmgren, T., 2001, *Aid and Reform in Africa: Lessons from Ten Case Studies*, Washington DC, World Bank.

DfID, 1997, *Ghana Civil Service Reform Programme*, DfID Evaluation Dept, London, DfID.

DfID, 2001a, *Working in Partnership with the Commonwealth Secretariat*, London, DfID.

DfID, 2001b, *Making Government Work for Poor People: Building State Capacity*, London, DfID.

DfID, 2001c, *Eliminating Global Poverty: The Middle-Income Countries*, London, DfID.

DfID, 2003a, *Better Govermment for Poverty Reduction: More Effective Partnerships for Change*, Consultation Document, London, DfID.

DfID, 2003b, Statement by Secretary of State, www.dfid.gov.uk/news/files/speeches/benn-micsstatement-nov03.

DfID, 2005, 'Commission for Africa report', London, DfID.

DFID (n.d.a), *Catalogue of Evaluation Studies*, London, DfID.

DfID (n.d.b), *Analysis of Incentives and Capacity for Poverty Reduction in Kyrgyzstan*, www.grc)-exchange.org/g_themes/politicalsystems_drivers.

DfID (n.d.c), www.dfid.gov.uk/mdg.

DfID/Foreign and Commonwealth Office/HM Treasury, 2004, *Partnerships for Poverty Reduction: Changing Aid Conditionality*, a draft policy paper for comment, London, DfID.

Dia, M., 1996, *Africa's Management in the 1990s and Beyond*, Washington DC, World Bank.

Diamond, L. and Plattner, M.F. (eds), 2002, *Democracy after Communism*, Baltimore, MD, Johns Hopkins University Press.

Diefendorf et al (eds), 1993, *American Policy and the Reconstruction of West Germany 1945–55*, Cambridge, Cambridge University Press.

Dobbins, J., McGinn, J., Crane, K., Jones, S., Lal, R., Rathmell, A., Swanger, R. and Timilsina, A., 2003, *America's Role in Nation-Building: From Germany to Iraq*, Santa Monica CA, RAND Corporation.

Docena, H., 2004, 'The other reconstruction: how private contractors are transforming Iraq's state and civil society', Focus on the Global South, www.focusweb.org/main/html/Article.289.

Dollar, D. and Svensson, J., 1998, 'What explains the success or failure of structural adjustment programs?', World Bank Development Research Group, Washington DC, World Bank.

Doornbos, M., 2003, 'Good governance: the metamorphosis of a policy metaphor', *Journal of International Affairs*, **57**, 1, pp. 3–17.

Dowden, R., 2005, 'To save Africa we must listen to it', *New Statesman*, 14 March.

Dower, J.W., 1999, *Embracing Defeat: Japan in the Wake of World War II*, New York, Norton.

Drake, P.W., 1993, 'From good men to good neighbours 1912–1932', in Lowenthal, A.F. (ed.), *Exporting Democracy. The United States and Latin America. Themes and Issues*, Baltimore MD and London, Johns Hopkins University Press, pp. 3–40.

Dror, Y., 2001, *The Capacity to Govern*, London, and Portland ME, Frank Cass.

Duncan, A. (with Jones, S. and Dietsche, E.), 2003a, 'Drivers of Change: reflections on experience to date', discussion note of workshop held in Oxford, Oxford Policy Management.

Duncan, A., Macmillan, H. and Neo, S., 2003b, *Zambia. Drivers of Pro-Poor Change: An Overview* (short version), Oxford, Oxford Policy Management.

Economist, 2002, 'Yes, Ministro', 16 November.

Einhorn, J., 2001, 'The World Bank's mission creep', *Foreign Affairs*, **80**, 5, pp. 22–35.

Engberg-Pedersen, P. and Levy, B., 2004, 'Building state capacity in Africa: learning from performance and results', in Levy, B. and Kpundeh, S. (eds),

Building State Capacity in Africa: New Approaches, Emerging Lessons, Washington DC, World Bank, pp. 87–108.

Erdmann, G., 2002, 'Neo-patrimonial rule: transition to democracy has not succeeded', EU, 2000 europa.eu.int/comm./enlargement/slovakia.

EU, 2000, europa.eu.int/comm./enlargement/slovakia.

European Commission, 1997, 'Agenda 2000: Commission opinion on Slovakia's application for membership of the European Union', Brussels.

Eyben, R. and Lister, S., 2004, 'Why and how to aid middle income countries', Brighton, Institute of Development Studies.

Feeney, P., 1998, *Accountable Aid*, Oxford, Oxfam Publications.

Ferguson, N., 2004, *Colossus*, London, Allen Lane.

Finn, R.B., 1991, *Winners in Peace: Macarthur, Yoshida and Postwar Japan*, Berkeley CA, California University Press.

Flint, M., 2004, *Evaluation of DFID Country programmes. Country study: Brazil 1997–2003*, Oxford, Oxford Policy Management.

Flint, M., Cameron, C., Henderson, S., Jones, S. and Ticehurst, D., 2002, *How effective is DFID? An Independent Review of DFID's Organisational and Development Effectiveness*, East Kilbride, DFID.

Flint, M., Gray, J. and Jones, S., 2004, 'Evaluation of DFID Country Programmes: synthesis report', East Kilbride, DFID.

Foreign and Commonwealth Office (FCO), 2005, www.fco.gov.uk.

Fukuyama, F., 2004a, 'Nation-Building 101', *Atlantic Online*, January/February, www.theatlantic.com/doc/200401/fukuyama.

Fukuyama, S., 2004b, *State Building: Governance and World Order in the Twenty-First Century*, London, Profile Books.

Gaetani, F., 2003, 'Public policy management change in Brazil 1995–1998', *International Public Management Journal*, **6**, 3, 327–42.

Garner, C., 1997, 'Public service personnel in West Germany in the 1950s' in Garner, C. and Moeller, Robert G. (eds), *West Germany under Construction: Politics, Society and Culture in the Adenauer Era*, Ann Arbor MI, pp. 135–95.

Garnett, H. and Plowden, W., 2004, 'Cabinets, budgets and policy: political commitment to poverty reduction', in Levy, B. and Kpundeh, S. (eds), *Building State Capacity in Africa: New Approaches, Emerging Lessons*, Washington DC, World Bank, pp. 149–78.

Girishankar, N., 2001, 'Evaluating sector reform: guidelines for assessing country-level impact of structural reform and capacity building in the public sector', Washington DC, World Bank.

Goldin, I., Rogers, H. and Stern, N., 2002, 'The role and effectiveness of development assistance: lessons from World Bank experience', Washington DC, World Bank.

Goldman, R.W. and Douglass, W.A., 1983, *Promoting Democracy: Opportunities and Issues*, New York, Praeger.

Goldsworthy, D., 1995, *Good Government*, London, British Council.

Goldsworthy, 2001, 'Public service reform: a pro-poor perspective,' unpublished paper.

Gould, J. and Ojanen, J., 2003, *Merging in the Circle: the Politics of Tanzania's Poverty Reduction Strategy 2003*, Institute of Development Studies, Helsinki, Finland, University of Helsinki.

Grasso, P.G., Wasto, S.S. and Weaving, R.V. (eds), 2003, *World Bank Operations Evaluation Department: The First 30 Years*, Washington DC, World Bank.

Gray, P., 2003, *Hard Cases and Improving Governance: Civil Service Reform in the Russian Federation*, London, London Metropolitan University.

Grindle, M.S., 1996, *Challenging the State: Crisis and Innovation in Latin America and Africa*, Cambridge, Cambridge University Press.

Grindle, M.S. (ed.), 1997, *Getting Good Government: Capacity Building in the Public Sectors of Developing Countries*, Cambridge MA, Harvard Institute for International Development.

Grindle, M.S. and Hilderbrand, M.E., 1995, 'Building sustainable capacity in the public sector: what can be done?', *Public Administration and Development*, **15**, 5, pp. 441–64.

Grugel, J. (ed.), 1999, *Democracy without Borders: Transnationalisation and Conditionality in New Democracies*, London, Routledge.

Hanlon, J., 2002, 'Are donors to Mozambique promoting corruption?', www.mol.co.mz/analise/corrupcao/jhsheffieldb.html.

Haque, M., 1999, *Restructuring Development Theories and Policies: a Critical Study*, New York, State University of New York.

Hassan, F.M.A. and Ojo, O., 2002, *Lesotho: Development in a Challenging Environment: A Joint World Bank–African Development Bank Evaluation*, Washington DC, African Development Bank/World Bank.

Haynes, J. (ed.), 2001a, *Towards Sustainable Democracy in the Third World*, Basingstoke, Palgrave.

Haynes, J. (ed.), 2001b, *Democracy and Political Change in the 'Third World'*, London, Routledge.

Healey, J., Hoebink, P. and Cox, A., 2000, *European Development Cooperation and the Poor,* London, Macmillan/ODI.

Hearnden, A. (ed.), 1978, *The British in Gemany: Educational Reconstruction after 1945*, London, Hamilton.

Hencke, D., 2005, 'Anger as £700,000 of £3m British aid to Malawi spent on US firms', London, *Guardian*, 29 August.

Hibou, B., 2002, 'The World Bank: missionary deeds (and misdeeds)', in

Schraeder, P.J. (ed.), *Exporting Democracy: Rhetoric vs Reality*, Boulder CO, Lynne Rienner, pp. 173–92.

Hicks, U., 1961, *Development from Below: Local Government and Finance in Developing Countries of the Commonwealth*, Oxford, Clarendon Press.

Hinden, R., 1950, *Local Government and the Colonies*, a report to the Fabian Colonial Bureau, London, George Allen & Unwin.

Hogan, M.J. (ed.), 1999, *The Ambiguous Legacy: US Foreign Relations in the 'American Century'*, Cambridge, Cambridge University Press.

Holmgren, T., Kasekene, L., Atingi-Ego, M. and Ddamulira, D., 1999, *Aid and Reform in Uganda*, Washington DC, World Bank.

Hook, S.W., 2002, 'Inconsistent US efforts to promote democracy abroad', in Schraeder, P.J. (ed.), *Exporting Democracy: Rhetoric vs Reality*, Boulder CO, Lynne Rienner, pp. 113–27.

Hughes, M.L., 1999, *Shouldering the Burdens of Defeat: West Germany and the Reconstruction of Social Justice*, Chapel Hill NC, University of North Carolina Press.

Hurd, D., 1990, Speech given to Overseas Development Institute, London.

Hyden, G., Court, J. and Mease, K., 2003, *The Bureaucracy and Governance in 16 Developing Countries*, London, Overseas Development Institute.

Iliffe, J., 1995, *Africans, the History of a Continent*, Cambridge, Cambridge University Press.

IMF, 1997a, 'Good governance: the IMF's role', www.imf.org/external/pubs/ft/govern/govindex.htm.

IMF, 1997b, 'The role of the IMF in governance issues: guidance note', Washington DC, IMF.

IMF, 2004, 'IMF Country Report No 04/384, Lesotho', www.imf.org/external/country/lso.

IMF/World Bank, 2002, 'Review of the poverty reduction strategy paper approach', Washington DC, International Monetary Fund and International Development.

Jacobs, C., 1998, 'Institutional strengthening and technical co-operation: developing a best practice model', *Journal of International Development*, **10**, pp. 397–406.

Jenkins, K. and Plowden, W., 1995, *Keeping Control: The Management of Public Sector Reform Programmes*, London, British Council.

Jennings, R.S., 2003, *The Road Ahead. Lessons in Nation-Building from Japan, Germany, and Afghanistan for Postwar Iraq*, Washington DC, United States Institute of Peace.

Jonaityte, D. (n.d.), 'Review of the activity of the Konrad Adenauer Foundation in Lithuania', www1kas.de/stiftung/englisch/international.

Kaldor, M., 2002, *Global Civil Society*, Cambridge, Polity Press.

Kaufmann, D., Kray, A. and Zoido-Lobaton, P., 2000, *Governance Matters*, Washington DC, World Bank.

Kennedy, H., 2004, *Just Law*, London, Chatto & Windus.

Kiakwama, G. and Chevallier, J., 2001, *Aid and Reform: the Case of The Democratic Republic of Congo*, Washington DC, World Bank.

Kiggundu, M.N., 1998, 'Civil service reforms: limping into the 21st century', in Minogue, M., Polidano, C. and Hulme, D., *Beyond the New Public Management: Changing Ideas and Practices in Governance*, Cheltenham UK, Northampton MA, USA, Edward Elgar, pp. 155–71.

Kiragu, K., 2002, 'Improving service delivery through public service reform: lessons of experience from select sub-Saharan Africa countries', paper for meeting of DAC Network on Good Governance and Capacity Development, February, OECD, Paris.

Klitgaard, R., 1997, 'Cleaning up and invigorating the civil service', *Public Administration and Development*, **17**, 4, pp. 487–509.

Klitgaard, R., 1998a, *Applying Cultural Theories to Practical Problems*, RAND reprint series RP-694, Santa Monica CA, RAND.

Klitgaard, R., 1998b, *Including Culture in Evaluation Research*, RAND reprint series RP-695, Santa Monica CA, RAND.

Koenen-Grant, J. and Garnett, H., 1996, *Improving Policy Formulation and Implementation in Zambia*, Washington DC, Management Systems International.

Kuotsai, T.L. (ed.), 2000, *Administrative Reform and National Economic Development*, Aldershot, Ashgate.

Laking, R., 1999, 'Don't try this at home? A New Zealand approach to public management reform in Mongolia', *International Public Management Journal*, **2**, 2, pp. 217–35.

Lancaster, C., 1999, *Aid to Africa: so Much to Do, so Little Done*, Chicago IL, University of Chicago Press.

Larbi, G.A., 1998, 'Institutional constraints and capacity issues in decentralising management in public services: the case of health in Ghana', *Journal of International Development*, **10**, pp. 377–86.

Layard, R., 1994, 'The current state and future of economic reform', in TACIS, European Expertise Service 1992–94, First Review Exercise, Brussels.

Leftwich, A., 2000, *States of Development: On the Primacy of Politics in Development*, Cambridge, Polity Press.

Livingstone, G. and Bowcott, O., 2003, 'Aid cash diverted to Iraq', *Guardian*, 23 October.

Lowenthal, A.F. (ed.), 1991, *Exporting Democracy: the United States and Latin America. Themes and Issues*, London and Baltimore MD, Johns Hopkins University Press.

Lumsdaine, D.H., 1993, *Moral Vision in International Politics: the Foreign Aid Regime, 1949–89*, Princeton NJ, Princeton University Press.

Lux, S.J. and Straussman, J.D. 2004, 'Searching for balance: Vietnamese NGOs operating in a state-led civil society', *Public Administration and Development*, **24**, pp. 173–81.

McCarthy, S., 1994, *Africa, the Challenge of Transformation*, London, Tauris.

McCourt, W. and Minogue, M. (eds), 2001, *The Internationalisation of Public Management: Reinventing the Third World State*, Cheltenham UK, Northampton MA USA, Edward Elgar.

McCourt, W. (n.d.), 'Political commitment to reform: Civil Service reform in Swaziland', Institute for Policy Development, University of Manchester.

McLaughlin, K., Osborne, S.P. and Ferlie, E. (eds), 2002, *New Public Management: Current Trends and Future Prospects*, London, Routledge.

Mamdani, M., 1996, *Citizen and Subject: Contemporary Africa and the Legacy of Late Colonialism*, Princeton NJ, Princeton University Press.

Manning, N., 2001, unpublished e-mail.

Manning, N. with Barma, N., Blandel, J., Pilichowski, E. and Wright, V., 1999, *Strategic Decision-Making in Cabinet Government: Institutional Underpinnings and Obstacles*, Washington DC, World Bank.

Manning, N. and Parison, N., 2003, *International Public Administration Reform: Implications for the Russian Federation*, Washington, DC, World Bank.

Mason, J., Fapohunda, B.M., Onibon, F., 2000, 'Training for good governance and civil–military relations', Impact Assessment of the Office of Transition Initiatives/Nigeria Program, Arlington TX, PriceWaterhouseCoopers.

Mason, J.P., 1990, 'AID's experience with democratic initiatives: a review of regional programs in legal institution building', Washington DC, USAID.

Matheson, A. (n.d.), 'Building capacities for governance: Civil Service reform in Commonwealth countries', www.iog.ca/publications/ps_reform.

Mikesell, J.L. and Mullins, D.R., 2000, 'Reforming budget systems in countries of the former Soviet Union 2000', Indiana, Indiana University, School of Public and Environmental Affairs.

Minogue, M., 1998, 'Changing the state: concepts and practice in the reform of the public sector', in Minogue, M., Polidano, C. and Hulme, D., *Beyond the New Public Management: Changing Ideas and Practices in Governance*, Cheltenham UK, Northampton MA, USA, Edward Elgar, pp. 17–37.

Minogue, M., Polidano, C. and Hulme, D., 1998, *Beyond the New Public Management: Changing Ideas and Practices in Governance*, Cheltenham UK, Northampton MA, USA, Edward Elgar.

Mishra, R.K., 1997, 'National civil service systems in India: a critical view', paper prepared for presentation at Civil Service Systems in Comparative Perspective, Bloomington IN, 5–8 April.

Misztal, B.A., 1996, *Trust in Modern Societies: the Search for the Basis of Social Order*, Cambridge, Polity Press.

Moeller, R.G. (ed.), 1997, *West Germany under Construction: Politics, Society, and Culture in the Adenauer Era*, Ann Arbor MI, University of Michigan.

Montgomery, J.D., 1957, *Forced to be Free: the Artificial Revolution in Germany and Japan*, Chicago IL, University of Chicago Press.

Moore, M., 2001, 'Political underdevelopment: what causes "bad governance"?', Brighton, Institute of Development Studies.

Mosley, P., Harrigan, J. and J. Toye, 1991, *Aid and Power: the World Bank and Policy Based Lending*, London, Routledge.

Mulley, S., Welsh, J. and Woods, N., 2005, 'Meeting report: Good government and donor coordination', Ottawa, Global Economic Governance Programme.

Muravchik, J., 1991, 'Exporting democracy: fulfilling America's destiny', Washington DC, American Enterprise Institute.

National Audit Office (NAO), 2002, *Department for International Development. Performance Management: Helping to Reduce World Poverty*, London, NAO.

Ndulo, M., 2001, 'Constitution-building in Africa: assessing both the process and the content', *Public Administration and Development*, **21**, pp. 101–17.

Nottage, R., 1972, 'The Royal Institute of Public Administration 1939–1972', *Public Administration*, **50**, 4, pp. 419–46.

Nunberg, B., 1995, *Managing the Civil Service: Reform Lessons from Advanced Industrial Countries*, Washington DC, World Bank.

Nunberg, B., 1997, 'Leading the horse to water: transnational inducements to administrative reform', paper presented at Conference on Comparative Civil Service Systems, University of Indiana, Bloomington, IN, 8 April.

Nunberg, B., 1998, *The State after Communism: Administrative Transitions in Central and Eastern Europe*, Washington DC, World Bank.

Nunberg, B., 1999, 'Rethinking civil service reform', PREM Notes 31, Washington DC, World Bank.

Nunberg, B. and Nellis, J., 1995, *Civil Service Reform and the World Bank*, Washington DC, World Bank.

OECD DAC, 1997, 'Evaluation of programs promoting participation and good governance: synthesis report', Development Assistance Committee Expert Group on Aid Evaluation, Paris, OECD.

OECD, 2000, *Report by the DAC on donor support for Institutional Capacity Development in Environment: Lessons Learnt*, Paris, OECD.

OECD, 2001a, *Evaluation Feedback for Effective Learning and Accountability*, DAC Working Party on Aid Evaluation, Paris, OECD.

OEDC, 2001b, *Strengthening Trade Capacity for Development*, DAC Guidelines, Paris, OECD.

OECD, 2002, *Report on the London Meeting of the Donor Public Service Reform Working Group (22–23 April 2002)*, Paris, OECD.

OECD, 2003, *Estonia: Public Service and Administrative Framework Assessment*, Paris, OECD.

OECD, 2004a, *Lessons Learned on Donor Support to Decentralisation and Local Governance*, Development Assistance Committee, Paris, OECD.

OECD, 2004b, *Summary Record of the 28th Session of the Public Management Committee, 16 February 2004*, Paris, OECD.

OECD, 2004c, 'Bulgaria: public service and administrative framework assessment', Paris, OECD.

Okungu, J., 2005, 'Peer reform is testimony that Africa has resolved to tackle its governance issues', Nairobi, *Standard*, 15 July.

Overseas Development Administration (ODA), 1993, 'Taking account of good government. Technical note no. 10', London, Overseas Development Administration.

Page, E.C., 2003, 'Future governance: lessons from comparative policy. Pulling threads together', paper prepared for Future Governance Programme Final Meeting, December 3, www.futuregovernance.ac.uk/Papers/Dec3PaperFinal.PDF.

Painter, M., 2003, 'Public administration reform in Vietnam', in Cheung, A. and Scott, I. (eds), *Governance and Public Sector Reform in Asia: Paradigm Shifts or Business as Usual?*, London, RoutledgeCurzon, pp. 208–26.

Parison, N., 2000, 'Russia: Public Administration Reform: Issues and Options', paper given to Conference on Post-Election Strategy Moscow, April 2000, www.imf.org/external/pubs/ft/semoinar/2000.

Parison, N., 2002, 'Civil service reform: for real this time?', *Moscow Times*, 17 May.

Paul, S., 1998, *Making Voice Work. The Report Card on Bangalore's Public Service*, Washington DC, World Bank.

Pavignani, E. and Hauck, V., 2001, *Pooling of Technical Assistance in the Context of Aid Management Reform. The Mozambique Case Study*, www.sti.ch/scih/swap_country_mozambique.

Pei, M. and Kasper, S., 2003, *Lessons from the Past: the American Record on Nation Building*, Washington DC, Carnegie Endowment.

Peterson, Stephen B., 1997, 'Hierarchy versus networks: alternative strategies for building organisational capacity in public bureaucracies in Africa', in Grindle, M.S. (ed.), *Getting Good Government: Capacity Building in the Public Sectors of Developing Countries*, Cambridge MA, Harvard Institute for International Development, pp. 157–76.

Philip, G., 2003, 'International agencies and policy transfer: the case of the Mexican civil service reform', paper presented to ESRC Future Governance Workshop, Vienna, December.

Picciotto, R. and Wiesner, E. (eds), 1998, *Evaluation and Development: the Institutional Dimension*, New Brunswick NJ, Transaction Publishers.

Poate, D., Riddell, R., Chapman, N., Curran, T., et al., 2000, *The Evaluability of Democracy and Human Rights Projects. A Logframe-related Approach*, Stockholm, SIDA.

Pope, Jeremy (ed.), 1999, *The TI Source Book, 3rd edition 1999*, Berlin, Transparency International.

Potter, D.C., 1986, *India's Political Administrators, 1919–1983*, Oxford, Oxford University Press.

Putnam, R.D., 1993, *Making Democracy Work: Civic Traditions in Modern Italy*, Princeton NJ, Princeton University Press.

Reality of Aid, 2004, www.realityof aid.org/roa.php.

Reining, H., 1965, 'Organization of the Civil Service for social and economic development', in Krisberg, M. (ed.), *Public Administration in Developing Countries*, proceedings of international conference, Bogota, April 1963, Washington DC, Brookings Institution, pp. 103–13.

River Path Associates, 2005, 'Review of the Westminster Foundation for Democracy', www.fco.gov.uk.

Romero, S.E., 1999, 'Changing Filipino values and the redemocratisation of governance', in Hang, Sung-Joo (ed.), *Changing Values in Asia: their Impact on Governance and Development*, New York, Japan Center for International Exchange.

Rose, R., 1993, *Lesson Drawing in Public Policy,* Chatham NJ, Chatham House.

Rose, R., 2000, 'What can we learn from abroad?', *Parliamentary Affairs*, **53**, pp. 628–43.

Rubienska, A. and Bovaird, T., 1999, 'Performance management and organisational learning: matching processes to cultures in the UK and Chinese services', *International Review of Administrative Sciences*, **65**, 2, pp. 251–68.

Santiso, C., 2002a, 'Governance conditionality and the reform of multilateral development finance: the Role of the Group of Eight', G8 Governance, Number 7, www.g7.utoronto.ca/governance/.

Santiso, C., 2002b, 'Improving the governance of European foreign aid. Development co-operation as an element of foreign policy', CEPS Working Document No 189, www.eldis.org/static/DOC11400E.

Santiso, C., 2003, 'Another lost decade? The future of reform in Latin America', *Public Administration and Development*, **23**, pp. 297–306.

Schacter, M., 2000a, 'Monitoring and Evaluation Capacity Development in sub-Saharan Africa: Lessons from Experience in Supporting Sound Governance', Washington DC, World Bank.

Schacter, M., 2000b, *Capacity Building: a New Way of Doing Business for Development Assistance Organisations. Policy Brief No 6*, Ottawa, Institute on Governance.

Schick, A., 1999, 'Why most developing countries should not try New Zealand reforms', *World Bank Research Observer*, **13**, 1, pp. 123–31.

Schiller, C., 2000, *Improving Governance and Fighting Corruption: An IMF Perspective*, Washington DC, Organization of American States.

Schraeder, P.J. (ed.), 2002, *Exporting Democracy: Rhetoric vs Reality*, Boulder CO, Lynne Rienner.

Sebastian, L.C., 'Values and governance issues in the foreign policy of Singapore', in Sung Yoo, Han, *Changing Values in Asia: their Impact on Governance and Development*, Tokyo and New York, Japan Center for International Exchange, pp. 219–50.

Select Committee on International Development, 2002, Sixth Report, *DFID: Departmental Report 2002*, House of Commons.

Select Committee on International Development, 2003, Eighth Report, *DFID: Departmental Report 2003*, House of Commons.

Sen, A., 1999, *Development as Freedom*, Oxford, Oxford University Press.

Shah, S., 2002, 'Governance and Public Sector Reform' in *PRSPs: Achievements and Challenges*, Washington DC, World Bank.

Short, C., 1997, 'Democracy, human rights and governance', speech at the University of Manchester, London, DfID.

Short, C., 2002, 'Reform of EU aid programme is overdue', *Guardian*, 29 July.

SIDA, 2002, *Supporting Ownership: Swedish Development Cooperation with Kenya, Tanzania and Uganda, Vol I: Synthesis Report*, Stockholm, SIDA.

SIDA, 2004, *Strengthening Public Employment Services in Armenia, Georgia and Moldova*, Stockholm, SIDA.

Singh, K., 2003, 'Aid and good governance: a discussion paper for the reality of aid', www.realityofaid/roareport.

Sotiropoulos, D., 2004, 'Democratization, administrative reform and the State in Greece, Italy, Portugal and Spain. Is there a "model" of South European Bureaucracy?', LSE, April.

Stevens, M. and Teggemann, S., 2004, 'Comparative experience with public service reform in Ghana, Tanzania and Zambia', in Levy, B. and Kpundeh, S. (eds), *Building State Capacity in Africa: New Approaches, Emerging Lessons*, Washington DC, World Bank, pp. 43–86.

Stiglitz, J., 2002, *Globalization and its Discontents*, London, Allen Lane, Penguin Press.

Struyk, R.J., 1997, *Making Aid Work: Lessons from Successful Technical Cooperation in the Former Soviet Bloc*, Washington DC, Urban Institute.

Sung Yoo, Han, 1999, 'Asian values: an asset or a liability', in Sung Yoo, Han, *Changing Values in Asia: their Impact on Governance and Development*, Tokyo and New York, Japan Center for International Exchange, pp. 3–9.

Sutherland, S.L., 1999, *Supporting Democracy: the South Africa–Canada Program on Governance*, Ottawa, International Development Research Centre.

Swann, S., 1999, *Reflections on the Allied Occupation of Japan*, London School of Economics, SunTory-Toyota International Centre for Economics and Related Disciplines.

Thomas, M.A., 2002, 'Can the World Bank enforce its own conditions? The World Bank and the enforcement critique of conditionality', Washington DC, World Learning.

Transparency International, 1995, *Building a Global Coalition against Corruption, TI Report*, Berlin, Transparency International.

Tsikata, Y.M., 2001, 'Ghana', in Devarajan, S., Dollar, D. and Holmgren, T., *Aid and Reform in Africa: Lessons from Ten Case Studies*, World Bank, pp. 47–100.

Turnbull, J., 2002, 'Solomon Islands: blending traditional power and modern structures in the state', *Public Admininstration and Development*, **22**, 2, 191–202.

Turner, I., 1989, *Reconstruction in Post-war German; British Occupation Policy and the Western Zones 1945–55*, London, St Martin's Press.

Turner, M. and Hulme, D., 1997, 'Governance administration and development: making the state work', Basingstoke and New York, Palgrave.

Uganda Debt Network, 2003, 'The Uganda Budget 2003–04. What relevance to the poverty situation?' Review Report No. 5, Kampala, Uganda, www.internationalbudget.org/resources/UDN03-04.pdf.

UNDP, 1997, 'Governance for sustainable human development', New York, UNDP.

UNDP, 1998, 'UNDP and governance: experiences and lessons learned', New York, UNDP.

UNDP, 2001, 'Reforming technical cooperation for capacity development', New York, UNDP.

UNDP, 2004, 'Public administration reform: practice note', New York, UNDP.

UNDP, 2005, 'Investing in development: a practical plan to achieve the Millennium Development Goals', New York, UNDP.

United Nations, 1997, *Future of the United Nations Development Programme: Initiatives for Change*, New York.

Unsworth, S., 2005, 'Focusing aid on good governance: can foreign aid instruments be used to enhance 'good governance' in recipient countries?', unpublished working paper, University College Oxford, Global Economic Governance Programme.

USAID, 2004, *USAID FY 2004 Performance and Accountability Report*, Washington DC, USAID.

Vanagunas, S., 1997, 'Civil Service reform in the Baltics', paper prepared for presentation before conference on Civil Service Systems in Comparative Perspective, www.indiana.edu/~csrc/vanag1.

Walker, D., 1999, 'Reform school', in London, *Guardian*, 29 September.

War on Want, 2004, 'Profiting from poverty: privatisation contracts, DFID and public services', www.waronwant.org/profiting.

Warrener, D., 2004, *ODI Synthesis Paper 3: The Drivers of Change Approach*, London, Overseas Development Institute.

Warrington, E., 1999, 'Efficiency first ... political education second', *Public Administration and Development*, **19**, pp. 487–506.

Watt, N., 2004, 'Copy can-do army, Blair tells the Sir Humphreys', *Guardian*, 25 February.

Welch, C. (1998), 'The IMF and good governance', *Foreign Policy in Focus*, **3**, 33, www.hartford-hwp.com/archives.

Westcott, C.G., 1999, 'Keynote address, workshop on Public Sector Reform, Washington, www.adb.org/documents/speeches/1999/public_sector_reform/nz_address.

Westcott, C., 2004, 'Improving public admninistration in the Asia-Pacific region: some lessons from experience', *International Public Administration Review,* **5**, 2, pp. 78–102.

Wimmer, A. and Schetter, C., 2002, 'What can aid donors do about governance in Afghanistan? State-Formation First: Recommendations for Reconstruction and Peace-making in Afghanistan', Bonn ZEF.

Wimmer, A. and Schetter, C., 2003, 'Putting state formation first: some recommendations for reconstruction and peace-making in Afghanistan', *Journal of International Development*, **15**, 5, 525–40.

Woods, N., 2000, 'The challenge of good governance for the IMF and the World Bank themselves', *World Development*, **28**, 5, pp. 823–42.

Woodward, B., 2002, *Bush at War*, London, Simon & Schuster.

World Bank, 1983, *World Development Report*, Washington DC, World Bank.

World Bank, 1989, *Sub-Saharan Africa. From Crisis to Sustainable Growth. A Long Term Perspective Study*, Washington DC, World Bank.

World Bank, 1994, *Governance: the World Bank's Experience*, Washington DC, World Bank.

World Bank, 1996, *World Development Report*, Washington DC, World Bank.

World Bank, 1997, *The State in a Changing World. World Development Report 1997*, New York, Oxford University Press.

World Bank, 1997, *World Development Report*, Washington DC, World Bank.

World Bank, 1999a, *Civil Service Reform; a Review of World Bank Assistance April 1999*, Washington DC, World Bank.

World Bank, 1999b, 'Monitoring and evaluation and governance in sub-Saharan Africa', Washington DC, World Bank, Operations Evaluation Department.

World Bank, 2000, *Reforming Public Institutions and Strengthening Governance: a World Bank Strategy*, Washington, DC, World Bank.

World Bank, 2001a, *Governance: the Critical Factor*, Washington DC, World Bank.

World Bank, 2001b, *Aid and Reform in Africa*, Washington DC, World Bank.

World Bank, 2002, *Governance and Development*, Washington DC, World Bank.

World Bank, 2002, *Reforming Public Institutions and Strengthening Governance: a World Bank Strategy. Implementation Update*, Washington DC, World Bank.

World Bank, 2003a, *Rethinking Governance*, Washington DC, World Bank.

World Bank, 2003b, *World Development Report 2004: Making Services Work for Poor People*, Washington DC, World Bank.

World Bank, 2004a, *2003 Annual Review of Development Effectiveness*, Washington DC, World Bank.

World Bank, 2004b, *An Evaluation of World Bank Assistance for Governance, Public Sector Management, and Institution Building in Transition Economies in Transition*, Washington DC, World Bank.

World Bank, 2004c, *OED*, *What Have We Learned? Some Preliminary Lessons from OED's Country Assistance Evaluations*, 14 September, Washington DC, World Bank.

World Bank, 2004d, *World Development Report*, Washington DC, World Bank.

World Bank, 2005, 'Capacity building in Africa: an OED evaluation of World Bank support', www.Worldbank.org/oed/Africa_capacity_building.

Yangzhong, W., 1999, 'Chinese Values, Governance, and International Relations: Historical Development and Present Situation', in Sung Joo, Han, *Changing Values in Asia: their Impact on Governance and Development*, Tokyo and New York, Japan Center for International Exchange, pp. 13–63.

Yudaeva, K., 2004, 'President Putin's Address to the Parliament: a Statist-Liberal Mixture', Moscow, Carnegie Moscow Center, Russia, 6, 06-07, www.carnegie.ru/en/pubs/briefings.

Yunus, M., 1998, *Banker to the Poor*, London, Aurum Press.

Zanini, G., 2002, *Assisting Russia's Transition: An Unprecedented Challenge*, Washington, DC, World Bank.

Index